# TELL ME
# WHAT YOU
# SEE

# TELL ME WHAT YOU SEE

REMOTE VIEWING CASES
from the
WORLD'S PREMIER PSYCHIC SPY

**MAJOR ED DAMES**
U.S. ARMY (RET.)
AND **JOEL HARRY NEWMAN**

**WILEY**
John Wiley & Sons, Inc.

Published by John Wiley & Sons, Inc., Hoboken, New Jersey
Published simultaneously in Canada

Photo credits: page 26 courtesy of the Open Clip Art Library; pages 30, 46, 70, 71, 72 (top), 73, 75, 77, 83 (bottom), 155, 161 from Ed Dames's collection; page 126 (top) U.S. Army photo by Monica King; pages 126 (bottom), 127 U.S. Congress photo; page 128 U.S. Navy photo by JOSN Oscar Sosa; page 160 U.S. Army photo; page 186 U.S. Army photo by Mr. Russell F. Roederer; page 225 Ben Schumin; page 236 Anthony Majanlahti; pages 253, 255 CIA; page 259 Zhenia Kapustina.

For general information about our other products and services, please contact our Customer Care Department within the United States at (800) 762-2974, outside the United States at (317) 572-3993 or fax (317) 572-4002.

Wiley also publishes its books in a variety of electronic formats. Some content that appears in print may not be available in electronic books. For more information about Wiley products, visit our web site at www.wiley.com.

*Library of Congress Cataloging-in-Publication Data:*
Dames, Ed, date.
 Tell me what you see : remote viewing cases from the world's premier psychic spy / Ed Dames and Joel Harry Newman.
  p.  cm.
 Includes index.
 ISBN 978–0–470–58177–3 (pbk.: alk. paper)
 1. Dames, Ed, 1949–  2. Remote viewing (Parapsychology)  3. Espionage, American—Miscellanea.  4. Parapsychology—Military aspects—United States.  I. Newman, Joel Harry, 1955–  II. Title.
 BF1389.R45D36  2010
 133.8′4—dc22
                                                                                    2010010783

Printed in the United States of America
10 9 8 7 6 5 4 3 2 1

*To Ingo Swann and the U.S. Army,*
*the father and the mother of remote viewing*

# CONTENTS

# FOREWORD

By George Noory

The first time I heard Major Ed Dames talk about remote viewing was back in 1996 on Art Bell's late night *Coast to Coast AM* radio show; he was that rare guest to whom Art would devote the full four hours of his program. At first I wasn't sure what to make of Major Dames, but being such a big fan of Art's, I knew that if Art felt Dames deserved the whole show he wasn't going to be some crank I'd just drift off to sleep listening to.

Here was a retired and decorated army intelligence officer discussing very scary things. He made uncanny predictions about the future, foretelling an event he called "Killshot," in which a large celestial body would pass by Earth, disrupting its electromagnetic field and leaving us vulnerable to an onslaught of life-ending solar flares. He followed that up with more chilling claims about upcoming terrorist attacks. He provided exact times and dates of great earthquakes, the rise of a global crop-killing fungus, and the next time a nuclear weapon would be deployed in anger. The predictions went on for hours. I never did get to sleep. I stayed riveted to that radio all night long.

Beyond his fantastic predictions, it was the psychic technique Major Dames used to arrive at them that fascinated me. He was an expert at remote viewing (RV), the ability to gather information about distant and unseen people and events without knowing anything about them. According to Dames, RV allowed your unconscious mind to travel at will to other places across time and space and, through a series of detailed organized steps, turn your mental impressions of the journey into sketches and bring that knowledge back with you. Amazing as it sounded, I was already familiar with the notion of taking a trip outside your body, and it was an experience I'll never forget.

As a young boy growing up in Detroit, I stayed home from school one day with a fever and suddenly found myself floating slowly up to the ceiling of my room. I remained there, hanging in midair for I don't know how long, bound by some unseen mechanism, looking down on myself sleeping in bed. While the incident frightened me, it also left me with the conviction that there were forces at work in the universe, unseen forces breathing a different kind of energy into the world—an energy that I wanted to learn more about. My impulse to investigate the paranormal took off that day, and with the support of my mother, who provided me with a copy of Walter Sullivan's *We Are Not Alone*, and a close relationship with my aunt, the renowned psychiatrist Shafica Karagulla, founder of New Age medicine, I began looking into the unknown.

My eventual choice of a career in journalism proved to be both a benefit and a drawback when it came to my interest in the occult. A lot of the time I had to keep it a secret. As a reporter I didn't openly broadcast my searcher alter ego, sticking instead to covering a wide variety of straight stories, moving around the country working as a news producer and director in Detroit and Minneapolis and earning three Emmys along the way. On occasion when I couldn't hold it in anymore, I'd tell an unusual tale or two, which led my colleagues in the newsroom to call me by the endearing name "Captain Bizarre." They just couldn't understand how a hard newsman like me, the last man to interview union boss Jimmy Hoffa before he vanished, could ever talk about things they felt weren't worth talking about. Going from missing mobsters to the Loch Ness Monster was too much for them to handle.

Liberation came when I turned host of my own radio show in St. Louis. Known as "The Nighthawk," I was finally free to cover paranormal topics the way I saw fit. The program caught the ear of Premier Radio Networks and I was invited to sit in on Sunday nights for my idol Art Bell on *Coast to Coast AM*. When Art retired, I had the honor of filling in for him full-time.

I held on to many of the regulars Art had hosted as guests on his show, hoping that one of them would be Major Ed Dames, or "Dr. Doom," as he was known. I wasn't sure if his allegiance to Art would make it difficult for him to come on my show, but I knew I wanted his unique in-your-face, no-sugarcoat style of presenting the dark side. As it turned out, Dames and I clicked from the start and he's remained a regular throughout my tenure on *Coast to Coast*.

With society going through this incredible time of change, Major Dames has proven to have his finger on the pulse of what lies beyond. Though not always correct in his predictions—thank God!—he's shown himself more often than not to be the real item and has been instrumental in informing and educating people about remote viewing by demonstrating clearly and concisely how anyone can do it. The unknown isn't so unbelievable in Ed Dames's hands. It's real.

In *Tell Me What You See*, Ed Dames and Joel Harry Newman take us on a fantastic voyage through true cases the major's worked on in his life, from his military black ops days as a psychic spy to his current role as one of the world's leading paranormal private eyes. Each story is more shocking and fascinating than the next. If you've never taken a trip like this before, better hold on for the ride. It's one you'll never forget.

GEORGE NOORY is host of the national syndicated radio talk show *Coast to Coast AM*. The program airs on more than five hundred stations in the United States and around the world and is heard by nearly three million listeners weekly.

# ACKNOWLEDGMENTS

Thanks to Lieutenant Detective Alan Johnson of the Lewiston Police Department, Asotin sheriff Wayne Weber, and Betty Wilks and the entire White family for their patience and cooperation looking back with us at a most difficult time for all of them. For all those looking with their hearts and minds for lost children.

A particular debt of gratitude is owed to these individuals without whose help and support the writing of this book would not have been possible: Dr. John L. Turner; Alan Nevins; Rick Rosenthal; Kerri Sandaine; George Yan; all the dedicated remote viewers military and civilian, past and present (and future); Sami and Matt Joynes for their timely "housepitality"; Feryat Newman for her endless patience and divine inspiration; and the incredible production team at Wiley, our gifted editor Stephen S. Power and his very precise assistant Ellen Wright.

Special thanks to George Noory for lending us a bit of his fame and humor at this precious moment in time and space, as all our moments are.

# TIME TO GO

*This has to be a bad dream.*

I'm alone in the desert, bleeding and filthy, my clothes torn, an unrelenting red sun overhead crisping me. It's as if the sky itself were on fire. Everywhere clouds of hungry flies swarm over a landscape dotted by sand dunes and dry brush. I can't breathe, paralyzed by a choking thick fog and the unmistakable smell of death.

I cross to the edge of a sloping hillside and look down. Spread before me is a scene straight out of Old Testament hell—corpses strewn like rag dolls as far as the eye can see, young men no older than my own sons, all with the same horrible grimace frozen on their faces. On the horizon, hundreds of tanks line up in attack formation, their engines idling. I recognize them as Soviet-made T-72s, but they're all rusted and in disrepair. There are more dead men in the tanks.

Strangely, there's no ocean of gore, no bullet holes, no wounds of any kind to indicate what happened to them. But one thing is for sure—they didn't stand a chance.

Then it dawns on me, not all at once, but in jumbled pieces cobbled together from many levels of perception. The inside of my head echoes with familiar sights and sounds. It's all beginning to make sense. I try to numb myself, to improvise a new me who had no hand in this, but I can't escape the truth. *This is my fault.*

I'm in Kuwait. I'm somewhere along the vast border with Iraq at the launch of Operation Desert Storm, the very moment our soldiers swept into the heart of Iraqi territory. It's January 1991, and Saddam Hussein continues tightening the noose around his defenseless neighbor to the south, thumbing his nose at a mountain of UN sanctions and resolutions. As the deadline for peace passes, the United States goes on the attack, joined by a coalition of thirty-four allied countries. It's an attack like none I've ever seen. Key fortified command and communications centers, missile sites, radar facilities, airports, runways, and Iraqi military forces all fall under around-the-clock assault. The sound of it is mind-numbing. I can hear the troops engaging, the muted *thump-thump* of distant mortar fire, the whirling blades of jet choppers, the screams of dying men. But something is wrong with this picture. *It can't be real.*

I can't be here. We had already won the war. It was over and done with a long time ago. And I've seen this horror before, only not in a way that most people would understand. I saw it *before* it happened.

The story begins on the other side of the world. I was in Washington, D.C., when the order came from Vice President Dan Quayle's office. By this time thousands upon thousands of Iraqi soldiers had abandoned their equipment and weapons in Kuwait and were in full retreat. We were at the doorstep of victory, yet one danger lingered—a threat so terrible it could bring the entire campaign to a standstill.

Quayle's people want my consulting company, PSI Tech, to psychically "see" if Hussein had left behind any weapons of mass destruction as he turned tail and ran. U.S. intelligence is sketchy, if available at all, the price for using tactics far removed from any previous standards of warfare. The basis for data collection in Iraq has been technology, not boots on the ground. Facts have existed as vague blips on a computer screen rather than evidence acquired from a real-time battlefield. Desert Storm is being touted as the first virtual war in history, a technological miracle. But at the end of the day, there isn't much to show for it. That's why they came to me. I'm the resource of last resort, the guy you call for help when no one else picks up the phone.

What I must do needs to be done quietly—no press conferences or Pentagon spokesholes grandstanding for CNN. PSI Tech is a private firm, but it's also a rogue operation I run from inside the military itself. We employ the best remote viewers there are, a handpicked group from the Defense Intelligence Agency's own Psi Spy Unit who signed up with me to moonlight as private psychic investigators. Only a select few know anything about us, the kind of people who talk but don't say very much. We're perfect spies who can uncover the most obscure and guarded enemy secrets totally undetected. A team of ghosts.

Desert Storm is the ideal mission for us. There will be no covert operatives or bribed tipsters used, no satellite photographs or ground maps or any other means of traditional intelligence-gathering. We will locate a target we know absolutely nothing about using only a pen and paper to record what we see in our minds. The classic remote-viewing case.

We go to work, running dozens of RV sessions night and day aimed at uncovering ghastly weapons no one else can, a nonstop process of collecting and analyzing impressions and senses, a patchwork of mental imagery converted into data in the form of sketches. Preliminary results show no missile silos or degassers or killer biological agents, nothing to indicate the presence of any WMDs. Or so it seems.

The evidence we find is far subtler and underhanded. My viewers turn up images of wild horses—herds of them galloping over miles of rolling hills and farmland. Some show simple laborers tilling the soil. There are page after page of drawings that to the untrained eye appear images of things peaceful and no threat to anyone. They could be pictures of a nice spring day in Montana, but they're not. The unit has also sensed huge slabs of reinforced concrete where no concrete should be, armed men in uniforms, in lab coats, vehicles barreling in and out of what look like caves and paths dug deep into the earth like rabbit holes. It's clear to us that Saddam's secret lies somewhere in these caves, in a man-made labyrinth hidden just below the surface. The dictator's picturesque garden is nothing more than an elaborate charade, a clever front for his chemical weapons program. I've seen this before in Russia and Iran, helpless animals used in experiments conducted beneath rural areas with no regard for the people who live there. The horses we view are guinea pigs, test things for antidotes to toxins created in underground labs built across the Iraqi countryside. There are no WMDs in Kuwait. There never were.

But there is something else.

Our psychic search has led to the discovery that the so-called Iraqi army is in reality a ragtag collection of forced conscripts and outcasts, half-starved young men yanked off the streets and from their homes at gunpoint, then dumped on the front lines to run interference for Saddam's elite Republican Guard. The poor bastards can't advance on our superior forces or turn back for fear of reprisals to their families. They're sitting ducks. No way out.

Quick confirmation follows. Once we pinpoint the exact nature and location of the targets it's no problem for the army to validate our findings. The armed units we saw in the tunnels were specialized sentries AI already knew about; the men in lab coats were biowarfare scientists and technicians; the vehicles, military convoys shuttling in supplies and personnel. High-flying spy planes and a few well-paid informers inside Baghdad's crumbling leadership verify this as well. Satellite reconnaissance picks up the distinctive outline of the bunkers exactly where we said they would be and they're blasted out of existence overnight.

Command's response to our intelligence about the Iraqi army is equally devastating. They react with overkill. Daisy cutters are used, a fuel-air weapon creating a deadly chemical aerosol that when combined with air and ignited explodes in a massive unstoppable fireball. The bomb sucks away all the oxygen around it, leaving an overpressure of more than one thousand pounds per square inch. All you see is a blinding flash of light, the blast wave, the blistering heat, and when the dust clears— no more air to breathe. It was this vacuum effect that did the Iraqis in. Only a tactical nuclear device can do more damage this way. I saw it coming, I saw the smothered men in the tanks just as I'm seeing them now. I knew daisy cutters would be used. I knew all of this would happen, it was remote viewing that set the table, and still I did nothing. That's why I'm here. *That's why I'm in hell.*

I hear a rumbling noise off in the distance now, the distinctive turboprop sound of a Hercules transport plane. It's getting closer, almost on top of me. It's more than a mile up, cruising at the optimal altitude for avoiding the shock wave of a daisy cutter. A parachute is released, a single huge bullet-shaped weapon attached to it. The hellish thing spews out a sickly blue mist as it descends, an ominous slurry cloud that disperses in every direction. I'm directly in the line of fire of the mother of all bombs and there isn't a damn thing I can do about it.

I feel as if I'm falling through myself, a heart-stopping plunge to I don't know where. Here I am, in the twenty-first century, believing in our greatness, how modern we are, space stations, cloning, smart bombs. Yet how do you deal with being cast adrift in time, flung headlong into the past or the future? How do you handle not knowing if you're about to live something, have lived it already, or are living it right now?

I look around me, feel the blood-soaked sand move under my feet. I keep repeating, "Wake up—wake up" over and over again. Suddenly, a brilliant white flash rips across the sky.

It's done.


"You all right, fella?" someone says to me.

I rub my face hard, try to get my bearings, try to shake off the glare of a thousand suns exploding in my eyes. Am I still in Iraq? Am I dead?

The man talking comes slowly into view as I focus better. He's in silhouette, shining a flashlight in my face. The dark of his shadow falls over me as he leans in closer. There's an unbearable pain shooting through my head.

"I asked you if you're all right," he says again.

"Yeah, just a little turned around," I answer.

"Turned around from where?"

I look at him and smile. "Do you have any aspirin?"

The man is tall and lanky, with the blackest eyes I've ever seen, his hair in a close-cropped buzz cut. He's got on a khaki uniform with a shiny silver badge and leather pistol belt hugging his waist. Even in my shabby state I can tell this guy's a cop.

"What you doin' out here, mister?" he says, more insistent now.

I don't respond. I'm alive. That's all that matters to me. I rub my face again and pinch myself to be sure. As my head clears, I notice it's the middle of the night. It's also ass-biting cold wherever I am. The pack of coyotes howling off in the distance tells me I'm not in Iraq anymore. There are no coyotes in Iraq. Killer snakes, wild jackals, and camel spiders the size of your fist—but no coyotes.

"You wouldn't happen to know today's date?" I ask.

Now it's his turn to say nothing. He just stands there waiting like an old debt. We check each other out, the night sky growing inkier as the moon sets. This man's not your average law enforcement officer. He's Native American, Navajo Nation to be exact. At least that's what it says on his Tribal Police badge and the side of his four-wheel-drive Suburban. I can only imagine what I must look like to him, my tangled blond hair, grubby pants, compass and binoculars slung over my oversized army-issue trench coat, and flap hat. I must look nuts.

"It's Sunday, December 21, 1991," he says finally, voicing each word as if they were convictions on a rap sheet. "You're in New Mexico, about five miles outside Chaco Canyon, in case you wanna know that too."

"*Chaco Canyon*? Are you sure?" I ask him.

"I'm sure."

What he says hits me like a pickax. Nearly a year has passed since the Iraq invasion, since I first saw it in my mind. I remember all of it now. Why I flashed back to Desert Storm, why I'm here. Why I'm such a mess.

I reach into my jacket pocket for my ID. Big mistake. He loosens the clip on his holster and eases his hand onto his pistol. I can't blame him for that. The way I'm acting, I'd probably draw on me too. He takes my ID and examines every detail written on the faded plastic card.

"Major Edward Arthur Dames," he says. "Well, you don't look like an army officer to me, *Major* Dames."

"That's very nice of you to say," I tell him.

He scowls and returns my ID card.

What more can I say? That in my head I was in Iraq when he stumbled onto me? That I remote viewed Chaco Canyon as the place to make one of the hardest decisions of my life? That a mental picture led me to here to the lizards and tumbleweeds? Better just to get him off my back. Say anything.

"Okay. I'm really out here looking for this thing that's interfering with our ballistic missile tests in the Pacific. An artificial construct of some sort, looks elephantine yet amoebic, with a giant electric proboscis."

"Huh?" he says.

"Oh, they're quite alien, not from around here."

I figure if he doesn't arrest me now he never will, but all he does is stare at me, a long hard stare into my eyes.

"Wait a minute," he whispers. "I know you."

If a man could jump out of his skin, his would be draped over a cactus. He shoots me a look; I know the expression well, a clean mix of shock and comprehension. The Navajo understand these matters. They're very quick to grasp what most people can't about what I do—a keen awareness of more things in heaven and earth than can be dreamt of.

He snatches hold of my hand and studies it, turning it this way and that. Stares at my eyes again, shining his flashlight at them as if trying to find something he missed the first time around. He mumbles, "Y-you're the one who—"

Without another word, he spins on his heels and bolts for his Suburban. He hops in, I hear the door slam, the rippling click of a key in the ignition. After a wildly eccentric U-turn, he's gone. The guy doesn't even look back, just guns the engine and roars off into the night. But he was right not to turn around. He knew me. We'd met before.

It was during the alleged hantavirus outbreak several years ago that we first crossed paths. I was living in Albuquerque and volunteered to help find the source of what was killing his people. The Centers for Disease Control claimed it was a virus, but my remote-viewing team and I found that the disaster was caused by deadly blue-green algae growing in cisterns where the Navajo stored drinking water. The images were clear enough, a soupy lime-colored scum blooming in standing water fed by the hot New Mexico sun. We gave our finding to the CDC but they buried it, wanting nothing to do with us. Bureaucrats would rather eat their reports than accept conclusions drawn from remote viewing. But cover-ups don't save lives, so my team and I drove from one pueblo to another around the affected area alerting everyone we could about the danger, making sure they cleaned up their water supply fast. Coincidentally, there were no more deaths after that.

When word got out about the unique methods we used to uncover the algae, the older Navajo began referring to us as "shape-shifters." We had accessed a place outside of normal time and space for answers, something their witches of tribal lore could do. They could also change shape into anything they wanted. When a shifter became a wolf, his eyes would appear dull and unreflective in light, the opposite of normal, in which they shine with an animal glow day or night. That's why my cop friend stared at my eyes so long, why he took off in such a hurry. That, and the fact that it was the dead of night. Many Navajos dread the night. It's when shape-shifters walk the earth.

I'm a little puzzled by the sense of loss I'm feeling as the cop's car gathers speed pulling away. What was it I felt while he was here? Maybe a sense of safety, maybe the sense of being protected for once and not the protector? He helped shatter my Iraq nightmare and snap me back to reality. I feel I owe him something for that. Now, as his rear lights dwindle in the distance, all I feel is alone. I'm alone again in the desert, and like most events in my adult life it was remote viewing that led me to a strange place looking for answers.

Since I was recruited into the army's prototype Psi Spy Unit in 1984, my world has changed in ways I never could have imagined. Experiences and ideas that once seemed outside the realm of possibility have become possible, almost routine. Many of the questions about life I thought I'd take to my grave have been answered. I wasn't in Chaco Canyon on a mission for the Central Intelligence Agency or Department of Defense or National Security Council or anybody else. I wasn't here to remote view a classified target or hunt down terrorists or locate missing hostages. This was personal. I came to find out if it was time to retire from the army, to quit the only life I've ever known.

*Retirement.* The very word sends shivers down my spine, images of a toothless old man in a rocker waiting for his Social Security check to arrive. That's not how a decorated intelligence officer was supposed to go out. I was at the top of my game, on a fast track to bigger and better things. Recently advanced to the majors' promotion list, I had just been assigned by the army to a strategic operations and counternarcotics unit called Team Six, a project so black, so deep cover that there was no congressional oversight of us whatsoever—not a very smart thing considering how it encouraged some in the unit to cross the legal line. We reported directly to the secretary of defense and no one else. Destabilizing enemy governments wasn't really a topic for open discussion. Team Six had the most creative and resourceful minds DoD could come up with from the ranks of those holding special security clearances like myself. I was in. So why did I want out?

What happened in Iraq is one reason. I needed to be reminded of that travesty to seal my decision about retiring. An overpowering sense of guilt settled over me after the war, the guilt of being ineffective, of not being able to do more to stop the wholesale slaughter of citizen soldiers. I had to do something to set things right again. That's why I lost myself in Chaco. The strain of getting my head around what took place had split me in half, landing part of me here and part of me in Iraq at the same time. Remote viewing a solution to my problem had resulted in bilocation, a visionary moment when you're seemingly in two places at once. You experience it cold and raw as if actually there, then return to the "real world"—if you know what you're doing. So here I was in the real world again traveling back in time to Desert Storm. Reliving the war so I could go on living.

Anyone who watched news coverage at the time knows what became of the Iraqis. What was left of them hobbled out of the desert begging to surrender to anyone who'd listen. The rest were like speed bumps lying in the way of our armored bulldozers and summarily buried alive. I still carry memories of the massacre like a bag of razor blades in my head. The entire affair was a disgrace and I detested my part in it.

My knowledge and experience in chemical warfare added another nail to my career coffin. I gave my full support to those in high places by recommending that pyridostigmine bromide be issued to help our troops overcome any possible chemical weapons Saddam Hussein might throw at them in the field. The FDA-approved drug was given prior to any possible exposure to the nerve agent Soman to help increase survival. Saddam had already used it on the Kurds with devastating results, so it wasn't much of a leap to think he'd miss an opportunity to kill Americans GIs with it. To my eternal regret, it wasn't Soman that we needed to fear. All too late we learned that pyridostigmine bromide was a key causal factor in Gulf War syndrome. The drug, in combination with breathing volatile aromatic hydrocarbons from oil fires set by the retreating Iraqis, exposed our servicemen and -women to immune system disorders, cancer, and a host of other grotesque health nightmares. What I did, as well-intentioned as it was, still haunts my every waking moment.

Pushed to the edge over Desert Storm and leadership changes at the unit I wanted no part of, I reached a breaking point where I could no longer support the policies of my own government. For a good soldier, that's the end of the line. The day I thought would never come had arrived.

It was time to make a decision.


They say your whole life flashes before your eyes when you're about to die, and in a way that's why I came here. This is where I needed to make my decision about retiring, to die a small death. There were still so many arenas I wanted to explore with this fantastic new intelligence tool. I had no license under any Department of Defense charter to remote view the future or the past or UFOs or any other phenomena existing outside what they considered "normal." It was just so much hocus-pocus to those not privy to my record of successes executing critical intelligence missions. I needed to be a civilian to carry on the work I'd started. I could serve my country more effectively outside the system than in. But after twenty years of service, it wasn't so easy to just turn my back and walk away. I needed some special help.

Chaco Canyon was what I came up with after weeks of remote viewing a site I hoped would inspire some answers in me. Apart from the rare natural beauty of it, there is something extraordinary about this place. The sky is so close here you can almost feel it brush past you, the folding back of day and night virtually unseen as one rolls into the other as effortlessly as a heartbeat. I sensed all this in my mind before coming, the soft red clay of the earth, the endless horizon, the rows of Native American ruins like an abandoned city on the edge of a dream.

Chaco is a place of ancient knowledge, much like the one we connect to in remote viewing that exists beyond the constraints of conscious thought. The people who lived here considered it sacred ground, the very heart and soul of their culture. When their civilization had run its course—as all civilizations inevitably do—the Chacoans scattered across the West, bringing what they'd learned to those in need.

I've lived most of my life as a spy, always on the outside looking in. It's time to become a part of things. It's time to go. I decide to retire from the army, to put my old demons to bed and bring what I've learned to an entire planet in need. But are they ready to listen?

# SURFING THE MATRIX

Picture this:

> Being unstuck in time.
> Sitting in front of a warm fire on a winter's night, then doing the backstroke along some amazing beach in Hawaii.
> Opening a door in Fresno and coming through a window in Paris.

All of it done at the same time, all of it done without ever going anywhere.

We've all experienced this at least once in our lives. The phone rings, but somehow you already knew it would. You even know who's calling. You have a feeling something bad is going to happen, or maybe a dream revealing an insight into your life or the future. Almost anything can trigger it. Photographs, a certain scent, a few random words or numbers, and the world unravels into moments. You're somewhere else.

It happened to the philosopher Emmanuel Swedenborg in 1789. He wrote in his journal of a casual dinner with friends and how he became terrified after "seeing" a hellish fire break out in his hometown of Stockholm—*more than three hundred miles away.* Though he couldn't explain it, Swedenborg insisted he knew exactly where the blaze started, the precise number of homes destroyed, and how many people were hurt. He could even feel the heat of the flames. When a messenger arrived days later with news of the distant fire, the old man's eerie vision was confirmed to the last detail, as if he'd actually been there.

Max Planck, the father of quantum theory, described this phenomenon as "the Divine Matrix," an energy field connecting everything in all creation, all that we love and hate and experience, the sum total of our innermost fears and desires. The renowned theoretical astrophysicist Stephen Hawking raised the stakes by calling it "the mind of God." To Carl Jung, the legendary psychiatrist and close colleague of Sigmund Freud, this very elegant mind-vault holding all of humanity's combined wisdom and symbols was the "collective unconscious." For me it's something more practical, an infinite storehouse of information where we can gain direct knowledge of targets. A tool to boldly go where no mind has gone before.

Call it the matrix, clairvoyance, ESP, remote viewing. It has many names, all of them rooted in one special place—a vast universal library where every thought, act, and idea that has ever existed or will ever exist is stored.

Imagine if you could tap into this wondrous place, use its awesome power to answer any question, find lost treasure, predict catastrophes, or even solve a murder. To touch a distant fire and not get burned.

I have.

•  •  •

What is remote viewing?

Best to explain what it isn't first. It isn't talking to the dead or raising spirits or channeling chatty ghosts. It's a structured technique the U.S. government poured millions of research dollars into with the goal of creating a new method of gathering vital intelligence.

In the early 1970s, the Central Intelligence Agency contracted with Stanford Research Institute to develop a reliable way of collecting accurate information on distant targets without actually being there. The prospect of intelligence officers psychically connecting with field agents or reading enemy war plans and smashing communication codes without moving a muscle was keeping the best military minds up at night. That both the Soviets and the Communist Chinese were actively recruiting clairvoyants and psychic wunderkinds for espionage and counterintelligence applications didn't help calm any nerves at the Pentagon either. No one wanted to believe the Commies could top us at anything, let alone using our brains. A paranormal cold war ensued that lasted more than twenty years, more than enough time for military research into psychic phenomena to move from the drawing board into the war room. Who could refuse such a low-cost radar system? Especially when you know your enemy has one.

What came of it was a set of protocols and a training program allowing almost anyone to uncover information and do it better than the most adept psychics in their deepest trance. The Psychic Spy Unit was born. We could describe the location of anyone and anything anytime we wanted. No target was too big, no obstacle too difficult to overcome, no unknown beyond the reach of our minds. We became trained psychics.

The ability to observe things not presently in front of you isn't something you just pick up. Premonitions and feelings of déjà vu sometimes reveal information without our really trying, but with no structured method to find it when we want, the data remain obscure until the premonition comes true or we come face-to-face with the event. If you could remote view your own death, the first thing you'd say before checking out might be, "Hey, I've been here before."

Remote viewing is about reaching beyond the five senses into the unconscious mind, to look inside and miraculously gather information stored like web pages on a cosmic computer. Even more miraculous is that we all have the innate potential to do this, a prescient sixth sense.

Animals have it. In the aftermath of the 2004 tsunami in the Indian Ocean when hundreds of thousands of people washed up dead along the shores of two continents, scientists were astonished to discover no animal carcasses in the flooded Yala National Park in Sri Lanka. While most visitors to the park that day perished, the local wildlife survived by fleeing to higher ground well in advance of the killer waves. It was as if they knew the disaster was coming despite no outward signs that anything was wrong.

The animals made it because of their sixth sense. Like us, they're born with a natural ability to sense impending danger, but they are more efficient at using it. There's no buffer zone between them and this hypersense, no analysis or imagination getting in the way of their connection to the matrix. Mother Nature sends them a direct message and they listen. Not us, though. We need to work at training our minds to connect correctly, to regain this natural and lifesaving "sense of the probable future."

Like accessing any Internet database, in RV you connect first by selecting a target, then choose a search term, direct the browser to a specific page, and record every bit of information you get. The difference with remote viewing is that it's your mind fetching the data, not Google.

We begin with the search term, a target cue that will focus a remote viewer's attention on what we're looking for. If the term is too abstract or general, the information that comes back will be abstract and general. Choose one that is specific, and the results will be limited to that specific term. Ask for information with the search term "dogs" and your mind collects volumes of data on all dogs. Focus the request on "beagles" and you've narrowed down the search.

The search term is a word idea that defines the target. It's filed in a case folder and stapled shut. This keeps the environment controlled and clean so as to bypass imagination and deliver up the facts in their pure form. No one is informed about the target term; there's no need to set anyone's psychic apparatus flashing with all the wrong signals. These strict measures are taken to avoid front-loading—bogging down the viewer with too many clues too soon. It would be like driving with your windshield covered in mud. You can't see a thing until the muck in front of you is cleared away.

We don't assume anything about the target in remote viewing, regardless of the available evidence or conclusions drawn by others. An RV session is performed blind. The viewer is taught that there can be no preconceived notions about the task. If you believe you know something, you're already off track, and an accurate transfer of information from the unconscious to the conscious mind becomes impossible. The arrogant part of the brain that thinks it knows everything blocks you out, distorting and contaminating the flow of data. The mind hates what it can't understand. It compensates by trying to make something out of blurred, indistinct images. Imagination must be separated out for a viewer to stay focused, to stop the mind from filling in the blanks with rubbish. Think of it as tuning in the flickering signal of a far-off radio station. Get the frequency right, cut through the storm of static, and the station comes in loud and clear. All it takes is training.

Next are the formally assigned target reference numbers, a set of two four-digit randomly chosen numbers used to further mask the target. The numbers by themselves have no real significance; they're essentially a file folder heading, an administrative tool permanently affixed like a label to the task at hand. The numbers are similar to a code name and only the project handler knows what they represent. If I wanted to know what happened to the Russian nuclear submarine *Kursk*, which went down with all hands on August 12, 2000, I would formalize the matrix search term by simply writing down the word "*Kursk*" and qualify it with the description "final cruise," then assign the reference numbers to formalize it as the target I'm looking for. When a trained remote viewer is cued with these numbers, they connect to the target unencumbered by any distractions, truly blind to what they're seeking. The numbers generate a signal line, a carrier wave of sorts, direct from the matrix to the viewer. This signal is maintained throughout a remote-viewing session.

When you're finished, you decode what you sense to uncover the essence of the target, the thing that makes it uniquely what it is. Armed with only these target reference numbers, the mind opens freely to a new and separate reality that leads us in the right direction. The numbers are your signpost.

This is Stage I in remote viewing, the all-important phase that allows the viewer to make initial target contact. It lays the foundation for all subsequent stages of the remote-viewing structure. Contrary to what most people believe, we don't cool down before remote viewing—no meditating or chanting or zoning out. No dashing off for a cold one at the corner bar. We're shooting for a concert pianist's state of mind here, a hyperattentiveness that eliminates all distractions. Forget about the boss glaring at you, the bills that need to be paid, or your mother-in-law coming to visit. The more the noise inside your brain fades, the stronger the signal line grows. After that, it doesn't matter if the target is in another room or on another planet. You zero in like a laser on sights and sensations existing anywhere at any time across the universe.

Stage I involves reaching out to the target, working your way from the general to the specific. It's where an ideogram is created, a spontaneous scribble the viewer makes at the start of a session. The ideogram comes from the immediate physical response of touching the target for the first time. The signal line travels from the unconscious as an impulse to the autonomic nervous system, the silent mechanism that runs our heart rate, digestion, and breathing without our ever knowing it. Your hand begins to twitch when the signal line connects. If there's a pen in it, you jot down the ideogram as a mark on paper. More complex data follow.

As odd as an ideogram appears, it is remote viewing's most essential component. Located within this jumble of scribbled lines is all the information you'll ever need. Producing it means the viewer has gotten the full package of data containing all the basic elements of the target. The ideogram represents a general gestalt of what we're searching for, a quick look at an organized whole greater than the sum of its parts. A wavy line could be a water gestalt if the target were an ocean or lake. An upside-down V might stand for a mountain. It's kind of like slowing down the film on a movie projector. Eventually you see the individual frames that make up the complete picture. An ideogram is the whole film in the can, but you can't see it until you search the movie frame by frame first. A remote-viewing session is our way of searching.

We have to go back to Jung and his idea of the collective unconscious to understand why most of us recognize a wavy line as a gestalt for water. According to Jung's theory, gestalts and archetypes are the originals after which all other similar things are patterned. They are forms without content symbol-izing the possibility of a real action or perception. Jagged lines might be lightning; horizontal ones land; a triangle the sail of a ship. Ideograms may seem like pointless doodles on a blank sheet of paper, but we gain experience about the target through them, experience that will lead us to exactly what we want. If the Lincoln Memorial were our target, a kinesthetic sense of rising high above the ground would envelop us at the start of Stage I, then we would descend rapidly to Lincoln seated on his chair, then back up again. We would feel the sudden lift and drop of flying. An ideogram of motion could be used to show it, maybe arrows pointing up and down.

This burst of motion feeling happens instantaneously in Stage I. It's in Stage II that we increase the connection to our target, obtaining additional information such as sounds, temperature, textures, and dimensions. We sense colors, luminescence, and contrasts. If Lincoln were our target again, we'd sense the coolness of the marble, his chiseled face, the craggy roughness of his beard. For some, Stage II images are as vivid as the colors of a painting, tastes as strong as eating a spicy hot meal. You hear and feel everything as if you were there, only you're not—at least not in the way most people think of being somewhere. You've entered the matrix with front-row seats to a show that never ends.

In Stage III we begin making pen sketches of the dimensions we sense, associating them with words like "low," "high," "wide," and "narrow." Together with the descriptive words, the mind-body connection increases with no thinking involved. We just draw what we feel.

At Stage IV we extract more detailed information about the target. We're working with a data matrix now, boiling down what we're perceiving, pulling it closer to us. The data here represent a higher level of contact where more detail presents to us, sensory and dimensional information as well as the emotional impact it's having on us. It's here that the first opportunity to use nouns comes up. Until now they were discarded because they couldn't be trusted, it's too early in the process to perceive. Remember, there are no conclusions, no thinking that we know something.

If we choose to move into Stage V we're basically pulling into a rest stop on the highway. We break our connection with the matrix and rely on memory more than perception. Our exploration of the target continues this way into Stage VI, where we have enough data to make an actual rendering of the target—a complete drawing, not a sketch. This is where all the work pays off. We've cut a swath to the target and won't need to go through the process again. Using only the target reference numbers, we can revisit the target anytime we want and in greater detail. Even the best psychics can't do that. They tell you what they see and that's all they've got. In remote viewing, *seeing* is just the beginning.

Sometimes during a session, the viewer's attention is so strongly directed toward the target that conscious awareness becomes split between their real location and the target site. Bilocation is a physical phenomenon; a person experiencing it feels that they can interact with their surroundings, experience sensations exactly as if they were there, even leave footprints behind.

One of the most interesting encounters I've ever had with bilocation took place in the winter of 1997 when I was living in Hawaii. Dr. John L. Turner, an engineering physics graduate of Ohio State University, where he also earned his MD, contacted me about a surgical case he was involved in. Turner, who for eighteen years was the sole neurosurgeon on the islands, had a deep desire to understand the paranormal ever since he read Jess Stearn's *The Sleeping Prophet*, a book about the famed American psychic Edgar Cayce. Among other things, Cayce was known for his precise psychic diagnoses of medical problems, accurately predicting diseases and correct treatments while in a dream state. Turner wanted to try to make psychic diagnoses using remote viewing. He had a patient with an acute leg pain that defied all normal means of diagnosis. Nothing seemed to work, and he couldn't figure out what was causing it. Once the patient agreed to my involvement, I stepped in.

Acting as the project manager, Turner followed my established remote viewing protocols by first devising a search term for the case—"cause of W.D.'s pain"—then furnishing me with a target reference number to keep the session blind. I immediately overlaid an image of myself to patient W.D. and began receiving a myriad of sensory hits. I had, for all intents and purposes, entered his body like the spaceship in the classic sci-fi movie *Fantastic Voyage*, where the characters are shrunken to microscopic size and injected directly into a stricken man's bloodstream. I was the ship.

Contact was made immediately. Drawing a stick-figure sketch of the patient, I felt around for the source of the problem and let Turner know where I was inside the body. As a trained remote viewer I went right to it—through the brain first, sensing its soft tissue, synapses firing electrical impulses like a generator. I moved down, drawing a line to the lower back, then to a smooth tubelike structure that curved in a helical pattern where a reddish-brown material appeared to be obstructing the flow of blood. It was as if I was seeing a dammed-up red river. I was sure this material was a fluid of some kind. It felt wet. Step by step I built an image of what was wrong with W.D.

The session was over in half an hour. When Turner examined my report, he immediately called the patient in to perform emergency surgery based on the information I had supplied. Afterward he said, "A remote-viewing session focusing on anatomic features revealed obstruction of flow due to an abscess cavity which may have impeded normal cerebrospinal fluid. The remote-viewing findings suggest a reddish-brown fluid as the etiologic agent. This was confirmed by MRI scanning, needle aspiration and surgery. Remote viewing shortened the delay in diagnosis and decreased medical costs of continued physical therapy in the patient."

In part because of our RV session together, Dr. Turner authored the book *Medicine, Miracles, and Manifestations: A Doctor's Journey through the Worlds of Divine Intervention, Near-Death Experiences, and Universal Energy* (Career Press). The book is a nonfiction narrative in which Turner describes his surgical career and spiritual quest into the field of integral medicine, a subject explored extensively by such noted physicians as Deepak Chopra, Mehmet Oz, and Dean Ornish.

Remote viewing can be an important tool in medicine, but our methods are different. For doctors, the rules are hard and fast, it's either this or that. We remote viewers simply observe and record. A typical RV session should take no more than forty-five minutes to complete. It's the only typical thing about it.

Perhaps the best way to understand remote viewing is to demonstrate how it works under serious real-time conditions. On March 11, 2004, at the height of morning rush hour, a series of coordinated bombs ripped through four commuter trains in Madrid, killing 191 and injuring scores more. Only weeks earlier a group of sixty students sat unaware of the coming terror at a Las Vegas hotel taking part in a remote-viewing workshop I was conducting. They were from all walks of life, ordinary working people, no different from the soon-to-be victims in Spain, except maybe for a shared passion about knowing the unknowable.

The Vegas workshop was an advanced class for students who had taken previous workshops with me and had gotten the basics of remote viewing under their belts. Because of this, I was able to make use of the higher-level term "open search" to get things started. Instead of naming a specific target for them to find, the "open search" term freed them to access anything within the universal library—to pierce the matrix as if it were a great cosmic piñata and see what fell out.

I asked one of my students to describe in his own words what happened that day. Independent contractor Bart Woodward from Tempe, Arizona, wrote:

> Our session began like so many others had in the past, Major Dames strolling to the front of the room then marking down the target reference numbers on a blackboard. As usual, the numbers were random to hide the target from us. All we got were the numbers, and that's all we needed. No hints or tip-offs or subtle suggestions were given. Our waking minds didn't have a clue about the target, but our sixth sense rightly connected to the matrix would soon tell us what it was. Using only the reference numbers, we trained our thoughts on something that had happened, was happening, or was about to happen. The numbers he gave us were *6213/5798*.

The major asks if we remembered to bring crayons to class and everyone laughs. As advanced RV students we knew accessing the unconscious mind in remote viewing takes a pen and paper, nothing more. We all knew this, the drill was routine for us. But not this time, there was nothing routine about this class. Something just wasn't right.

I can tell from the anxious expressions on many of the students' faces that this session is unlike any we've ever participated in before. A feeling of impending danger fills the room. It's so heavy it almost has a life of its own. No one is talking to each other, just shifting nervously in their seats, watching distantly, waiting for Major Dames to say something to cut the tension. Eventually he asks what we came up with. I know he's using a light touch at first to loosen us up. He jokingly wants to know if we dropped in on an alien world or a haunted house, maybe a gopher hole.

Dead silence is all he gets.

When some people do finally talk, they seem to all agree we're viewing a negative situation, a frightening scenario out of some awful action movie. Our pen sketches confirm this. Straightforward pictures of animals—big cats to be exact—terrorizing what looks like a panicked crowd of people. Nearly all of us drew rectangular shapes too. Long and narrow and boxy like skyscrapers or towers look, but with unique diagonal lines running across their exteriors.

I can see the major's face tighten when he looks at our sketches. It's hard hiding a mood shift from relaxed to edgy to a group of sixty people focused only on you. We were onto something big, but none of us knew exactly what.

Major Dames says he wants specific words to describe our emotions in relation to the event we're viewing. He asks the question so seriously that all casual classroom banter comes to a halt. He wants it now.

The answers again are nearly the same for all of us. Words such as "worry," "fear" and "terror." He asks us what's causing this fear. Once more the majority are in synch, a kind of psychic consensus is reached as we listen astonished. Phrases like "businesslike" and "organized" come up, "a group working together." The major wonders aloud if there's any motion at the site, any human activity. The room erupts.

"People running, scattering everywhere," a man at the back shouts.

A woman in a pantsuit leaps to her feet and announces, "I have a tube, like a snake with people in it and motion above them. They're all going in the same direction."

"Where are they going?" Major Dames demands.

"They're running from the tube towards a structure, a building of some kind. They're terribly afraid."

"Afraid of the big cats?"

A young man raises his hand and calmly states: "No, not the cats. It's not them. They're afraid of the *fire*."

The room falls silent. Major Dames steps away from the blackboard, moving through the room examining each sketch we made one by one. This session has hit a raw nerve with him, that's obvious. It's hit a nerve with all of us. I feel sick. I have to go, get out of this room, out of the hotel, this insane city. There are too many distractions here. The sound the door makes as I exit is like a steel casket slamming shut. And I'm not the only one who leaves.

A few days later, after he's had time to carefully analyze the information our class collected, Major Dames sends us all emails with a composite diagram of the session attached. The diagram is a kind of map laying out everything we see and feel in a remote-viewing session, a mind map where all roads lead to the target. What the template says, in no uncertain terms, is that we had uncovered a terrorist attack. A horrific bombing was about to take

A flag of Spain with a lion in the upper right corner remote viewed at my RV seminar in Las Vegas.

place, and according to Major Dames, we even found out where.

The big cats we drew were in reality lions symbolizing the national flag of Spain. The narrow rectangular shapes that touched the sky we saw in our minds, the famous towers of the Puerta de Europa with their unique exterior crisscrossed motif.

"Something terrible is about to happen," the major wrote, "but since determining the actual time of an event in remote viewing is currently unworkable, I don't know when."

He finished by telling us our data would immediately be forwarded to the local Spanish authorities as well as the FBI, CIA and other intelligence organizations. What they would ultimately do with it, he couldn't say. He had no control over that; in remote viewing you never do. Five weeks later, like so many others around the world, I could only sit and watch as the bloodbath in Madrid unfolded on the evening news. My darkest fears had been realized.

There was no need for me to explain to my students why nothing was done about the intelligence we uncovered before the Madrid attack. It's part of my regular curriculum to discuss how badly the authorities treat remote viewing. There's no reward for being right afterward, no party, no fanfare or parade down Broadway for us. No fingerprints left behind. What people can't pigeonhole they often reject. We were dealing with a system that treats what we do like watching someone have a seizure from behind a two-way mirror—uninvolved yet shamefully fascinated.

Our efforts more often than not wind up in the hands of people who never get the point, who discard them for no better reason than politics or outright contempt for the RV process. The results we deliver are hidden away forever like vague shapes in the mind waiting to be revealed in a pen sketch.

One by one my students checked in after seeing the attack on television, some crying, some amazed at how accurate our hit on the terrible tragedy was. But all of them were flat-out angry. Despite our accurately having predicted the carnage, nothing had been done about it. What happened in Vegas stayed in Vegas. All I could tell them was that maybe one day we'd know why no one acted, why so many innocent people died so needlessly. We'd just have to take a closer look at the problem. It's what we do in remote viewing.

# THE JERSEY DEVIL

A supposed creature of the New Jersey Pine Barrens, the Jersey Devil has haunted the state and surrounding areas for the past 250 years. Countless residents have witnessed seeing the beast over the centuries, and the very rumor of a sighting often sent whole communities into a frenzied panic, shuttering their homes and closing down schools and businesses.

Most believe the monster to be a legend cooked up by settlers who long ago left this desolate forestland. But there are those who would tell you that the mythical fiend was none other than young Edward Arthur Dames. That's me.

I was definitely what you'd call a troubled kid growing up, but I won't take any blame for the Jersey Devil's doings. Born in Hackensack, I spent much of my early childhood in Paramus, a good two-hour drive from the Pine Barrens. My family's house

Me in my high school days.

bordered backcountry similar to it, only not on such a grand scale. But to me it was huge; the isolated woods around our home were like getting locked in a big candy store. The countryside had everything back then before invading developers turned it into a shopping mall mecca—slow-moving streams, slimy peat bogs, and eerie carpets of gnarled vines. It was a curious boy's dream come true—my own Disneyland in the backyard. It was heaven to me, but hell for my neighbors.

Vandalism was my stock-in-trade. I spent endless hours in the bogs alone or at the head of a band of fellow savages burning down trees and turning headstones over in cemeteries. Fun for us was damaging other people's property wherever we could find it. Constantly in trouble with the law and school officials, I became the king of detention and a poster boy for juvenile delinquency. Still, whatever punishment they meted out, none could match the abuse I suffered regularly at the hands of my father.

There isn't a time I can remember when my dad *didn't* beat me. His weapon of choice was a trusty two-by-four; no belts or switches would do. He'd bash the living hell out of me with that cursed piece of wood and I never knew when or for how long the pummeling would go on. There were no lengthy lectures about bad behavior being the cause of the beatings. Dad needed no excuse for coming after me. He was the boss and that was that. Live with it. I've been told that my rage was a by-product of his abuse, a way to take my anger out on others.

It wasn't until much later in my life that I found out his father had treated him in much the same way, as did his father's father before him, and so on. I was caught up in the proverbial "cycle of violence" so many therapists speak of, and being just a boy there wasn't much I could do to break it. My mother was no help, even when he began focusing his attention on my younger sister, Eva. I hated myself for not even being able to protect a little girl. The guilt I felt I buried deep inside my psyche until the day my father died. We were all afraid of Arthur Dames. He was a very scary man.

The forest was my sanctuary. I would sneak out of the house and run away, staying there as long as I could, sometimes after the sun went down. I loved climbing trees and would always shoot for the biggest ones I could find and sit up in them for hours dreaming about being anywhere but where I was. I learned about hunting and how to be quiet, using stealth to catch rabbits and salamanders. This was my first military mission, building traps, using nets and slingshots to take down my prey. Hunting gave me a feeling of control I could get nowhere else. As much as I loved animals, they became the primary target of my need to dominate, to make someone else the victim for a change.

When I was ten, my family picked up and moved to San Diego. I had severe bronchial problems in cold and wet New Jersey and they thought the move would do me good. Nobody knew at the time it was my mother's relentless chain-smoking that caused my breathing condition. We also had family in San Diego, which made relocating even easier.

We loaded everything we had in this world into our old Packard and headed out on the open road. We really didn't have all that much. My father was a mechanic and did okay financially because he worked so hard all the time, but rich we weren't. The move west was the most incredible adventure I'd ever had. Old Route 66, the people, the truck stops and diners, the cars whizzing by at breakneck speeds of fifty miles per hour!

Now when I look back, I know why the trip to San Diego has remained etched in my memory for so long. It was one hell of an adventure for me. I learned something about myself on the road. I needed adventure. I needed to know that a challenge was waiting for me around the bend, a contest I could lock horns with and win. The bigger the challenge, the more required of me in conquering it.

My first impression of San Diego was sheer ecstasy. At least the countryside was. There were no more secluded forests hiding the sun like back in New Jersey. I no longer had to escape home by hiding in the shadows. Here there were wide-open spaces as far as I could see, sunshine so bright it blinded you, and mountains and trails and more mountains and trails. And there was something entirely new I'd never seen before—a desert. Gone were the harmless creatures of New Jersey. Here were the kinds of animals that drive a young boy wild, snakes and soaring hawks and weird lizards that scampered around at your feet. It was paradise to me.

The friends I began making at school and in the neighborhood were equally intriguing. Jack Lee was a boy hunter like me, only he had the most amazing collection of guns. No wire traps or carrots on a string for him; he had a British .303 Enfield rifle, a Ruger .22 pistol, and a treasure trove of the nastiest shotguns you've ever seen. To top it off, he was an expert at homemade explosives and timers. We built every pyrotechnic device imaginable, and made regular runs across the border to Tijuana, Mexico, for heavy-duty fireworks. Jack and I were bosom buddies, inseparable. We were like one person when it came to making trouble. He was the badass friend your mom wanted you to avoid like a case of bubonic plague—the archetypal "bad influence."

Being with Jack provided a fresh new inventory of ways to make people's lives miserable. Having guns and bombs at my disposal was a dream come true. I planted incendiary devices in garbage dumps, shot out streetlights, set fires in and out of the classroom. Most of the irrational things I did in New Jersey I took with me to California, only now I was older and more dangerous. And I was growing progressively worse.

There was no letup in the beatings at home. Bizarre things were going on now between my father and sister too, things I didn't understand but knew were very, very wrong. Much as I tried, there was nothing I could do to stop any of it. I continued to bury my emotions and unload what I felt on everyone around me. There was no empathy for others in me; it was as if someone had stolen it. People and animals were playthings to help me cover up what I was going through.

Once, on one of those long summer days that seem to last forever when you're a kid, I experienced my first encounter with a place outside myself. I crawled up to the top of a huge oak tree and lay down on one of the branches. It wasn't the most comfortable place, but before I knew it I had fallen fast asleep. The sun was so warm and I was so tired. I'm not sure how long I was out, but when I awoke my whole world had changed. Instead of being an intruder here and everywhere else I went, I felt something I had never felt before. A sense of belonging, of being one with everything, swept over me. I was part of nature, at unity with all I could see and touch. I no longer had an identity of my own. Edward Dames had vanished; I wasn't just some anonymous boy hiding from his dad anymore.

Though I had no idea at the time, this was my first brush with the matrix. And while I couldn't understand all the information racing through my mind, I knew I had changed. Tormenting animals was the first destructive pattern to end. I could no longer hurt them just for the sake of hurting them. It would be like harming myself. I even became a vegetarian, which I remain to this day. Familiar ways of being had become alien to me. I remember walking home and noticing how the trails I'd hiked every day since the moment we got here seemed somehow foreign to me now. Everything was new.

Well, maybe not *everything*.

I had changed, but my father didn't. The beatings were like clockwork, regular as ever, as regular as his hot coffee in the morning. And the anger and resentment I harbored still burned deep inside me. It would take more than a sudden tree branch revelation to put that fire out.

Ironically, it was being a battered kid that eventually saved me. My high school principal, Mr. Metz, took things to the extreme with a drubbing of his own that transformed my worldview. Back then corporal punishment in school wasn't only legal—it was expected. Mr. Metz was a consummate professional at it, a prim and proper Quaker who had zero tolerance for hooligans before "zero tolerance" became an overworked expression. One day, after classes were over, he finally had enough of busting Ping-Pong paddles on my butt and decided to cure me once and for all. A three-quarter-inch plywood paddle custom-made in the school's wood shop was the medicine he had in mind. I guess wood was the preferred material for thrashing problem kids in those days. After eight prior whippings, on the ninth try Mr. Metz used his super-paddle on me. One swat with the edge of that medieval instrument and I was paralyzed. He hit me so hard I couldn't walk straight for weeks. A welt the size of another head swelled up on my rump. It scared the daylights out of me.

Following the punishment, whenever an opportunity to slam a locker door on a fellow student's head arose, you can bet I thought twice about it. All I had to do was remember that doomsday paddle and the right decision became a no-brainer. Finally

I got it right. This wasn't a pointless beating like my father's; Mr. Metz wanted me to do well. He would spend hours talking to me man to man about what I was capable of and how much he believed in me. I wasn't just a dumb loser to him. From that moment on I ceased being a fighter and arsonist. Academics and sports became my new emotional outlet, and I have Mr. Metz to thank for it. If not for his unique style of persuasion, I probably would've landed in prison one day. He literally beat the *me* out of me. It saved my life.

Much to my surprise and that of everyone else who knew me, I became quite the excellent student and an even better athlete. Science and chemistry were high on my list and I took up running and skin diving. My long-running love of the ocean took root when I learned how to dive, the sea my ultimate sanctuary. No one could find me down there; I was safe.

Being short in stature, I had always found ways to compensate that involved some sort of violence. But that changed along with everything else. I was turning my life around by getting into my studies and building myself up. Soon I was setting physical fitness records at Santana High School and being voted the captain of our cross-country team. I discovered a benign method of venting my restless energy through physical training and mental discipline. No more bullying.

I began to enjoy solitude and find new ways to escape the harsh realities of my home life. Part of my dream world included short-wave radios, which I learned how to use as soon as I was old enough. Hearing broadcasts from such mysterious places as the Sudan and France was like getting messages from another dimension. The different variety of languages and music was thrilling, especially Arabic music. For some reason its rhythmic melodies appealed to me, haunting and exotic. I was sitting in my room in the dark hearing people from places I'd never been before, perceiving things intangible and remote. Without knowing it, I had touched the matrix again. I wasn't there, but my mind was, just like in remote viewing. And my mind discovered something equally as exotic around this time: girls.

To be more exact, girls discovered me. I was short—nothing could change that—but I was in great shape and rapidly becoming the "little" big man on campus because of my athletic prowess. When my winning ways in track and field were announced over the loudspeaker at a football game, I suddenly discovered how popular I really was. Martha Cross, the city of Ramona's Apple Day Queen and one of Santana High's best-looking girls, took notice of me. She was statuesque, with an incredible hourglass figure and very, very blonde. Martha Cross asked me to a movie. She asked *me*! None of my friends could believe it. I couldn't believe it. I was in love. But being in love required some fast growing up on my part. I was sixteen and Martha seventeen, so I of course began making plans for our future together. What teenager doesn't? But there was some personal business that needed tending to first.

On one particularly hot afternoon as I came running down Rattlesnake Mountain, I saw my father going at it with my mother. Rattlesnake was a summit nearly a mile high that I ran every day for a workout. But it wasn't only for exercise that I went up Rattlesnake; something strange would happen to me every time I was there. The world would seem to move in slow motion, unhurried and self-propelled, coasting smoothly as if every surface were level and glassy. My thoughts made sense after a run there, my head clear. That day when I saw my father threatening my mom again I knew exactly what had to be done. With no hesitation at all, I reared back and raised my fist to hit him. We looked at each other—it couldn't have been more than a second or two, but for me it took forever. We looked into each other's eyes and for the first time in my life he stopped. He stopped. A moment later he turned and walked into the house, slamming the screen door behind him. The whole thing was surreal.

My mom later told me that he hadn't fought back because he knew he'd kill me if he did. But I see it differently. I was as strong as an ox and built like a boxer by this time, and I think he understood I would have killed *him*. Violence was all he understood and I was damn ready to dish some out. He knew I meant business; I wasn't about to back down like I had a million times before. And I was right. He never lifted a finger against my mother or me again after that. Like a passing storm, my nightmare had come to an end. It was over.

The time for me to leave home was at hand. Escaping into another world through ham radios and athletics was no longer a workable choice. I needed to fly, and the fastest way to take off was to become a soldier.

A military career was inevitable for me. My family had a long and sometimes illustrious warrior background. My father himself had been in the navy and served in Korea, and my uncle John Pennington from my mother's side was a genuine war hero. While serving as a torpedo man on a submarine in World War II, he dove into fifteen-foot-high seas to rescue a B-25 pilot after he had to ditch in the Pacific. Comic books of the time told his story to a whole new generation of young Americans. My great-grandfather John Spofford was a legend too, a merchant mariner who captained a Gulf Oil tanker loaded with high-octane fuel for our allies in World War I. Putting out to sea sometimes with only half a crew, he routinely braved raging storms and a fleet of killer German U-boats to deliver his cargo. He was also from my mother's side of the family, as was the frontiersman and conservationist John Chapman. During the War of 1812 it's said that he hiked more than thirty miles, warning settlers across the Ohio Valley of imminent Indian raids. Chapman later became known to history as Johnny Appleseed.

Yes, I'm related to Johnny Appleseed.

The reason I know more about my mom's genealogy than my father's is because his were mostly ne'er-do-well cowboys and horse thieves who were nearly to a man hanged for their crimes. He rarely if ever spoke to us about his family's history. They just didn't live long enough to have one.

There was only one thing holding up my enlistment now. Part of me wanted to go to college to study biochemistry, another said be all you can be in the army. The Vietnam War was kicking into high gear and I wanted to win medals, to be a hero like my grandfather. My first choice was Special Forces, the hardest bunch of wise guys in the military, but I was too young to get in. Later I received an appointment to the Air Force Academy, but I was afraid I'd miss the war by the time my academics and flight training were over. Martha didn't care much either way. She was like me, the child of blue-collar workers, most of whom got factory jobs or joined the military out of high school. We wanted to get married as soon as possible, so I needed to make a decision. A long hike into the mountains with my buddies was a good place to think it over, she told me. I should know what I wanted by the time I returned. Martha was great when it came to helping me get my thoughts straight. I tend to overcomplicate things.

Mountains have a weather system all their own, and it suddenly took a turn for the worse the day we went hiking. While my friends ran for cover, I remained outside, mesmerized by the approaching storm. I was so curious about everything back then that I didn't have the sense to come in out of the rain. All I recall was a bright flash and then smashing face first into the hard ground. I had been hit by lightning, a dazzling bolt out of the clouds searing my clothes, dropping me like a rock. As I lost consciousness, a swirl of images danced before me. Men in army officers' uniforms—a hand drawing a dark tower—a great fish with amazing golden eyes.

Though I was hurt pretty badly, I wanted more, to go deeper into this dream place to find out what it meant. The experience triggered something in me. I became obsessed with stories about UFOs and Bigfoot and other paranormal subjects. I couldn't get enough of it; there weren't enough books or television shows out there to quench my thirst for what most people view as crazy. Martha thought I was crazy too and getting crazier all the time. We got married anyway. Apparently she liked crazy.

Fresh out of high school, I followed in my family's footsteps by joining the army. The way I saw it, I'd be living my dream and not living at home. The next thing I knew, I was in airborne infantry training at the height of the Vietnam War, all excited about going into battle. But as usual, the moment I made a plan a surprise hit me out of the blue. This time it was a chance to hook up with the Army Security Agency. With them I could work in army intelligence, the plum of military plums. Here was the challenge I was hoping for. I took an aptitude test, on which I scored well, and because of my extensive shortwave radio knowledge and being self-taught in Morse code, the army changed my occupational specialty and transferred me out of infantry. But they tricked me. With visions of becoming a codebreaker swimming in my head, I was shipped off to Fort Devens, Massachusetts, into the much less glamorous Morse Intercept School. I became a high-speed Morse intercept operator, or "monkey," as we were lovingly called. Why monkey? Even a monkey can type out Morse code.

The unbearable monotony of long shifts sitting at a radio receiver is hard to describe. Day after day, your ears plastered to your headphones, listening to the scratchy Morse streams of *dits* and *dahs* your low-tech enemies use to keep from being found out, and then typing what you have into some ancient manual typewriter that ought to be in a museum. All I wanted to do was throw the stinking thing through a window. But instead of going insane, I broke the army's Morse code speed record and was finally noticed by ranking officers. I was only eighteen years old, but it didn't come a minute too soon.

As an honors graduate, I was informed by my commander that I'd been promoted to specialist fourth class and that I was heading off to Taiwan. I'd never heard of Taiwan and asked if it was in Thailand. They ordered me to shut up and get packed.

I eventually learned that Taiwan is a country and I was going there to intercept Communist Chinese communications. At first I wasn't too happy about it. I wanted to hit the front lines, but my commanding officer convinced me of the importance of my work and how it was better than sitting in a stinking mud hole in Vietnam trying to pick up the muddled transmissions of people trying to kill me. Here I would be listening in on a much bigger and deadlier enemy, the ChiComs—Chinese Communists. If not for my being an honors graduate, I never would have been tapped for this assignment. I got lucky, or maybe command saw something in me they wanted to keep around a little longer. A dead monkey serves no one.

I sent for Martha and we found a place to live in Grass Mountain, an upscale area of Taipei. It was gorgeous there, but she wasn't too overjoyed about the move. If they had posted me to the dark side of the moon she couldn't have felt more isolated. Coping with this strange new world was very hard for her. She knew no one, had no family or friends and not much to do. Martha was a small-town girl, and Taipei was no small town. It was tough for her to adjust, but she did her best. I caught her alone crying sometimes.

I had my work to keep me busy, and plenty of it. Intercepting code from the Chinese mainland turned out to be more interesting than I thought, gathering intelligence about infantry division movements and nuclear weapons tests. I turned what I found over to agents at the National Security Agency, who now knew me by name. They liked what I did. Considering that the NSA was home to the best and brightest codemakers and codebreakers, the right people were beginning to take notice that I existed. I was putting my intelligence to work.

I drove myself to do more, even learning how to speak Chinese. It wasn't easy, but I was having the time of my life. I was working as an electronic spy, living in a far-off place, was married to the most beautiful girl anywhere, and serving my country all at the same time. It didn't get any better than that. Still, Martha was deeply unhappy, and I didn't know what to do about it. She was lonely there, and I was involved in things I couldn't talk to her about. I couldn't talk to anybody about them.

The quality of my work got me into a specialized course with the NSA in Tokyo, and I spent several weeks there, learning about delivering critical strategic and tactical information to key war planners and war fighters. I immersed myself in all its intricacies, but it was Martha I was thinking of. *I'll make things better for her, for us, when I return. I swear this.* But as they say, "If you want to hear God laugh, just tell him your plans." When I finally got home I accidentally discovered a package of love letters Martha had been writing to a guy she met in Taiwan, an American like me. I thought I would die when I saw them. I tried to understand why she did it—maybe she even had good cause—but it was the lying that hurt me the most. I dealt all day long with lies in the intelligence business and it was the last thing I needed at home.

I went crazy when I found the letters. I couldn't sleep or work. It was a shock that took me forty years to get over, laying bare other deep-rooted issues I had. Martha abandoned me in much the same way my mother had, when I needed her most. I was destroyed internally. From that moment on I was different. Not the most trusting guy to begin with, now I trusted no one. Martha and I divorced.

My work in Taiwan continued and I became a shut-in, a hermit devoted to work and little else. But my friend Moose wouldn't have it and forcibly hauled me out of my room and into the city's nightlife. I was never what you'd call a partier, but the local clubs and discos in Taipei were hard to resist, especially hanging around with a guy named "Moose"—the lights and food and dancing, the beautiful women, a seductive game I had never played. I astound myself even saying this, but it didn't take long for me to fall in love again. Perhaps it was loneliness, maybe missing being with one special person, I don't know, but I fell head over heels for the lovely Hui-Ping Wang from Taipei. Her English name was Christine.

Christine was from a well-to-do Chinese family who right off the bat found me totally unacceptable. I wasn't an officer or a college grad, which meant I wasn't good enough for their little girl. Working class was what I was, an enlisted grunt. We would never get their blessing to be married, so I grabbed her one night and off we went to elope. The war in Vietnam raged on as a backdrop to our love, but it would rage on without me soon afterward. I learned that my marriage to a foreign national had disqualified me from continuing my relationship with the NSA. I would have to wait five years to regain my Top Secret Special Intelligence clearance. That door had closed in my face—but others opened.

An officer has more opportunities than an enlisted man, so if my quest for super-spooky spy assignments was to be successful, I was going to have to get commissioned as one. I was accepted to Cobra gunship pilot school, but a pilot's shelf life is limited. If I lived through the war, all I'd be flying when I hit a certain age was a desk. In military intelligence you rise in your career as you get older and more experienced. An office job is not where they want you. The field is where you live, and the work just keeps getting better and better.

Crushed after toiling at one mundane assignment after another and with my hopes of advancement slowly evaporating, I surprised myself and everyone else I knew by humbly exiting the army with an honorable discharge. I couldn't allow what had happened with Martha to happen again. My marriage to Christine was primary and it had to work. I wanted children, a house, a dog and a cat, a normal life—everything that had been denied me up to now. I had to find a new career to keep it together. I was all of twenty-four.

UC Berkeley was my next stop. I attended on a state scholarship and focused on pre-med and biophysics with a minor in Chinese language. Berkeley had been a hotbed of politics and drug culture, the Free Speech Movement, but I wasn't part of it. I guess you could say I missed the sixties altogether, but there was a reason why I kept my nose clean. I might have quit the army, but the army had never quit me. Should I want one day to return to the service, my behavior as a civilian would come under close scrutiny. Military intelligence was very tough back then, no games. To move up the ranks into an intelligence position you needed to be as shiny as a silver dollar with a spotless record. MI would deny you entry for something as insignificant as a traffic ticket. Being careless was frowned upon, and I wasn't about to cut myself out of a career for making a lousy left without signaling. I still wasn't sure I'd be reenlisting, but if I ever did, I needed to know I wouldn't hit a brick wall when I got there.

While at Berkeley I began experimenting with Zen meditation and my interest in the paranormal expanded. I started taking part in things I used to only read about. Psychic phenomena fascinated me; the possibilities of making new discoveries seemed endless. The drive to achieve in me intensified, compelling me to make a clean break with civilian life. After pursuing a biophysics major I switched gears again by checking out engineering, but that didn't cut it either. I decided to drop out of Berkeley altogether. My marriage was already hitting the skids, and this drastic move completely turned everything upside down. Not having a suitable career path was unacceptable to Christine. In her culture, with its strict traditions, your life is mapped out from the day you're born. There's no word for "waffling" in the Chinese dictionary. Not knowing what to do is unheard of.

I made up my mind—or, more correctly, took a stand. I decided to follow the path I had mapped out for myself, the one I had veered from before I got married to Christine. Tradition or no tradition, this was what I wanted. I joined Berkeley's ROTC program and entered San Francisco State College as a Chinese major. Christine wasn't exactly blissful about it, to say the least. The military life was no life to her. She pressured me to become a doctor, a scientist, anything but a soldier again. But the army had always been home to me. I was a fish out of water anywhere else, especially someplace like Berkeley. Even though I wore my hair long, I couldn't seem to fit in there. Students recognized me as army just by the way I walked. I had grown up in the military, so it was kind of hard for me to hide who I was. To her credit, Christine made a good effort to understand how I felt. That I wasn't returning to the military as an ordinary enlisted man helped a lot. I was an ROTC Distinguished Military Graduate now commissioned as a second lieutenant in military intelligence. I had done it. I was an officer and back in MI where I belonged. Christine was okay with both. The world was my pearl for now, and Germany was where I was assigned. The sky was the limit—and the goal.

I was soon trained as a tactical electronic warfare officer, the first in the 2nd Armored Cavalry Regiment's history, assigned to Nuremberg to intercept and jam Russian and Czech communications. I took on the additional duty of nuclear weapons control officer. I didn't have my finger on the big button, but I could send off a half-kiloton nuclear artillery shell if ordered. It's like tossing an atomic hand grenade, a truly wicked device. Nuclear weapons—not bad for a crazed kid from Paramus! Even Jack Lee would have been envious of the toys I had now.

Time passed quickly, and before I knew it, Christine and I had hit the ten-year mark in our marriage. We decided to have children. Our relationship was on the rocks over my workaholic ways, and we believed adding a child would help out. Love is the perfect fixer. We planned to have our first by timing its birth as close as possible to when I was stationed at home and could be with her. The army lent a hand by ordering me to report to Fort Huachuca, Arizona, for advanced intelligence training. The move would keep me on base for a while. Time to have a baby.

It was at Fort Huachuca—"Fort Wegotcha," as we fondly called it—that the vision I had after being struck by lightning as a kid became a fantastic reality. I still remember it, my waking dream, seeing a room filled with uniformed top brass who wanted something from me. And this was exactly what happened when I attended a special class designed to teach intelligence officers how to think out of the box.

All my old friends were at the school, all of them MI captains now like me, and there were several generals in the room—just as it was in my vision. I had been given a glimpse of the future long ago and there it was standing in front of me in all its fruit salad glory. Two real-life army generals. It made me want to get hit by lightning more often.

One of the officers was Brigadier General Stanley H. Hyman, known for using intelligence to predict enemy plans with an extremely high degree of accuracy. The other was Brigadier General Sidney Weinstein, our school's commandant and the man who later became deputy chief of staff for intelligence. The class started off with an announcement that General Hyman had just received his second star. Hyman immediately shouted to Weinstein, "Hey Sid, guess now we know who the smartest Jew in the army is."

God, I loved this job.

As the captain giving the lecture put half the room to sleep droning on about living systems theory, I stood up to get my two cents worth in. I explained very matter-of-factly that what the captain was trying to say was simply an analog model of how energy flows in and out of complex organizational systems in a non-equilibrium thermodynamic way. I sat down.

The captain's jaw dropped and he looked at me. He was quite emotional, almost on the verge of tears. I suppose he couldn't believe someone actually got what he was talking about. I could see now that everyone in the room was staring at me too, even the generals. I wasn't sure if that was a bad or a good thing. All I knew was that I liked the attention.

That night, I celebrated getting noticed a little too much at a formal dinner given in the generals' honor. There we were, officers and gentlemen, including the women officers, all clad in our dress blues with our elegant significant others. A group of

West Pointers sang the West Point school song and everyone went bonkers for it. I raised my hand and heard my friends in the back groan. They knew that when Dames raised his hand there was bound to be trouble. I asked if it would be okay if I sang my alma mater's theme, the Berkley ROTC song. I was, after all, a Distinguished Military Graduate from a very prestigious university on a par with the haughty West Pointers. I was just as good as these old-school soldiers they all seemed to adore. The crowd admired my school spirit, so, accompanied by yelps of approval, I broke into song:

> My mother's a whore in Chicago,
> My father's a pimp in D.C.,
> My sister goes down for a quarter,
> And I'm in the R-O-T-C!

Someone grabbed the mic out of my hand and they dragged me off. I guess they didn't think I carried a tune very well. Lucky

Relaxing with my sons Enoch and Aaron near the Capitol.

for me I didn't wind up in the brig, because my son Enoch was born just a few weeks later. It's good that he wasn't around for my singing debut.

I heard from the top brass a few months later, called into a private closed-door meeting. They informed me that I had been recruited by a scientific and technical military intelligence "black unit" to direct clandestine operations against high-value foreign targets. My orders at Systems Exploitation Detachment were simple and direct: prevent technological surprises in future wars. It was my duty to make sure no commander in the heat of battle would ever be stuck asking, "What was that?" or "What just happened?"

It was also my job to pick targets and direct my agents on gathering intelligence successfully, to make good use of my tradecraft to penetrate and expose exotic weapons programs being developed by Soviet and Chinese scientists. As they were telling me all this, I nodded and did my best to keep a straight face, no reaction or emotion on the surface. Inside was another matter. This was the dream assignment I'd been waiting for, the first step into the arcane secrets of the intelligence world. Nirvana. Or the closest thing to it.

For three years I remained in deep cover, traveling around the world under assumed identities, posing at different times as a professional toxicologist, research physician, and information science manager. I conducted regular debriefing sessions with foreign émigrés and defector scientists to confirm if they were really switching sides or acting as double agents. I also squeezed them for secrets, matching wits at every turn, pitting my guile against theirs. It's the part of this work I confess to enjoying the most. It's what being a spy is all about. Playing the game. The one who gets what he wants without the other knowing is the winner.

During one interrogation, a Czech man told me about a psychic project in his country, how intelligence about the United States was routinely being gathered this way. The Soviet Union was backing a psychic spy program targeting our classified equipment and operations. Amazingly enough, my superiors confirmed this. They also shared with me the bombshell that we had for some time employed a similar intelligence-gathering team of our own. The problem with our psi program was that few high-ranking officers were willing to risk their careers over the stigma attached to joining it. This came as no surprise to me. Truth be told, I had already heard about our Psi Spy Unit and was keeping my interest in it under my hat for the same reason. I knew discussing anything that even smacked of the paranormal could get me booted out on my ass permanently. But the fact is, while serving at SED, I had asked for the unit's assistance in penetrating places no agents on the ground could ever hope of going. What they supplied was incredible; real-time intelligence of targets they knew nothing about, all gathered in their minds. I was sold.

Once you've lost your virginity it's impossible to get it back. All I could think of was transferring from SED to the Psi Spy Unit. There was nothing in my army career that could ever measure up to it. I wanted to be a part of this so much that I began a relentless campaign to join the program, sounding out my superiors practically on a daily basis. Who wouldn't want to be a psychic spy? It's like asking a boy if he wants to be Batman. To me, the RV Unit was the super-sexiest job that could ever exist, a way into the sanctum sanctorum, the deepest well of military intelligence. I threw everything I had at them—the data I compiled as an interrogator at defector debriefings, my experience as an intel analyst, my work on the Soviet biothreat, my own experiences with the unit tasking them on top-secret missions. I didn't stop.

One night, at around 2 a.m., I received a mysterious call at my home. I knew who it was, but Christine didn't. She handed me the phone, frightened by the raspy voice on the other end. She was trembling.

"Go with the man who's coming to your house," the voice said. "Do what he tells you to do. No questions."

"Got it," I said.

Dial tone.

I knew at that moment my life would never be the same. As the morning sun rose over Fort Huachuca, I officially signed on as the newest member of America's Psi Spy Unit.

Ingo Swann is a New York–based artist and one of the world's most gifted authentic psychics. He was also the man behind the curtain at the RV Unit, the one who pushed all the buttons. Based on protocols originally developed by René Warcollier, a French chemical engineer in the early twentieth century, Swann's genius was discarding the conventional model of RV experimentation to develop a new way of doing things. He had been a research subject at Stanford Research Institute in the 1970s and had escaped from the typical guinea pig role by threatening to resign if his handlers wouldn't acknowledge his ability to break down and understand psychic functioning.

Swann refused to play along with the old-school approach of doing what you're told and keeping your ideas to yourself held over from when the CIA was in charge of the program. He wasn't about to become another burned-out casualty of the system like so many who came before him. His knowledge of psi pioneers such as Warcollier put him a notch above those who were running the show at SRI. Ingo later documented his psychic data gathering system, and remote viewing as a learnable and trainable skill was realized. His blueprint for framing psychic phenomenon into a viable tool is called coordinate remote viewing. Instead of dropping off into a meditative state to produce dreamlike images in the mind, CRV uses a site address, a geographic map coordinate. A remote viewer's quick response to the address is reported in an exact format to cut down on interference from his imagination. It would be like trying to remember where the bank is as opposed to having a map to get you there. It was this breakthrough in psychic intelligence-gathering Swann originated that we use today.

He's the father of our field and is credited with coining the phrase "remote viewing." His model is the bible on how the collective unconscious communicates information to conscious awareness.

Swann's innovation was the claim that the ability to remote view is an innate faculty like language, and like language it must be learned to be effective; it was a milestone. To test out his theory, the army put together a team of trainees with Swann acting as teacher and mentor. Ingo agreed to the program, but insisted that there be no natural psychics like himself in the unit. He wanted army officers, soldiers with no preconceived notions who were about as psychic as rocks and totally open to learning his new technique. He wanted trainable shamans in uniforms. A short time afterwards, the army sent six officers and one civilian to study with him as a prototype psi spy trainee group. I was one of them.

My first meeting with Swann was okay, but a little tense. A prickly man who suffers no fools, and reclusive by design, he's the type who feels as comfy dressed in Bermuda shorts and a straw hat as in a three-piece suit, a master chameleon. He's a hefty bearded combination of Ernest Hemingway and Indiana Jones with a voice like Truman Capote. Referring to him as a "psychic" was a no-no at the unit; he prefers "consciousness researcher." I'd call him King Arthur if that's what he wanted.

Swann and I soon hit it off, and it wasn't long before I become his protégé, not because I was the best remote viewer in the unit, but because I loved it even more than he did. This wasn't pseudoscience to me, or an experiment, or just a new spy tool. I genuinely loved RV and saw the infinite possibilities it had to improve the lives of ordinary people. But used strictly as a military instrument, it had no equal. I saw the supporting evidence with my own eyes, findings verified and replicated over and over again. In one session, Ingo made several reports on the surface, atmosphere, and weather of Jupiter. His statement that the gas giant had planetary rings like Saturn was controversial, but their existence was later confirmed by NASA's Voyager probe.

Other results our team achieved were just as amazing, actually better, beyond anything we anticipated. Under Ingo's guidance, we began producing psychically derived data with incredible consistency and accuracy. As the newly appointed operations and training officer for the unit, I had them apply their remote-viewing skills to the toughest national intelligence problems. These included locating and tracking international terrorists and their hostages, uncovering the Soviet nuclear testing area at Semipalatinsk, hunting down Libyan strongman Muammar Gadhafi before the 1986 bombing of his headquarters, identifying a KGB colonel caught spying in South Africa who'd been smuggling information using a communications device masquerading as a pocket calculator. And though Ingo didn't "see" it coming beforehand, he was there to help celebrate the birth of my second son, Aaron. Things were finally going my way, so I of course mucked it all up.

My interest in the paranormal resurfaced again. It actually never left. Under the guise of "advanced training," I used my position as training and ops officer for the Fort Meade remote-viewing program to secretly task viewers against such off-limits targets as aliens, ancient civilizations on Mars, and UFOs, among many others. The results were startling, never-before-seen images flashing before unprepared minds. Some couldn't handle what they saw; no training in the world could have prepared them for it. Some wound up in hospitals, some talking to themselves. But I continued the research, pushing remote viewing and the men who were willing to go with me to the very edge of the envelope. News leaked out about what I was doing and I was called on the carpet for it, but that was the least of my problems. Soon there might not be a carpet to be pulled out from under us. The unit was in trouble.

As a result of increasing turmoil and turnover in the ranks of top intelligence leadership in the late 1980s, "channelers" and other psychic charlatans were recruited to work with the trained pros of the RV Unit. The so-called witches of remote viewing were turning us into a cheap Vegas lounge act. Worse yet, a host of ugly politicians wanting an inside track about their political and personal futures began using the team like a private psychic hotline. Add to this a deepening regret over my role in the Gulf War and you have my volatile state of mind at the time. Rather than being forced to stand by and watch as everything I believed in collapsed before my eyes and risk the loss of remote-viewing technology, I retired with the rank of major from the U.S. Army.

In 1992, because of my obsession with remote viewing and my wife's insistence that I get a "real job" after I retired, my marriage to Christine dissolved. I had asked her to keep up with me and she couldn't. It was no fault of hers; I can barely keep up with myself most of the time. Remote viewing isn't for the fainthearted, and certainly no easy way to make a living or support a family. As much as it hurt, we were done.

I moved with my sons to New Mexico, where I created a civilian remote-viewing training course and continued working with my company, PSI Tech, pioneering private commercial remote-viewing services. Not long after, we were on the road again like the Beverly Hillbillies, moving to Beverly Hills, California, where I recruited my original army remote-viewing team's best and brightest again to join me. I decided to grow the business after I met Joni Dourif, the ex-wife of actor Brad Dourif. Our stormy relationship began when she became my partner at Psi Tech, developing our training program. My new role as the preeminent teacher of remote viewing took shape and Joni and I moved in together. The training tapes we produced were an instant hit, and with much press ballyhoo the name Major Ed Dames became a household word wherever remote viewing was spoken. Or whispered.

I began teaching to packed houses at venues around the country. The concept that anyone can be taught to become a psychic was very appealing. Meanwhile, PSI Tech clients now included leaders of Fortune 500 corporations, academics in science, medicine, and law, and top individuals from the private sector who agreed to undergo my firm's specialized training. Things were sailing along nicely when disaster hit. Isn't that how it always works?

We had just moved the company to Maui when a break-in took place. All our confidential files and remote-viewing data were stolen. Joni accused me of doing it, and things heated up. Our relationship ended several years later in acrimony and lawsuits surrounding ownership of the company.

As bad as that was, good things kept happening as well. I continued my long-running relationship with Art Bell, the host of the wildly popular *Coast to Coast AM* radio talk show. The topics I discussed defined me to millions of listeners as Dr. Doom, the bringer of bad tidings. Among my many successful predictions: a killer plant pathogen spreading from Africa; the financial meltdown of the U.S. economy; and the "Killshot"—a deadly solar flare set to strike Earth. Art's audience loved every minute of it and I became a regular guest. My appearances were the highest-rated of any celebrity on the program. I guess I became a star.

Hollywood came calling soon after and I was recruited by Tom Cruise's production company to become a consultant on their feature film *Suspect Zero*. I also got my first acting role, playing an FBI profiler, which isn't very far off from what I really do. A profiler enters into the psyche of a criminal to determine who that person is and how they'll act in a given situation. Where the profiler bases his judgment on an analysis of the crime committed, we as remote viewers go straight for direct knowledge. We're in the room when the deed is done, we see what the bad guy sees, feel what he feels, know what he knows. We're watching him.

Coaching Sir Ben Kingsley on what it takes to be a remote viewer was my main job on the set of *Suspect Zero*, and the British actor turned out to be a natural. Who would have thought Gandhi would make such a great psi spy? My showbiz career continued as

I did guest shots on the network television show *In Search Of* and A&E's *Real Premonitions*, as well as a host of others.

Entertainment was fun, but it was work that attracted me the most. I was exploring the world of the paranormal at levels I hadn't since the heyday of the Psi Spy Unit. Living on Maui, I created the private intelligence group Matrix Intelligence Agency, which uses remote viewing to solve the unsolvable, to find what can't be found—missing kids, unsolved crimes, lost treasure, you name it. But our doors are not open to everyone. The mystique of intelligence work is what propels the public's interest in me, but I have limited resources, so I have to be picky about what cases I take on. MIA's primary mission is based on my belief that we will one day be confronted by a nuclear terrorist attack, an attack we will prevent by exposing those planning it.

There it is. A quick thumbnail of the major events in my life, all except for one.

Several years ago, as my father lay ill and dying in some hospital room, I learned that aside from beating me, he had done unspeakable things to my sister, Eva. Things he'll never have to pay for now. It makes me sick just to think about it. Too young to fully understand the nature of this evil at the time, I still remember feeling how wrong it was in my gut. Yet I blocked the truth from my mind anyway, reversing the flow of responsibility that comes with knowing. Eva needed my help and I didn't give it. Like my mother, I was too frightened to do anything, a pretty lame excuse now when I look back on it. But I was just a small boy; that has to count for something. At least that's what I keep telling myself.

I was obsessed throughout my youth with becoming strong, so strong that it would prove to my father I was more of a man than him. But I never took the time to see what he was doing to my sister. I should have been strong for both of us.

I swore the moment I put my father in the ground to make things right somehow, to bring my knowledge and experience to bear by helping those with nowhere else to turn. I dedicated my skills to create a living hell for the monsters who torment the innocent. When a criminal looks over his shoulder, he'll find me there looking back. A world with no secrets means no place to hide, and to a low-life murderer or child molester, that's a world of pain.

As a remote viewer it's my duty to expose the truth no matter the cost, to get to the bottom of things and let the chips fall where they may. How people use what I provide is their business. Knowing the truth and doing something about it are two very different things. I choose to take the risk, to believe what I see and feel. To teach it to others. The pulse of every secret around every dark edge is out there waiting to be found. It begins when you stop being afraid.

It was fear that created the Jersey Devil and helped it flourish for more than two centuries—a fear of the unknown, of the unexplained, an irrational dread of things that go bump in the night. My job is about penetrating the unknown, making damn sure I bump into everything there is, day or night. Denying the truth is no longer an option.

Not on my watch.

# FOR CHRISTINA

I knew nothing about Christina White that early July morning in 2004. Nothing about how she was kidnapped and killed or about her grieving family, or the fact that in over twenty-five years nothing had happened with the case. She was never found. I had no clue her short life would soon connect with mine, as so many others had in the past—children who, like her, simply vanished one day with no rhyme or reason. Kids who just fell off the earth.

All I knew watching the sunrise over the sleeping sands of Wailea was that another night had passed in paradise. The moon was still up, suspended like a great Chinese lantern, the air windswept and fresh. It was that perfect moment when darkness collides with dawn. The world holds its secrets in the morning. All light seems fleeting, creating a sense of certainty well defined but just out of reach. Familiar things

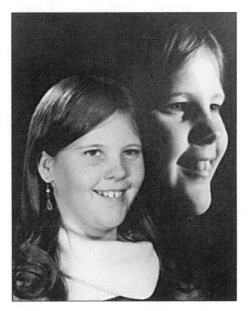

Christina White.

become foreign, a jumble of chance shapes that stir us, urge us to consciousness. Time to wake up.

So I woke up, and did what I do every morning. I had some coffee, ignored the usual phone and email messages that were piling up, then headed out to the beach before the tourists took it over. I free dive, have done ever since I was thirteen. In this sport, you have no air tanks or depth gauges or anything else to keep you safe. You just take a long breath and plunge into the murky unknown, you and freedom and the big deep blue. In the warm waters off the Maui coast lies the true essence of remote viewing—*no think, no thing, no one*—nothing to distract you from entering another world. When I was a young boy, the ocean was a way to escape reality. Now it's a way in.

Diving and remote viewing are very much alike. One opens a door to the secrets of the sea; the other, mysteries of the unconscious. The gateway to both lies at the surface, masked by things you can easily see and understand. For a freediver it's the waves and wind, your fins moving, the second skin of a wet suit if you have one. In remote viewing it's the images of daily life, the routine things we accept without question. A run-down house, a smoke-stack, a rich field of wildflowers, perhaps the face of a young girl you've never met before.

Like freediving, RV involves a structured technique, a set of rigorous protocols designed to get you there and back in one piece. It's a disciplined ability anyone can master, a method of acquiring information that normally has no venue of expression except in rare moments of revelation or dreams. Learn it, and you become extremely aware of everything around you, moving past shadows into a boundless dreamscape of strange and fluid forms. You see as if through a glass darkly the patterns of another dimension distant in time and space. Interpret these patterns correctly and you're in. The matrix is open for business.

That morning in July 2004, I got home around ten after freediving for two hours. I'd hit about thirty meters and figured I'd call it a day. The sea can be a very unforgiving place with no air to breathe. One misstep on a breath-hold ascent and you black out. Quietly and unnoticed, you're dead.

There was a lot more work waiting for me today than usual. I had spent the night before as a guest on Art Bell's radio talk show, which meant tons of extra email. Being on *Coast to Coast AM* attracts all sorts of souls trying to reach me for one reason or another—some personal, some for business, some I really can't talk about. But one particular letter that morning stood out among the rest. It nearly jumped off my screen. A retired cop from Colorado was asking me—imploring me—to help solve the mystery of a missing girl from Washington State. Christina White.

The cop's name was Paul Ramsay, an ex-officer from Eagle Rock who had quit the force after the Kobe Bryant debacle. The special treatment the basketball star received had sickened him, and the ease with which Bryant's high-priced defense team outmaneuvered bumbling prosecutors had pushed him over the edge. He just couldn't stomach all the political crap anymore, and that was something a grizzled old army spy like me could understand.

Ramsay said he'd met Christina's older sister at a local hospital where they both worked after he traded in his badge for a new career as an emergency room tech. The morbid story she told about the abduction shocked him and he'd been itching to do something about it for a long time. When he heard details about my Project Goldeneye on the program the night before, he'd felt compelled to write.

Goldeneye's mission was to find kids who can't be located by traditional means, namely through remote viewing. I named it after the vision I had when I was hit by lighting as a boy, the fish with huge golden eyes that I saw. As a freediver I have always searched for this kind of fish; their eyes reflect everything they see right back to you. Golden eyes never lie.

Ramsay said that to date, ongoing police investigations had uncovered nothing. Not Christina, not one new piece of evidence, nothing. The case remained open on the pretty twelve-year-old who'd left home one chilly spring afternoon and never returned. Worse yet, the animal responsible for taking her was still at large. The very idea that this guy was out walking the streets free as a bird was keeping Ramsay up at night. He wanted me in on this. To him, I was some kind of occult super-detective, a cosmic Columbo. He wanted my team of remote-viewing investigators and me to uncover the truth, to come to the town of Asotin, Washington, where the troubles began. Where he hoped this nightmare would come to an end.

The former cop was stunned when I got him on the phone. I suppose he didn't think I'd call, at least not this fast. His voice was a little higher up on the register than I expected, but he sounded very strong and in control of himself. He thanked me for contacting him, said how much it meant to everyone involved. I asked

him if he had anything on Christina for me. He drew a long
breath before answering.

"I won't waste your time, Major Dames," he said. "All I have is
this short article from a local newspaper."

"Send it along, every little bit helps," I told him.

Again he took a breath, this time followed by a surge of emotion, which seemed out of character for him. "So, we'll be seeing
you in Asotin—I'll make all the arrangements—you won't have
to do a thing."

I hesitated now. He was moving too quick. Pushing too hard.
Desperation is no place to start anything, particularly something
so complicated. It had taken thirty years for this horror to find me;
I might have to give it a little longer.

"Get back to you on that, okay?" I said.

End of conversation.

Ramsay's background material showed up a New York minute
later. It wasn't very much, only a weathered blurb scanned from
the *Lewiston Morning Tribune* dated April 30, 1979. There was
nothing here of any real value to me, simply a statement of fact. A
frightening moment frozen in time forever.

ASOTIN, WA.—A County sheriff's posse has launched
a search for a 12-year-old Asotin girl who disappeared
Saturday night. The missing girl is Christina White, daughter of Betty Eminger. The girl was last reported seen at the
Asotin County Fair.

I got really pissed when I read this. It's that anxious instant
when you look at something already knowing what it is. Though
I couldn't be sure if Christina was alive or dead, the story conjured
a rush of murderous scenarios in my mind. I could see her at
the county fair, the sound of laughter and music everywhere, the
Ferris wheel creaking round and round. She's so happy eating her
kettle corn by the handful, playing with her friends. To her, this

is a place filled with magic, not dread. How could she know she's being followed, hear the overlapping rhythm of the man's footfall just behind her? He's the dark one, the lover of shadows and dense life, the swarming air of children. His victims. He's watching her; I can feel it. Watching and waiting. I imagine Christina lying in the darkness where he took her, where she fell spread out on the floor of some dingy room, face buried in cold wood. Or was it something even worse?

A lengthy web search turned up nothing, not so much as a mention of her name anywhere, as if she never existed, completely forgotten by the world. It took a couple of hours more of this, but I eventually found what I was looking for. A picture, a grainy out-of-focus black-and-white photograph featured on some online sleuthing site with a host of other lost kids. It's Christina, maybe the last picture ever taken of her. A chill ran through me. Some images stay with you, especially those of children who get stolen and hurt. There she was, still carrying some baby fat, smooth skin, long hair, bright eyes beaming with typical adolescent excitement about everything. The photo was at once private and thoroughly public, a singularly iconic image of childhood innocence. The face of purity before evil took a hand.

What the picture captured—what lingered—was a shared intimacy with others now being shared with me. This photo would prove important over the course of any future investigation. It reminded me of what needed to be done here. What *had* to be done. It also made me madder than hell.

Still, I hesitated, but not because it was a kind of case I hadn't worked before. I'd used remote viewing to find missing kids for years, their broken bodies, who did it to them and why. I hesitated because of the pain that such a search could cause families should it prove unsuccessful. As a father, I know having a child disappear is the worst possible torment anyone can go through. When children are abducted they're inevitably killed after being sexually abused by the monsters who took them. That's why

I launched Project Goldeneye in the first place. It was a human monster hunt.

But like any hunter, you must be careful not to become the hunted. There's a power curve on the part of some parents I get involved with that isn't always pleasant to be around—for them or for me. It begins with grief, when the official police investigation has gone cold and they're at their wit's end. Most know their case will fall off the radar, but there isn't much they can do about it. They can only stand by as the press heaps endless attention on them for a worthless week or two while the story grabs ratings. Then when nothing turns up and interest begins to wane, they watch helplessly as their child is kicked to the curb, exiled to the back of some milk carton or a sad footnote on an obscure web page. "We'll get in touch when we have more" is the usual law enforcement refrain.

Parents are freaked-out angry after that. They want justice, but it never comes. It's an act of desperation by the time they call on me. I'm the proverbial last resort. Most are grateful when we step in, but that can change fast. Since you're the final hope, you're the one who takes the full brunt of their rage if you come up empty-handed. You said you'd find their baby and didn't deliver. They begin despising you, a sentiment I completely understand, but one that makes getting the job done even tougher. Ever try helping someone who's trying to bury you?

It's the same with the police. That's why I make it a rule to work only with those who ask for our help. The rest are loath to even mention us; they resent people like me right from the get-go. We're lumped into the same category as some demented B-movie medium living in a tacky trailer on the outskirts of town, the kind that latch on to vulnerable families under the guise of caring, only to revictimize them when their so-called results turn out to be crap. The kinds of phonies who give people like us a bad name. The police rightfully don't want these creeps in their knickers, but they're not always on their game either. Sometimes cops won't even cooperate with each other, let alone with me.

A good illustration is the case of JonBenet Ramsey, the tiny beauty queen found brutally murdered in her own home the day after Christmas. Her mother, Patsy, once lamented in a TV interview that "the truth will prevail," but she certainly didn't get to see it. She passed away waiting for a call that never came. Four separate law enforcement agencies fought over that case and nothing happened. It was classic Keystone Kops as the public's shock over the crime soon began to share equal time with its growing dismay at the inept police investigation. Then here I came, a decorated military officer who'd located hostages and terrorists around the globe, telling them how it was done. If I succeeded, it meant they hadn't done their job right, that remote viewing could accomplish what tough detective work could not. Cops don't take very kindly to that sort of thing. They usually run your butt out of town. Things never got that far since they refused my offer to help.

Too many cases ended this way with Project Goldeneye. There was Leah Freeman, the fifteen-year-old whose body was found in a wooded area outside of Coquille, Oregon. Stephanie Condon, only fourteen when she disappeared while babysitting. Ashley Pond and Miranda Gaddis, the seventh graders whom searchers discovered buried under a concrete slab in the backyard of their killer's ramshackle house. We weren't exactly warmly welcomed on those investigations but volunteered anyway, supplying ground and aerial reconnaissance teams in support of law enforcement and the National Center for Missing and Exploited Children. But that didn't matter. My team still became the focus of public outrage when things didn't work out. The documented success we enjoyed on similar cases in Japan seemed to mean nothing to anybody. It was somehow our fault these heinous crimes went unsolved, our failing that the authorities went out of their way to block us at every turn. When stacks of hate mail addressed to "Hey Asshole" hit my doorstep, I thought it best to end operations on Project Goldeneye permanently.

But my conversation with Paul Ramsay moved me. His desire for a full accounting of what happened to Christina was genuine. I didn't need remote viewing to see that it was coming from the heart. That he was a cop who actually *wanted* to work with us ratcheted up my interest. It was always better that way. When my people rolled out onsite with bundles of equipment, he could explain what we were doing to the local police, maybe even get them to listen to us for a change. With a trained cop aboard we had a very capable search-and-rescue man, someone who knew how to keep people alive when they're busted up, should some-one be injured during an investigation. Most importantly, law enforcement usually has the complete confidence of families, as was the case with Ramsay and Christina's kin. He said they would support us no matter what happened, an enormous weight off my shoulders.

The more I thought about it, the better this all sounded. Normally time is of the essence when I'm asked to help with a miss-ing persons or abduction inquiry; it's all too often a race against the clock. But that was thankfully not an issue here. Because of the strange circumstances surrounding Christina's disappearance and the eagerness of the individuals involved to solve it, I decided to take the case. It was unlikely any progress would be made finding her if I didn't, and all other options had been exhausted. We defi-nitely had our work cut out for us on this one. It was the coldest damn case I'd ever seen.

I logged on to my Matrix Intelligence Agency website. My inves-tigative team had to be brought in, the wheels set in motion for Christina. Ramsay couldn't have picked a better time to get us. We were currently between assignments for various clients, coming off work on approaching catastrophic earth changes and a form of bovine AIDS that could be transmitted to children. We had also recently dropped the bombshell that North Korea would test its first nuclear weapon by the end of the year. The press of course ignored us, but much to the chagrin of my critics and the Korean dictator Kim Jong Il, our prediction was right on the money. The nuke blew several months later, just as we said it would.

Matrix is a private consulting group, a think tank's think tank where I serve as executive director. It's here that clients commission my team for a variety of projects involving remote viewing and where I host all pro bono work.

I generated a search term, "Christina White/now." The term pointed to the target and was for my eyes only. Next were the target reference numbers, two sets of four random numbers my people would use like a road map to lead us to Christina. These numbers *were* Christina. For this case they were *9290/4097*.

Stage I of remote viewing was now in play.

From talking with Paul Ramsay to tasking my team ran about two days. It took that long for them to drop what they were doing in their lives and come work with me for free. The Matrix team is an all-volunteer psychic army.

The payoff came on my computer screen. Sketches on the White case began streaming in from across the country. It didn't take a brain surgeon to interpret the drawings, connect the dots, and there it was—tracts of open land, mountainous vistas strewn with rocks and boulders. But this was no desolate moonscape. The terrain from my unit's sketches all shared a similar theme—a deserted landscape completely overgrown with tall weeds and grass and dense foliage, each area ringed by rolling hills to one side, tree-lined paths shrouded in darkness to the other. And there was water.

The "feeling component" of remote viewing was coming in strong as well, written down in words in the order each viewer perceived them, descriptors like "flowing and cold" and "wet to the touch." More followed. One team member repeated the feeling of something "gritty and earthy" close to the target, the sound of "rhythmic rustling." Another heard a "metallic noise" accompanied by "grinding" and the clamor of rushing liquids. My first impulse was to say this was a place of water where something mechanical was involved, but I stopped myself. Though a real-time picture was emerging of a possible crime scene, the clues by themselves meant nothing. It was like trying to decipher a jigsaw puzzle using only the individual pieces. As the project manager, it was my duty to make sure everything fit. To see the big picture.

Based on my review of the team's sketches, I found that what they'd uncovered about the target wasn't very encouraging. Among the many impressions they'd viewed, the one thing missing was a real person. We didn't have a human here, there was no sense of personal movement, of a life being lived like yours and mine. There were no common everyday emotions. A young girl would be playing with her friends, talking about boys, eating, sleeping—something. What we had was a non-being, an absence of humanity. I was left with only one conclusion.

Christina White was dead.

The phone rang. The noise rattled me and I quickly picked it up. "What took you so long?" I said.

It was Brent Miller, one of my best RV investigators, someone who had worked his way up from a wet-behind-the-ears scrub to a full Matrix member. I didn't recognize his voice at first; it was tortured like the bending of natural law, like a rock or a tree stump trying to speak. Brent was clearly upset.

"This person we want, it's a little girl—yes?"

"Yes," I answered. "Go on."

"She's been missing for a very long time."

"That's right."

An extended silence passed between us before another word was spoken.

"She's gone," Brent whispered.

"I know."

"So what are we going to do about it?"

"Let's bring her home."

More silence. "Yeah. Bring her home."

All I could think after we talked was how the accuracy of remote viewing still knocked me off my feet after all these years. Armed only with numbers, Brent already knew what the target was. I had much the same conversation with other team members that day, keeping the dialogue to a minimum. I would see them soon enough in the town of Asotin, Washington.

Last light drained into the Blue Mountains, turning their tops a soft cold purple. A slight red-orange shaft of sunshine still prevailed as lines of dark clouds lingered overhead. It was almost sundown when I arrived in Asotin.

A storm was coming.

I pulled my rented car up to the motel we'd all agreed to stay in. It wasn't very fancy, but it had a small conference room where we could meet for more session work. I like Asotin. It reminded me of how Paramus was before the developers ruined it. Nestled on the banks of the Snake River, it's a quiet village, a popular last stop for tourists to fill up on gas and beer before heading out to visit Hells Canyon along the Oregon-Idaho border, the kind of classic small town you see in a storybook, with a general store and quaint little post office and gleaming white church with a pointed steeple. The church stood out to me; it seemed uneasy perched along the main road, its perfectly coiffed grounds uncomfortable being so close to hot greasy blacktop. The situation was not an easy fit for the old place; it belonged to another time.

The name Asotin comes from the Native American Nez Perce tribe's language, meaning "place of eel." There was once an abundance of eels here, but now it's all steelhead trout and sturgeon waggling downriver. No more eels. Not many Nez Perce left either. Asotin is also home to bighorn sheep and elk, as well as the Asotin County Fair, complete with a rodeo and rodeo queen, livestock auction, and full dress parade. The fair's mission statement is posted all over town every April to let everyone know exactly what they're in for. It reads, "To provide recognition and inspiration to county youth and youth leaders for encouragement toward greater achievement."

Christina was lost at this county fair.

My room was okay, slightly grimy around the edges, but okay. I made the mistake of opening the refrigerator door and peering inside. Somebody had left some food the cleaning staff obviously missed, and a strange hissing sound was escaping from some half-eaten meat wrapped in an old Ziploc bag. It was a sickening crackly noise, like what a body decomposing might sound like in slow motion, the freeze-dried sizzle of molecules breaking down, solid matter resolving to free vapor. There was a single hair in the bag too, a thin brown hair that if I touched it would mean sharing an intimacy with some faceless fry cook's or waiter's life. I'm not all that picky as a rule; no one who's served in the military has that luxury. Still, I couldn't help think but what strange passage this hair made to get into my fridge, from one person to another across stretches of space-time and places and diseases and unclean foods. You could remote view the entire universe in that hair, but I was tired and all it did was make me want to puke.

It was after seven and the bloated clouds outside had turned progressively darker. They were almost black now, and the temperature had dropped. I could feel the approaching storm, a feeling similar to what happens when you encounter static electricity, like when you take the clothes out of a dryer and separate the socks from the shirts. There would be lightning: the hair on my body stood on end and my fingers were tingling. I was right; a second or two later it struck, a razor-sharp bolt out of the sky branching out many times like the limbs of a tree, generating a rumbling thunderclap reverberating down the canyons outside. A soft raindrop ping hit the window ledge in countable taps at first, then banged everywhere, quickly filling up the motel's plastic drains and downspouts. A passing housekeeper told me what an unusual storm this was considering the season, but I'm used to *unusual*.

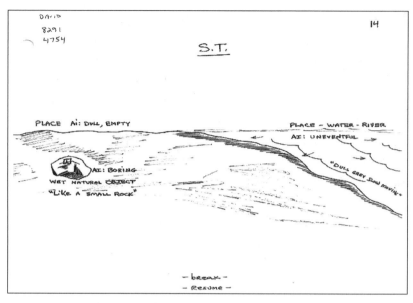

A remote-viewing sketch of a body of water that later matched up to a photograph of the Snake River.

A photo of the actual Snake River site located by remote viewing.

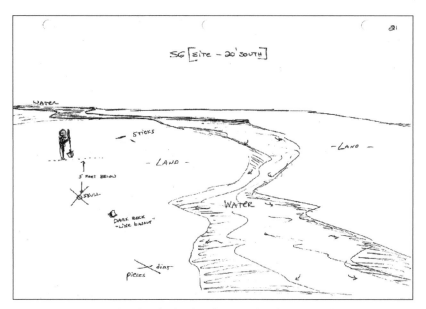

A remote-viewing sketch of a body of water that later matched up to a photograph of the Snake River.

A photo of the actual Snake River site located by remote viewing.

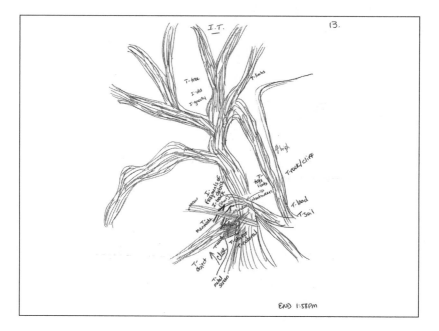

A remote-viewing sketch depicting tributaries of the Colorado River flowing into the Snake River. This sketch was one of the first in the Christina White investigation and shows from a high vantage point the general area where her remains were interred. The image later matched up to satellite a topography map of the area.

A satellite topography map of the general area where Christina White's remains were believed to be. The map clearly shows the arms of the Colorado as seen by the Matrix Intelligence Agency team.

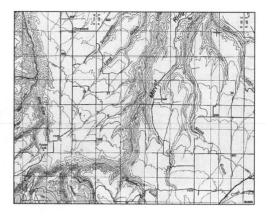

The white church, the site I remote viewed and where it was believed at first that Christina White was killed.

I composed my face and walked into the conference room. They were all waiting for me, my investigators, seated in armchairs around a large oak table in the center of the room. There was Brent Miller, a software engineer from Las Vegas with an IQ of about 180; Alex DiChiara from Sausalito, a former Greco-Roman wrestler into commercial real estate management; and Joe Bush, a master gunsmith and father who part-times as a real bounty hunter. Sitting next to Joe was Dawn Stoltz, from Virginia Beach, where she owns a massage therapy business.

To look at them, you'd never know each was living a double life—one the world and their families saw, and the other they secretly shared with me. They were Bruce Wayne and Batman, Clark Kent and Superman. They did what every ordinary person does: had regular workaday jobs, wives and husbands and children they cared about. They saw movies and had Sunday picnics in the park. But when there was a case, when the Bat Signal flashed on a cloud calling them to the rescue, they came with no questions asked. I have walked into their workplaces, stood silently in a corner waiting for them to notice me, then offered little else than a nod or a wink and they immediately understood why I was there. It was a call to arms.

Each member of my team had taken last-minute red-eyes to get to Asotin; they wouldn't miss this mission for the world. And they were all here as volunteers paying their own way. This is how it works at MIA. The expense is ours wherever the job takes us. My people had worked their tails off to get here, taking 120 hours of training with me, spending six months on probation until I could be sure their remote-viewing work was top-drawer, always consistent and dependable. I never take in any professional psychics. They can usually locate a target but couldn't tell you exactly where it is to save their lives. It would be like sending a Delta Force squad into a jungle hotspot blindfolded. They need to get the target site down cold or it's a bloody massacre. I don't like massacres.

We only had forty-eight hours in Asotin; that was all that time and money would allow. Two days to find out what happened to Christina. As we were getting started, Paul Ramsay strolled into the room bigger than life. He had to be six feet five at least, a good 250 pounds, a real bruiser. Paul shook *your* hand, not the other way around. He'd be joining us as an adjunct team member, an observer and liaison with local authorities should the need arise. And we'd be able to bounce our hypotheses off him, see if the crime theories we came up with were feasible. He could also alert us to what laws we were breaking along the way. There's no escaping that in this line of work. Being crafty comes with the territory.

We'd already determined in private remote-viewing sessions that this was the right state and region where Christina White vanished. The next step was narrowing down the target to specific geographic or man-made landmarks that would ultimately lead us to her remains. It could be a stadium or a roller coaster or Mount Rushmore, we just didn't know. We needed to identify

Matrix Intelligence Agency investigators (left to right) Alex DiChiara, Brent Miller, and Dawn Stoltz, and former police officer Paul Ramsay.

a landmark and get an anchor hold on it. Even working blind, if the team followed the protocols correctly, we should be led directly to her.

The team knew the routine. They picked up their pens, wrote their name, date, and time, and then launched immediately into Stage I. The search term I used for this session was "Christina White/nearest significant feature." The target reference numbers were the same: *6213/5798*. They had two seconds.

The ideograms came one after another in machine-gun blasts. Flashing, fleeting. Riveting. What started off as a series of squiqqly and straight marks later took on the form of recognizable shapes. The first contained sloping lines spiraling from the tops of the pages to the bottom. Brent said they were cables or wires because they rolled from a great height going down. Dawn had the same thing. Definitely wires of some sort, according to them.

I told them to try again. To define it more. They repeated the process, their eyes dropping down, pens to paper, moving in automatic response. Joe's eyes lit up with that eureka look in them, convinced that what we were seeing were just ordinary telephone lines. Alex leaned over and added his usual cynical punch line. "No way it's a phone line," he said, smiling. "We're positively looking at a ski lift here. I'd stake Brent's life on it."

Brent didn't laugh and neither did I. The consensus was a ski lift. Where they got the idea that this was a democracy I don't know. Agreeing on things doesn't count for much here. I told them all to stop what they were doing. There was a serious speed bump they were hitting, a stumbling block that could muck up the session. It's called analytical overlay, or AOL, data that results when a viewer attempts to interpret what they're seeing by themselves, imagining the target out of step with the structure we're using. This kind of data is almost always wrong. Analyzing what you see on your own clogs up the perception equipment. A mystical indigestion sets in, halting the flow of information, rendering you inert to any new data. The forces behind imagination are powerful. They have to be dumped right away for this thing of ours to work.

"No boulders in the river, guys," I warned them. "Declare your AOLs and chuck them. Just draw what you see."

More sketches. A clifflike structure with wire mesh appeared. They all had it in one form or another and it was clear enough to make out, the crisscrossing lines, the feeling of tensile strength. I would have said it was the kind of mesh they use to hold back rain-soaked hillsides, but I wouldn't have said it to them. No AOLs, thank you.

On top of the cliff was an old house, no mistaking it, even the worst artist in the world can render a drawing of a house. Still not enough. None of the drawings were enough. They could be anything—the cliff just a cliff anywhere, the old house an old house in any town. Uncovering the exact location of a target requires

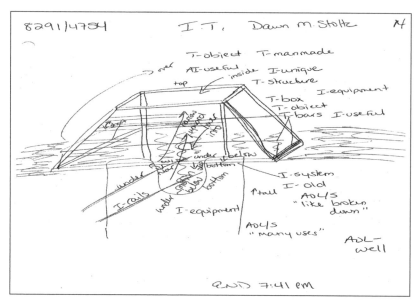

An RV sketch of a house and wire fence near a cliff as seen by the MIA team.

A photo of the actual house and wire fence near a cliff as seen by the MIA team.

navigating through complex issues like homogeneous terrain, buildings and lakes and cars and holes in the ground that all look the same. We have to cut to a specific building, what city or town it's in, a specific car, and so on. We must pinpoint unique geography and significant features. And we have to take our time doing this, can't ram it through. This is the roughest part of remote viewing. There can be no stupid mistakes, no rush to judgment. We need to narrow everything down to find a unique feature that exists nowhere else. Something special.

Then it happened.

The team produced a strange corkscrewlike object in their sketches. I told them to redo it, draw it a few more times. Again and again the feature appeared. They were all connecting to the same image, as if they were one person—no variances, no shades of gray. I told them to describe what they sensed. The goal here was aesthetic impact, to put them in the picture as an FBI profiler would. To find out how the site made them feel as if they were physically there. I gave them fifteen seconds max for this.

"Metal or heavy plastic," Dawn said. "It's shiny and reflective. I'm sure of it."

Brent raised his head and looked at me. "It's something going around and around, the sound of wind moving through it. Maybe a vacuum hose?"

Alex didn't think so. "No. It's a lot bigger and nastier," he said. "I'm not sure if it's pouring or sucking things in. Wait a minute—" He began sketching the movement he meant, using arrowheads to illustrate the direction the object was taking.

"What are we looking at?" I asked.

No one answered. The sound of the rain falling outside and the low rumble of thunder was all there was. I turned to Paul Ramsay. He shrugged and said nothing. His expression told me he was just glad to be here. Glad *we* were here.

"Water. Running water and concrete holding it back," Dawn said. "I can feel it."

"Is it the Snake River?" I asked her.

"No. Not the river. Something man-made."

Alex smiled again. "And it's cold," he said.

"She's buried near water," Brent concluded.

I shut my eyes and leaned back in my chair. It was time to call it a day. I halted the session because the team was trying to wrap things up, to reach a conclusion with the information they'd collected. That's a huge no-no. This is what the mind does when trying to solve an unknown. It proclaims with certainty that the problem must be this or that, or something else. Not in remote viewing. Thinking is forbidden. What you see is what you get. Just the facts.

I instructed everyone to get some sleep. They were going to need it. The aftereffects of a remote-viewing session can be like a hallucinogenic hangover, leaving you fried and on edge. Everything becomes more intense afterwards. A door closing can sound like a steel bank vault, a few birds chirping like a flock of thousands shrieking in the forest. Concentrating that much force on nearly imperceptible visions leaves you stumbling and spent, "bouncing off the walls," as we old psi spy veterans used to call it. Normally after an hour or so you're good as new, but there have been those who didn't quite make the trip home with all their luggage. Knowing exactly when to quit is a very important component of remote viewing. The session was over. We'd head out bright and early tomorrow to see what we could find in the "real world."

The next morning was fabulous, with no more rain. It looked like summer again in Asotin, the warm sun baking the rocky, grassy slopes so prevalent here. If I didn't know any better, I'd have sworn I was back home in the high desert of California where I grew up. Where I *had* to grow up.

We took two cars, Paul on point with me. What was still unknown was how far apart the features we had viewed back at the motel were. This was our first time scouting the area, so they could be within a few yards of each other or hundreds of miles apart. We drove speculatively past several nearby towns to see if we could spot anything familiar, to see if we were at least in the right neighborhood. The surrounding communities all looked much the same, sparsely populated, with well-maintained houses and white picket fences and garage doors. There were lots of families and pets and kids, lots of kids. The mellow machinery of small-town life worked like a charm here, but strip away the façade and who knew what lay beneath. In the case of Asotin, it was a killer for sure.

We kept going, from the end of one village to another. Some in the team wanted to turn back. They wanted to blink and find themselves at the hotel surrounded by familiar things, not seated in a cramped rental car on some wild-goose chase. But we continue to even remoter areas, the air outside growing still and thick as we moved, as if existing under a spell. I could hear a small dog barking in the distance.

This went on for too long, but after searching across state lines for what seemed like years, we finally located the first feature. There was the clifflike structure covered in wire mesh that we had sketched—*exactly* as we had sketched it. There was a graded hillside with steel webbing being used to hold muddy ground back from the highway. Construction crews were still working it, adding more wire to the slipping hillsides. The discovery electrified the team. It didn't matter whether you believed in remote viewing or not. There it was. A tangible excitement swept through us, an energizing mental current like a glowing chord passing from one person to another. It was the thrill of first contact, as landfall must have felt to Columbus. And this was just the beginning.

I felt Dawn grip me near the elbow, not so much in a gesture of surprise but one of physical support. I turned to her, and she had the pallor of someone about to pass out, a half-creamy white with just a hint of purple. She batted her eyelashes a few times and then focused in Brent's direction. So did I. He was pointing to a bluff directly above us. There was something there that I didn't know what to make of at first. It needed a more careful explanation than I could provide at the moment. How was it possible, this thing right where it should be, as if inserted there on purpose?

It was the mysterious house Brent had drawn, sitting like some grand brooding conscience along the brow of a craggy bluff. We looked at one another, as if to remind each other of the nature and being of real things. This house was the real thing, right down to lines of the roof, the tall grass around it, and the clouds floating above. It was perfect.

"You're not gonna believe this, guys," Joe said, his husky voice landing like an anvil. "Look over there—"

We did a one-eighty, expecting something, but getting more than we expected. I felt like that occasional hospital patient who gets to leave with good news after a serious illness. You know the type, shaking the doctor's hand, everyone's hands, laughing hysterically at everything. We had hit the mother lode, the jackpot only other people win. A remote-viewing *trifecta*. To nail one target is difficult enough, but to get three?

There, across the river, were the cables Joe had sketched earlier, the same cables we had thought were connected to a ski lift. Not so. They belonged to a power tower, steely gray high tension electrical lines angling across the wild Snake River. It was a pretty good call considering Joe had never been here. Considering none of us had ever been here.

Except for me.

The tower looked exactly like the one I saw in my mind after lightning landed me on my back when I was a boy. I had thought it into being in the shallowest sort of illusion and now there it was, as real as our mission to find a little girl. The same dark tower. I kept this to myself, but inside a volcano was about to blow, with that feeling *you can do no wrong*. My life had come full circle just when I needed it to.

Despite all we'd accomplished on the road today, we were still not entirely convinced this was the right place. That's a good thing. In the heat of battle, people sometimes see what they want to see. Accepting these objects at face value would have been a dumb blunder, the kind of mistake amateurs make. We needed to find that last unique feature, the one that confirmed we were getting closer to Christina, the feature that would close the book on this session and any lingering doubts anyone might have.

I walked to the lead car to check the Google satellite and topographic maps I made against local ones Paul had brought us. They were the usual assortment of gas-station-style road maps for tourists, ones that couldn't always be relied upon to give you an accurate read. But if I had my bearings right, I should be able to locate the final link by comparing them. Suddenly, it hit me.

"Everyone back in the cars," I told them. "Now."

We drove a short distance over a winding road. Paul was trying to control himself, but his foot was like a brick on the accelerator. I knew as an ex-cop he was trained in high-speed driving, but this was like riding a bullet taking wide turns as it twists through the air. Luckily, Dawn rolled down her car window and shouted, "Over there!"

It was totally unnecessary; there was no need for her to shout anything. Everyone could see what she was charged up about. We all were. It was the *corkscrew*, the one that Brent had drawn so exquisitely before. Our caravan screeched to the side of the road overlooking a flat stretch of land and we exited the cars and hurried toward it, practically tripping over one another, as if whoever got there first would win a prize. The only prize worth winning here was being right. As it turned out, we could all chalk one up for the team. The corkscrew was the pump from a wastewater treatment plant where flow from the city's sewers is reclaimed before returning to the Snake River. We'd done it. What should belong to the world of dreams was again made real, something you could touch with your hands. I loved this water pump. It told me we were on the right trail. A trail we weren't alone on anymore.

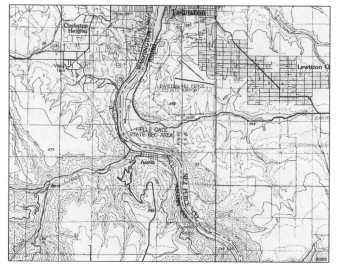

A TopoZone map of the Snake River with the wastewater
treatment site described by the MIA remote viewers, narrowing down the location of Christina White's remains.

I explain a point to *Lewiston Morning Tribune* reporter Kerri Sandaine.

A woman was approaching us, neatly dressed, with bright curly red hair, attractive. Paul immediately moved in her direction, cutting her off before she could get any closer. They talked in hushed tones for a minute or two, then Paul returned. The look on his face told me this couldn't be good.

"Her name is Kerri Sandaine," he said. "A reporter from the *Lewiston Morning Tribune*."

My mind raced. "How in the hell did they find out we were here so fast? We just got in last night."

"Small town," Joe said. "Probably folks heard about us over lemonade at the corner drugstore."

"Yeah. I'm surprised the mayor and school board aren't here too," Alex added.

I shot him a look. Not funny.

"She wants to talk to you," Paul explained. "And she isn't the type who takes no for an answer. I can get rid of her if you want me to."

I thought it over fast and waved her on. There was little else I could do. We exchanged pleasantries. Then it was all business.

"You're looking for Christina White, aren't you, Major Dames?" she asked me.

"Uh-huh," I answered.

My answer made her bear down even harder on me. I guess she expected more than an "uh-huh." She had a nice smile.

"Will you be using the same remote-viewing techniques you did at the Defense Intelligence Agency's Psi Spy Unit back in the 1980s?"

"You did your homework," I said.

"Yeah. Some of us hicks even have computers."

I could hear chuckles rising behind me, but that was fine. The break in the tension was good for us, a relief considering the horror we were trying to uncover. Kerri stepped in closer, not at all shy. I liked her.

"You know," she said, "people in these parts generally don't believe in all this psychic stuff. Think you can prove them wrong?"

"We're not psychics," I told her. "Everyone has a right to be skeptical until we deliver something, that's only fair. We're confident we will."

Paul Ramsay interjected now, his large frame gently nudging Kerri away from me. "If anyone can find Christina, it's Major Ed Dames," he said firmly. "Count on it."

I took Kerri by the arm out of earshot of my team. There was a small favor I wanted from her and I didn't want anyone else to know I was asking for it. I wanted her to keep our arrival in town on the QT the best she could. Having a crowd of uninformed bystanders wouldn't help anything, could even make things dangerous. Kerri nodded and said she'd try, as long as I cut her a deal. The deal was to keep her up to date on our movements in Asotin and give her an exclusive on the story. No problem there. She already had that.

"But don't blame me if half the town already knows," she added. "You seem to attract a lot of attention."

"I bet you do too," I said.

She smiled and walked off, looking over her shoulder at me. Then another nice smile. We might have found an ally here. That she found me irresistible was good too. Joking.

The day was almost over and we needed to get back to the motel for another RV session, the one designed to pinpoint where Christina's body was. No joke there. Twenty-four hours left.


The wind kicked up strong at sunrise, rustling loudly through the trees a few yards off from the motel. The whooshing sound it made startled me and I stopped to listen. I had to listen. It's a funny thing about wind, how it strips away your confidence and belief in things, how it works its fingers into your muscles and bones to the very marrow, forcing you to feel what can't be seen, revealing the hidden weakness of everything around you. And this wind was like no other I'd ever heard before, more like a voice, the voice of a young girl urging me to silence. Be still.

There was a sense of renewed hope among the team this day. Leaning on our previous successes, we'd use the water treatment plant as a checkpoint to conduct the final batch of RV sessions. With the station as our guide, I generated the final search term: "Christina White/present location/nearest recognizable feature."

Now we could target the most recognizable objects nearest the actual remains. Since the team had located the previously identified features, we should be gradually reducing the area in which we had to search. They began surfing the matrix for clues, for patterns to move us to the next step. I watched and waited. The room was so quiet you could hear a pin drop on the moon.

In this final stage of remote viewing I was hoping against hope that at least one of my investigators would bilocate—that is, lock onto the target with such intimacy and immediacy that they, or some inner part of them, would transcend the barriers of time and space, become present both *here* and *there* at the same time. I needed them to soar into the air and look down like a bird from a thousand feet up. To draw me the curves of the meandering Snake River, the imposing black transmission towers, the highway, the mysterious old house, and the water treatment plant. I needed them to see the world as an eagle would. If they couldn't, and everything wasn't where it should be, then it was back to the drawing board. We'd have to say, *Maybe Christina's not here.* Maybe she was moved somewhere else after she was murdered. And I knew she was murdered, though no evidence to that effect had come up. I just knew.

The team's sketches were nearly identical again. And there was more. They'd identified the nearest features to the corkscrew—a small pile of junk containing metal objects strewn helter-skelter on top of them, and a cubical structure with a described use for storage. The last item was a filthy old mattress. It boggled the mind to think about that one. The horror continued.

Dawn detected a flash of wispy colors, insectlike, a swarm of butterflies maybe. She moved through the scene, viewing the discarded rear axle of an abandoned car and some crushed beer cans among a pile of rocks. Don't ask me how a massage therapist who'd never worked on a car before even knew what a rear axle looked like, but it didn't matter. All I cared about was the map we were making to our missing girl.

We raced to the cars and hit the road back to the water treatment plant. It was sizzling hot outside and we were dressed in shorts and T-shirts with hats and backpacks, like we were on some freaked-out psychic safari. Up ahead were some thick woods containing mazes of paths overgrown with vegetation bracketing the pumping facility—the exact same surroundings we viewed in the first session. The rugged nature of the area forced us to continue on foot; there was just no other way to get up there. There's never a horse around when you need one.

Paul reminded me that we were on county land and could be arrested for it. Great. He also informed me that Christina's mother was aware of the search and was praying for us. She hoped we'd find her daughter and bring the family closure. My skin crawled when I heard that. I hate that word "closure," especially when one is dealing with an insurmountable tragedy. A family loses a child, the bad guy is caught convicted and executed, and then some bonehead pipes up with, "At least the family has closure." From what I've seen in my life, there's never any closure. Old wounds have a way of staying open.

Now that we'd narrowed down the remains to a few hundred square feet, we headed into the dense foliage. It had been so long since Christina was reported missing that there was no telling how difficult these last key features would be to identify. The sheer amount of plant life in the area would make it hard to spot the specific arrangement of objects we were looking for. We could be several feet from her remains and never know it. The search had us scouring through sharp brambles and weeds about 350 feet north of the sewer plant in thick brush near the Snake River. It was rough ground even for the heartiest of hikers, which most of my team are not. But we kept going anyway. This was what we came here for.

About an hour passed and still nothing. But things changed fast after that. Joe thought he'd sniffed out something, a horrible smell coming from a shadowy corner over by some trees. It had been too long for any odor to rise from a fully decomposed body, but no clue could be overlooked. On further examination, the smell turned out to be nothing more than a dead rabbit. It was completely stiff and dead, eyes perfectly round like glazed marbles and its head small and shrunken. I imagine it wept when it died, a high-toned vertebrate cry like the melancholy prayer of a violin. Despite what most people think, I believe animals know when they're about to die. All living things do.

Dawn shouted to us. She'd found something too. I ran to her. There among a mass of butterflies and crushed beer cans was a tilted oblique box and mattress—the same objects she remote viewed this morning. It was no surprise to me. Vegetation comes and goes, it's ephemeral, but solid things stay the same. They can rust and rot, but they remain basically the same. I told Dawn to go round up the rest of the unit. This was it.

If we were dealing with a crime scene we could reconstruct it here. Abductors typically choose such concealed sites because they want the child's body decayed by the time the remains are found. In these types of cases the bodies are never buried; the killers are too clever for that and are usually familiar with the terrain. They know when and how to cover their tracks, allowing nature to take its course and lend them a hand. It's how they get away with it.

Out of nowhere Kerri Sandaine showed up again. She was alone this time, no other reporters, just as she promised.

"You find anything?" she asked.

"We think we have a crime scene," I said, standing near the ratty box springs and old file cabinet. "We think the child's remains are here."

The obscene mattress grossed her out, but Kerri offered to help with it anyway. We lifted it up first—there's no telling how deep the remains were if they were interred here. The chances were slim, but we were hoping they were close enough to the surface to be easily recovered. Paul removed the heavy crisscrossed pieces of metal covering the mattress. A collective sigh went up when nothing was found underneath, just dirt and rocks, no remains. It appeared that the phenomenal results we had reached in blind RV sessions had led us to Christina, but recovery was proving easier said than done.

We began digging, everyone pitching in with shovels and pick-axes, raking leaves, clearing dirt away from the site. Paul eagerly took on most of the heavy lifting, which was fine by us. One trench after another, we dug and dug. Still nothing. It was very frustrating. I wasn't so sure anymore if the remains were under these objects or several feet away.

Dawn dropped her shovel and recoiled from one of the pits. Her face was white as a sheet. She'd found a small tattered jacket, the kind a little girl might wear, a purple-and-pink jacket with a manufacturer's label from the 1970s on it—the same decade when Christina disappeared. Then an even more shocking discovery was made. A *bone* was uncovered within several feet of the ragged old coat. I touched it, lifting it from the ground and holding it up for everyone to see. Kerri and Paul stared wide-eyed at me. They knew as well as I that I'd be in a world of trouble if this bone turned out to be evidence and I'd tampered with it. They advised me to immediately call the proper authorities to cover my butt. But I didn't. I made a command decision instead. We'd bring the objects to a lab for analysis, I told them. No coroner, no cops. Paul thought it over and reluctantly agreed. The bone didn't really look all that human anyway, and the jacket seemed too small for a twelve-year-old. And since I'd already put my hands on them, what harm could there be in keeping all of it under our control? There was a lab in town at the regional medical center, so we'd give the items to them and see what they came up with. It was all we had, not very much. But it was something.

More bad news followed. Kerri said the Snake River, which ran just feet away from our search area, had a long history of flooding out. Periods of heavy rainfall and the spring runoff of mountain snowpack had caused Asotin and several other counties to be declared states of emergency many times in the past. A flash flood struck the creek once, killing two young children, both members of the same family. The seasonal flooding consistently affected growth, some years washing away vast amounts of dry land, depositing fresh new sediment in others. With this cycle going on for who knew how long, there was no telling exactly how deep or misplaced Christina's remains could be. Even worse, they might have just washed downstream on a lazy summer afternoon much like today.

As discouraging as all this was, my team was still willing to continue. They were ready to do whatever it took. But as always, I was telling God my plans and I could just about hear him laugh. He had something else in mind for us today.

A chopper suddenly appeared overhead throbbing like a giant appliance. The ABC NEWS markings on its side were visible even from where we stood. And if that weren't bad enough, Kerri told me that news stories about us were bound to start coming out in the local media now. We'd be the best-unkept secret in town. She must have remote viewed the situation, because more unwanted attention showed up before she finished her sentence. A contingent from the Army Corps of Engineers arrived and ordered us to cease all digging operations. We were on government land, they said, so we should pack up and leave or face the judge at the county seat. We might even spend a night behind bars if we didn't play our cards right. The looks on their faces told me they meant business. They'd actually do it. If the corps had been this serious about Hurricane Katrina, New Orleans never would have submerged, families wouldn't have suffered on rooftops, and the Superdome wouldn't have devolved into chaos. It seemed to me they were going a bit over the top for a simple case of trespassing. It made me wonder—*Is there more going on here?*

The impact of their stop order reverberated like a plane crash—not a crash landing, mind you, but a full-blown crash. You can prepare for a crash landing; there's at least some time before it happens to consider your options. A crash is too sudden; there aren't any what-ifs involved. Not a damn thing you can do about it.

Despite local support and the assistance from people in power Paul'd spoken with, the corps's order proved a fatal blow to our recovery operation. The digging came to an end. We loaded up our gear and headed for the cars. No words were exchanged between any of us. What was there to say?

I remained behind for a few minutes more listening to the wind howl down the canyon. No matter how right it is, no matter how much it screams its case or argues its rights to this site, the truth cannot be denied. Christina was here, I was sure of that. As sure as I was that this wasn't over.

Not by a long shot.


The drive back to town wasn't a total loss. It was so beautiful here, the wide vistas of natural basalt, the mountains and water and blue sky. I found myself thinking about the eels that once ruled the waterways. Would they ever return? There was some talk about folks wanting to reintroduce them to the Snake River, but so far it was just talk. Life in Asotin is about tradition and people here cared about nature, but not in a tree-hugging sort of way. These people were farmers, and how can you not care about nature if you're a farmer? I crossed my fingers for the eels.

I turned to Dawn as we headed down the road back to the motel. She looked at me and began to laugh. She told me one of the locals threatened her with bodily harm if we told the world what a perfect place Asotin is. Seems they didn't want any of our violent city ways infiltrating their Eden. She didn't have the heart to tell them they were too late. It was violence that brought us here.

The country road we were on began sloping downhill and curving to the left on a steep grade. When we came around the turn I saw that sparkling white church again with its high steeple rising over the road near the end of town. But it looked different somehow in the low light, spooky and haunted, one of those places I used to whistle past when I was a boy to get my courage up. A kid's worst nightmare.

The good-byes at the motel were quick. There was no need to make this more painful than it was—not because we were parting company, but because we hadn't found what we came for, except for the bone and jacket, which didn't get my hopes up. The ground truth of finding Christina's remains had eluded us. It wasn't anyone's fault; she'd been missing for far too long. We would have had to dig up the whole bloody river valley to find her, and there just wasn't enough time. It's always like this. When you're sleep-deprived and crazed, the race feels like it's never going to end, the back-and-forth of it moves at a hyper pace. But when it's finally over and you haven't accomplished anything, you realize things are ultimately tied to the cycles of the moon and sun. Time isn't on your side. There just wasn't enough time for us.

I put on my best supportive smile and waved as the team headed out to the airport for their flights. Paul took off in his car too; he'd join me the next day once more to tie up some loose ends in town. It began raining again.

The storm this night was more humid than the last one. It was so wet even the walls of my room were perspiring. Outside was a downpour, the streets empty, people scurrying in and out of the motel trying to stay dry. I looked at myself in a small mirror propped up on the night table under a lamp. Then I thought, *What am I doing?* No matter what happened out in the field, I had never before abandoned my role as commander. I could smoke, get drunk, hang out until the sun comes up, but I had never tolerated failure, on the part of my team nor on myself. So why was I doing it now?

We might not have been able to find Christina, but what about her abductor? When we discovered that the cause of death was murder, we could have turned our attention to the event itself, found out the nature of the killing and who the perpetrator had been. It's not hard in remote viewing to determine if they were a family member or someone else the victim knew. Their current location and daily routine is also accessible. I could have tasked my people with that job, but uncovering hard evidence had to come first. Without it, nothing else would follow. Putting the cart before the horse doesn't cut it with the cops. I couldn't very well claim I had the killer when I didn't yet have the victim. Anyone who's ever watched *CSI* knows there's no crime without any proof—no murder without a body. That's how it works in the real world, and in that regard our primary mission had failed.

The secondary target still remained, harder and more challenging even than the first, a dynamic encounter far removed from anything in the real world. Searching for Christina's remains involved something tangible, something you could hold in your hand. I needed to hunt down an idea, a thought, a pattern of energy stored within the matrix. I decide to break my own rules. I was going to remote view what actually happened to Christina. And I was going to do it alone.

The storm was in full swing now, the huge weeping willows out front casting swaying shadows on the wall in my room. The wind was fast and urgent, conveying a sense of primal fear and warning. Spread out across my bed were the case notes and maps I'd made, a pen and a blank sheet of paper—the mind traveler's tools to navigate the unconscious. There was this feeling in me that I couldn't shake before I got on with it, something about that white church that stuck in my craw and wouldn't let go. I'd start with a site. The search term I used this time was "Christina White/death/location."

I wanted to know what went down and where it was that Christina spent her last minutes on earth. This was what I told myself, my mind, to reconstruct an event from the past as if I were really there when it happened. To stretch the boundaries of perception not only beyond those of simple geography, but across the fabric of space-time itself. I put pen to paper and it came—

Detergent.

I sketched boxes of liquid soaps and sprays and air fresheners. I could smell the institutional odor of cleaning materials hanging in the air. The chemical stink of it filled my nostrils until I felt like gagging. I drew a steeple. It was a church—my white church? I had something, but I sensed it wasn't the *same* church. Gone was the striking whitewashed paint job that first caught my attention. This church was made of stone. It was Gothic, castlelike, a brooding redbrick structure. I was somewhere else, but there was no doubt that this was a church. There were long billowing curtains drawn near the rectory, and a closet nearby. I was inside looking in the direction of the smell, all the while being many blocks away from it, my physical body sitting on an unmade bed in some cheap motel.

It was dark inside the church, only a naked bulb hanging from the ceiling flashing on and off intermittently on its own. I saw some benches, an old pair of running shoes, and a kid's bike that had been taken apart piece by piece lying there on the floor. From what I could tell, it was a girl's bicycle. And it was red. Blood red.

I saw a little girl, about ten. She was *not* Christina, I could make that much out, but mostly her face was a fast blur. She entered and then left quickly, her feet barely touching the floor, ghostlike. There was music, lively music, a band with drums and a guitar and saxophone—a cabaret show of sorts. The sound of it rushed into the air, looping deeply inward to the arching ceiling above me then swiftly returning to earth. But why was there music in this church?

I heard a frightening sound after that, a shuffling noise, as if someone were dragging something heavy across the floor coming toward the door. My first instinct was to take cover, but this had happened so long ago that I stifled the urge to conceal myself. *I'm not really here*; I had to remember that. I kept repeating, "Don't move. Don't move."

The dragging halted just outside my view. It was quiet for a second before the thumping of someone rummaging around inside the closet began. Impressions surged into my brain: fingers—sweaty palms—a man—faded blue jeans.

The man fell to his knees and began cleaning in frenzied obsessive strokes with a filthy rag. The burled wood on the floor was a disturbing taunt to him, the more he washed the more the swirls in the grain grew with every conceivable variation of hue and texture. But no matter how hard he scrubbed he couldn't get rid of the elusive stain. The light overhead was blinding him, a knife of white dawn with edges hacked out by notches of darkness. Lit-up surfaces broke into clumps and patches and broke again and shrank and vanished and strange tints of red spread like ink around him. He stopped and turned. He looked at me. He looked up from the grimy floor and leisurely glanced over at me. *He knows I'm here.*

Jesus. He had no eyes. Only a grotesque pair of hollow black sockets.

"You have my eyes," he hissed.

He reached for me. I jumped back, taking the lamp and mirror along with me. They slammed with such force to the floor that they broke instantly. The sound of it snapped me back. I'd lost the moment; I was in the motel again, in my room. I looked down, my reflection staring back at me from the broken shards on the hardwood. Millions of Ed Dames faces in every piece of shattered glass, each becoming a distinct mirror while still a part of the whole, the way a single drop of seawater holds the same elements of the entire ocean. A priest once told me that God created nature in such a way so that one pattern would fit all. If you could recognize yourself in that pattern, then you would know who you are. *Is this who I am?* Jagged and ruined, a little wild-eyed, but not too crazy.

Yeah. That's me.

The storm finally let up, the hard rain more of a light drizzle now. I looked out the window. There was a bird on the window-sill outside in the night and I wanted to believe it saw me too. Imagine what an impossible world it would witness, me standing there straight as a board bathed in sweat. I was so flat I could be a perch for it to rest on. But I was back to normal, and that was good enough. And now I know why birds sing after a bad storm. They understand the passing of suddenness. A return to what they know. I moved toward it to touch it, but the motion of my hand frightened the bird away. And then it was gone. The terrible images were gone too, together with the demon I conjured up from hell. I was exhausted, but it was all clear to me now. I knew what had happened to Christina.

My flight back to Maui was in a couple of hours, but I need to make two stops first. One was to Asotin's sheriff, Wayne Weber, the other to Betty Wilks, Christina's mom. There were some questions only she could answer, dark places only she could shine a light on. Betty had always been in the back of my mind; the sensibilities of the mother are always important. I never gloss over that. We had resurrected a very difficult time in her life, and it was only right now that I was paying my respects. Perhaps with her help I wouldn't have to walk away leaving nothing behind. Paul would meet me there, it had all been arranged. My date with the cops I went to alone.

At the station, Sheriff Wayne Weber was very polite as he escorted me into his office—a professional courtesy given that Paul was once part of the law enforcement family. Still, with all the hoopla surrounding my team and me being in Asotin,

I wouldn't blame him if he were a little upset, which of course he was.

"Why did I have to find out from the local paper that you were in my jurisdiction?" he asked. "You should've contacted me first. My door's always open to anyone who wants to help."

"Even remote viewers?" I asked.

"Especially them," he said, smiling. "Whatever that is."

Chief Weber apparently had some history with Christina. He was just a deputy when she vanished, and he had long wanted to collar the guy who did it. According to him, she wasn't the only young lady to meet with foul play in the area. There was a series of five serial killings from the late 1970s and early 1980s in nearby Lewiston, Idaho. Kristen David, a twenty-two-year-old University of Idaho student who disappeared in 1982, was believed to have been murdered by the same person who killed Jacqueline Miller, eighteen, and a thirty-five-year-old man named Steven Pearsall. They were all at or near the vicinity of the Lewiston Civic Theater the very same night they vanished. Eight days after her disappearance, Kristen's headless torso and legs were found along the Snake River in Clarkston. Her head and arms were found the next day. My heart jumped when I learned this. The poor kid was found along the Snake River. Exactly where we believed Christina was. Where I *knew* she was.

Authorities in Lewiston had a longtime suspect in mind, but never arrested or publicly identified the individual, Weber explained. They couldn't because the evidence that pointed to him was circumstantial. I hesitated to inform the good sheriff that evidence gathered in remote viewing is regarded by most as about as circumstantial as things get—if they bother to call it evidence at all.

"Do you know what I do, sir?" I asked him.

"Sort of," Weber says. "Can't say I understand it."

I grinned. "Not many people do."

"My sister-in-law reads tarot cards like nobody's business, though," he added, his face brightening. "She could tell you what you had for breakfast this morning. Amazing how she knows things. She knows *everything.*"

I settled back in my chair and leveled a stare at him, the kind that means, *Let's get down to business.* He seemed relieved by that, not the type of man who enjoys small talk. The feeling was mutual.

"Information has come to light regarding our visit here," I told him.

"That wouldn't have anything to do with the bone and jacket you found, would it?"

I froze. *He knows.* I didn't know how he found out, but it was more than likely Kerri Sandaine who rolled over. It was understandable. Withholding evidence is no laughing matter. I was waiting for Weber to slap the cuffs on me.

"In case you want to know, I've seen the lab results," he said.

"Yes," I answered nervously. "I'd like that very much."

"The bone was inconclusive. Probably came from an old coyote or mule deer. Hikers out by the river find ones just like 'em all the time washed up along the banks."

I nodded, still waiting for the steel bracelets.

"Like stiff sponges, bones," Weber continued. "Absorb just about anything. The cotton from that jacket will too. Both of them contaminated with foreign DNA, I suspect. But I'll look into it some more. Bet you're disappointed."

I nodded again. Wiped the sweat from my face. I'm thinking, *He isn't going to lock me up over this! I'm not going to jail today.* I was beginning to like this small-town sheriff.

"Got anything else?" he asked.

A loaded question. I wasn't sure what to say or how to say it. But I couldn't let this dead-end here. I had a cop's ear, and he was cooperating with me. It was now or never.

"What would you say if I told you that Christina was murdered in that white church at the end of town?"

Weber looked at me, expressionless. His eyes were piercing, but his face was deadpan. "I'd say that's impossible," he answered finally.

"And why is that?"

"Been shut up for years after it got damaged in a flood. Locked up tighter than a drum. A jewel thief couldn't get in there if he tried."

I believed him. The church I remote viewed was made of stone, a fact I couldn't escape. It couldn't have been this one. I'd driven from one end of Asotin to the other and never saw a church made of stone anywhere. Then it hit me. If I was wrong about this, then I was wrong about the killer too—and the little girl I saw, that phantom little girl. But how could I be so far off the mark? It had never happened to me before.

Sheriff Weber poked more holes in my theory. "We have a suspect you know, in Christina's case," he said. "The last one to see her alive."

"How do you know that?"

"Because he told us."

Weber said the suspect was a man who lived several blocks down from the Whites' home. Weber wouldn't give his name because he'd since left town, and like the police in Lewiston, there wasn't enough to charge him with. They had to cut him loose. Weber stared at me for a moment, then reached into his drawer for something. It was a plain envelope with a letter inside. He tossed it onto the desktop and motioned for me to open it. I hesitated.

"Not to worry. We dusted for prints already," he said.

I read the letter. It was anonymous, no date, no signature, neatly printed on the kind of plain white paper you could buy in any stationery store anywhere. The person who wrote it claimed to know who took Christina, someone very close to her. I connected with the word "her" instantly.

"This suspect of yours, did he by chance have a daughter?" I asked.

"As a matter of fact he did," Weber said, raising an eyebrow. "They used to play together. We think Christina stopped by to see her after the county fair, when she was feeling sick. The daughter would be about thirty now."

I looked at Weber. He looked at me. Bingo.

"Are you saying it was the killer's daughter that wrote this letter?" he said.

I nodded.

I could barely contain my excitement at this point. Weber had just confirmed what I remote viewed back at the hotel. Confirmed and accepted. I started breathing faster.

"But it's not enough," Weber added.

"Not enough?"

"For a warrant. There isn't a judge in the county who'll get behind what you say, not unless you have something more solid to back it up. Do you?"

I folded my arms, looked at him. "There has to be a way."

Weber dashed off a note to himself. He shook his head. "Damn interesting, this remote viewing. Yes, sir. Makes my sister-in-law's tarot stuff look like child's play."

My instinct was to grab him and the both of us track down the suspect and drag him in ourselves. In a perfect world Weber would probably have gone for it—he had that look in his eyes, the look of someone who doesn't always follow the letter of the law. I know that look. But it was not to be.

Weber wouldn't budge without a warrant, and I had no idea how long that would take to get. My time in Asotin was over, so I thought fast. Maybe there was still some way to salvage the work we'd put in here. If we could find Christina, if there was a body or identifiable remains, then we'd be in business.

I asked the chief if he could somehow arrange for Paul and me to return to the dig site, if through his good offices we could get permission from the Corps of Engineers to try one more time. He shook his head and grinned that grin again.

"Not a snowball's chance in hell you'll get to snoop around up there anymore," he told me. "The Feds are real touchy about that particular stretch of land out by the water treatment plant. The Army Chemical and Biological Defense Command stockpiles twelve percent of the nation's chemical munitions upriver from here."

He went on to say that the chemical depot's deadly stash consisted of rockets, land mines, and bombs containing nerve agents like GB and VX, not to mention containers loaded with the blister agent HD, more commonly known as mustard gas.

I got it. If any of their charming inventory found its way into the water supply or was unearthed by a couple of curious remote viewers, there'd be hell to pay. Talk about your conspiracy theories.

"No way I'm stepping into this one," Weber said. "I like my job as sheriff."

"I understand. I can't ask you to do any more than you have. You've been great."

The chief rose from his chair and thanked me for helping to renew interest in Christina's disappearance. He asked that I forward any new tips directly to him in the future. I didn't know what to say. None of this made any sense. There wouldn't be any new tips coming, not now, not ever. We both knew who the killer was, but the law said hands off. It really sucked.

Weber extended his hand to me. "Nice talking to you, Major," he said. "Wait till I tell my sister-in-law I met Major Ed Dames. She'll flip."

"Don't bother," I said. "The way you say she reads tarot cards, she already knows."


I heard the screen door slam behind me when Paul and I entered Betty's house. The place was modest, just off the main road, walking distance to the center of town. There was nothing special about it, real Americana at its best. I felt her and her husband's eyes burning a hole in me as we walked in. It had been a long time since I notified the next of kin of a death. My legs were rubbery and about to give way under me.

Betty was open and appreciative to us, but the way she reacted when I told her that her daughter was gone was typical. It's how most families react when informed about the loss of a loved one—a little anger, a little falling apart, a desire to pretend nothing happened. There's always still some ray of hope that they may yet be found alive. We sat together in the living room and she offered Paul and me tea, managing a slight smile as we talked. Betty didn't know it, but her next words could have been the most important she'd ever spoken.

"I was just wondering," I asked. "Did Christina have a bike? A red bike?"

She looked surprised, her eyes widening. "Why yes," she said. "She did. Bought it for Christmas. How'd you know it was red? She loved that bike so much."

A tear welled up in her eye as she explained how Christina was riding that bike the day she left, how she loved to think she was silent and wispy when she was on it, barely stirring the air as she went.

"Did the police ever find it?"

"No. Or my baby."

I took a time out now to allow Betty to compose herself. Much as I hate doing this, I had more questions to ask. Hard questions.

"Did you know that man, the man who lived—"

Betty stopped me now, her face flushed with anger. "The man who killed my little girl," she said. "It was Lance Voss. He was our neighbor—our neighbor."

At last, the suspect had a name.

There was flesh on his cruel bones. *Lance Voss.* I asked Betty if there was anything unusual about him, something out of the ordinary that stuck out in her mind.

"Yes, he's a very clean man, always washing this and scrubbing that. One time his hands were as red as beets when I saw him. Oh yes, he was a musician too. Played the saxophone." Betty sighed and took a long sip of her tea. "Would anyone like a cookie?"

Paul and I declined the cookie. "One more thing," I said. "Did he ever play at a church here in town?"

Again, Betty took a few moments to think it over. "No, never. But he played at the Civic Theater in Lewiston. It used to be a Methodist church. Does that help?"

I nearly passed out when she said that. I had the suspect, the little girl, and now the church. Everything I remote viewed was on the mark. Voss was the man I saw, he had to be. It all added up. But one question remained.

"Do you happen to know if the Civic Theater is made out of stone?"

"Why yes, as a matter of fact it is," Betty said. "What a strange question. Why do you ask?"

I drew a breath before answering her. Paul noticed me do it, but pretended not to.

"No reason in particular," I said.

Betty shifted nervously in her chair. "Doesn't matter. It won't bring my baby back, will it? Nothing will now."

I could only watch as this broken woman cradled her head in her hands and wept. How could I tell her what I knew? Even the police couldn't bring Voss in. He was a suspect, not a criminal in the eyes of the law. What I remote viewed wouldn't change that. There was nothing more I could say. Death is a hungry ocean where the slightest disturbance attracts the nibbling of tormented beings. Why hurt this broken woman any more than I had? Best to leave things just as they were.

I explained I had to be going and offered Betty my deepest apologies for not bringing her daughter home. She thanked me, told me I'd done more to put her mind at ease than anyone else had over the years, then proceeded to give me a big hug. It's not easy to break the heart of an old soldier, but she managed somehow. Time to be going.

Paul crossed the room to say good-bye. He lowered his huge arm on my shoulder and offered that knowing look cops get when they sense you're not being completely honest with them, when you're holding back, handing them a load of crap.

"Is there something you're not telling me, Ed?" he said.

"Not a good question to ask a retired spy," I answered.

The big SOB nearly snapped one of my fingers as we shook hands. "Maybe some other time," he said, still smiling.

"Yeah. Count on it."

I was almost out the door when Paul handed me the morning paper. He told me to have a look at the lead story by Kerri Sandaine. We made page one.

ASOTIN, WA.—Ed Dames and his psychic Cohorts have left town after several days of working on the 25-year-old disappearance of Christina White. He and his team of "remote viewers" came up empty-handed. They did not find the girl's remains or her 10-speed bike.

I didn't want to, yet I laughed anyway. I'm pretty sure my people wouldn't like being called "Cohorts," but at least they got my name right. Actually, Kerri got it all right as far as she knew. Sheriff Weber and I knew better.

Outside, a hot summer breeze fluttered across Betty's sparse lawn. I stopped to listen, to breathe in the clean air of Asotin. For some reason, I reached into my wallet for the picture of Christina I'd carried with me since this all began. It wasn't just her life the bastard took who did this to her; it was everything she was and could have been, a lost childhood that in some ways reminded me of my own. Only I was still here, still in the dance. Still thinking about her. Thinking about my little sister Eva. I wanted to let go of the photograph, allow the wind to carry it off, but I slipped it back into my wallet. This was where it would stay.

For Christina.


With information provided by Major Ed Dames and his Matrix Intelligence team, the suspect in Christina White's disappearance was linked to the murders of Kristen David and Jacqueline Miller. Lewiston police lieutenant Alan Johnson confirms that Lance Voss, in the context of interviews conducted with him regarding the Civic Theater slayings, remains a "prominent person of interest" in both cases. Voss has reportedly taken up residence in Raleigh, North Carolina, where state authorities, as well as Lieutenant Johnson, continue to monitor his whereabouts.

Christina White's case remains open.

# THERE BE WITCHES HERE

January 29, 1989. 17:45 hours, Romeo Time

Blood.

It was in the air.

There was no mistaking the smell of it, sickly sweet, acrid and coppery with a hint of rust and salt. A unique thing with a unique smell, strong and out of place like an orange in an apple orchard. You grow accustomed to it working in a field hospital. In the heat of battle, the stink is obscene.

I could feel it on me too, caked up in rotting blotches. A chalky mix of fear and torture around my eyes and lips. The bloody crust that builds up after a merciless beating, pooling in the corners of your mouth.

More smells. A sheep and goat stench, matted dank wool. The odor of spoiled milk swirling in days-old coffee. And I smelled gasoline burning, singeing the inside of my nose.

I was remote viewing a life-and-death situation for the Psi Spy Unit, breaking down the barriers of yesterday and today by being in two places at once. The place I was in now was a darkened office at the Defense Intelligence Analysis Center (DIAC) in Washington, D.C., headquartered at Bolling Air Force Base. The other place was what I was psychically trying to find.

Earlier RV sessions had revealed a rural village somewhere in eastern Lebanon's Bekaa Valley. The Bekaa, a fertile region that once provided grain to the provinces as part of the Roman Empire, now existed as a perilous no-man's-land overrun by bands of marauding terrorists and opium growers. It was here somewhere that the Shiite killers also known as Hezbollah were holding Lieutenant Colonel William Higgins. It was Higgins's lifeblood I was remote viewing.

Yanked from his vehicle while driving the coastal highway between the cities of Tyre and Naqoura in southern Lebanon more than a year earlier, Colonel Higgins had been serving as a senior military observer attached to the United Nations at the time he was captured. He was returning from a meeting with a local leader of the Amal movement, a rival Shiite group fighting an ongoing battle with Hezbollah for ultimate control of Beirut. Hezbollah, after holding Higgins for more than a year, had communicated to us their intent to kill him under the guise of retaliation for Israeli attacks on their strongholds. It was a lie. They'd murder an American just for the sake of murdering an American, Israel or no Israel. What was more of a lie was that Hezbollah had Higgins at all. We knew for a fact that he'd been turned over to an ally of theirs, an even more extreme group called the Organization of the Oppressed on Earth. They were the same charming people who brutally hijacked a TWA airliner in 1985, releasing most of the 152 non-American passengers and then murdering U.S. Navy diver Robert Stethem in cold blood. Stethem was beaten to a pulp, shot once in the temple, and his body dumped like a pile of trash on the tarmac of Beirut International Airport. These Oppressed Earth people were now threatening to kill Higgins. It was our mission to locate the colonel before they could harm him, to pinpoint his exact position so a rescue mission could be mounted in the hope of saving him.

As always, the Psi Spy Unit worked alone; no other intelligence agencies were involved, no high-tech gadgets like satellites or drone reconnaissance planes were used, nor devices that would pick up data from a transmitter he might be carrying. We would find him from more than three thousand miles away with our own special tools—our minds, pens, and blank sheets of paper.

The Defense Intelligence Analysis Center's office was a perfect spot from which to remote view. Windowless, with a décor made up of plain cork bulletin boards covered in endless bureaucratic notes, it presented no outside distractions whatsoever. More of a mausoleum than a military installation, it was an ideal setup for us. My senses were on edge for this mission and I didn't need anything sidetracking me. Saving a fellow soldier's life was why we were here. He'd do the same for me if the roles were reversed. We take care of our own.

As the RV session rolled on into the night, more physically terrifying intelligence came in. I could feel what Higgins was feeling at this moment, as if inhabiting his body. There was no doubt in my mind that my wrists ached from the ropes binding him. They burned when I tried to move, the rough thread that was cutting into Higgins's skin was seemingly cutting into mine as well. It was the agony of festering wounds opened by incessant whipping and beatings. They were torturing him.

I was hungry and scared—*he* was hungry and scared—but at least the unbearable pain had stopped. There could only be one explanation for this: the colonel's tormentors had taken a break to give him time to suffer alone. They wanted him to feel what they had done before laying into him again, the sting of the lash on his skin, the wretched bite of broken bones. They wanted him to understand what fragile creatures we are when surrounded by a world of hostile facts. The facts of William Higgins's life had been boiled down to only one now. Despair. I sensed it in him; despair over missed loved ones, the warmth of a wife's intimacy, the laughter of his children. Despair in the belief that he would never share any of it with them again.

What was missing in this session was a visual lock. If I could sense nearly everything Higgins was going through, then I should be able to see what he was seeing as well. Images in remote viewing are never photographic; they're blurred and indistinct, grainy and out of focus like a photograph of something moving. I could see none of this, only pitch black. I concluded that Colonel Higgins must be blindfolded, his immediate surroundings shielded from him in darkness. This was bad news for us. We needed some sort of landmark to anchor his exact position. It could be anything—the angle of the sun through a window, a sofa or chair, the color of chipped paint on a wall. Without a familiar marker to go on, saving Higgins could prove extremely difficult, if not impossible

Paul Smith shifted his chair closer to me. Paul was a colleague of mine, one of six who made up the Psi Spy Unit. He'd be acting as monitor on this session, a sort of psychic manager interfacing between the viewer and the outside world. It's the monitor who finds opportunities to go deeper by collecting data a viewer working alone inevitably misses.

Earlier in the week it was I who played monitor to Paul as he remote viewed the step-by-step action from the time Higgins was kidnapped through his journey into the Bekaa Valley. It was Paul's duty to help me pin down Higgins's whereabouts—not where he was yesterday, not this morning, but right now. We were running out of time.

"Try a movement exercise," Paul said. "Go a hundred yards to the left."

I heard his words and in my hyperconscious state I also heard the buzz of the fluorescent lights above him, an ant crawling across my desk, and a man wiping his hands at the other end of the building. At this stage of remote viewing everything seems larger and louder than life, and I can actually move anywhere in relation to the target. I could take my focus off Higgins and shift it an inch, a mile, or a hundred yards as Paul asked.

"Draw what you see," he said now.

I slid my pen across the paper to move me away from Higgins. The sound it made was like a knife slicing through sandpaper. Paul inched closer.

"Tell me what you see."

"A building, a white building," I answered. "A man dressed in a khaki shirt holding a gun. There's a child with a ball, but I'm not sure if it's a boy or a girl."

"What else?"

"Goats, lots of goats. Wait, wait a minute."

An image popped into my mind that didn't jibe with the rest of the picture. I wanted to be sure before I told Paul what it was. I had to get it right.

"I see a small plane landing, and I smell smoke."

"A plane?" Paul asked. "With the goats?"

"Yes. And smoke."

"Okay. Go a hundred yards above the plane."

I trained my mind's eye above the target and looked down.

"Draw what you see," Paul said.

Without thinking, I began to sketch buildings and a long narrow road, a small river.

"There are rocks jutting out from a hillside—no, not rocks—they're too smooth and regular to be rocks. They're more like columns, pillars."

We looked at each other. The pieces were coming together. I wouldn't normally come to a conclusion at this point; it's too fast, too early in the process. But there was no time to question what I saw, no time to analyze every bit of data. We had to move now. A man's life hung in the balance.

I determined that Higgins was being held in a small village. The lives of the people here were simple: goat farmers, kids playing with simple toys. The man with the gun inspired mistrust in them. He wasn't from around here, didn't belong in this village with his big-city ideas and corrupt political energies. I could feel they wanted him and his people gone, but were too afraid of what might happen if they ordered them off their land. They were terrified of them.

The gunman and his crew had erected a makeshift airstrip near the river to fly in more like him. The smoke I picked up was from one of their small planes landing close by. As to the pillars I saw, I would have staked my commission they were the columns of a Roman ruin, pockmarked and spotted with fungus and moss, the names and dates chiseled across them barely legible, yet I was sure they were in Latin. There was a deathly silence here that had held its ground for centuries, a defiant silence like the one that soldiers maintain before they go into a desperate battle. It didn't matter if it was today or a thousand years ago, this was what a fighter did to prepare for what awaited him. It's what a Roman soldier would have done.

Paul wasted no time checking my analysis against the operational maps and detailed satellite imagery taken of the area. They were nearly one and the same, like Xerox copies. They clearly showed a village in the valley some twenty miles outside the town of Zahlah where the ruins of the ancient Roman city Riyaq lie. The ruins were the key. This was no coincidence, no chance finding. We had our target.

We had found Higgins.

Paul and I nearly fell out of our chairs, but there was no time to celebrate. We had to forward our intelligence to Dr. Jack Vorona and get word to the commandos waiting in the field to launch the rescue mission. Vorona, a former nuclear physicist and high-ranking Pentagon scientist, served as the chief of DIA's Scientific and Technical Intelligence Directorate. He was in charge of overseeing the funding and tasking of our unit. He was also the go-to guy with the final word on what intelligence made it up the food chain to the Joint Chiefs and secretary of defense. While I had no doubt that Vorona would pass our critical information upstairs, I was really worried that the man he had chosen to lead the Psi Spy Unit would throw a wrench into it. He'd done it before.

Fern Gauvin was a retired army intelligence officer who ran covert operatives in Europe before joining up with the civilian defense establishment and the RV Unit. He had more experience here than anyone else, having worked both as a viewer and a monitor, but to me Gauvin was a nine-to-five suit more concerned about career advancement than a soldier's sense of mission and duty. As branch chief he was technically our leader, but when it came to the day-to-day operations, everyone knew I was the man in charge. I was the ranking active military officer before either Vorona or Gauvin came aboard, and the unit's only "waterwalker." That meant I was one of the untouchables, an officer who shot up the ranks with top ratings, got the sexiest, most sought-after assignments, and was on track to make general. Gauvin couldn't lay a hand on me officially, but he could still make my life very miserable. The bastard was like an itch you can't scratch.

The whole staff was aware that there was no love lost between Gauvin and me. We had worked together in the past, but since he transferred into the unit the animosity we had for each other had grown by leaps and bounds. Being administrative chief wasn't good enough for him anymore; he also wanted full operational control. He wanted my job and figured success with our search for Colonel Higgins would be the perfect vehicle to get it. It would also establish credibility for the natural psychics he had brought with him to the unit—a group nobody except him even wanted near the program—the "witches," as I called them.

Ever since the Psi Spy Unit had moved from the army's Intelligence and Security Command to the DIA, those of us who came before had held the firm belief that the only dependable means of gathering data psychically was through coordinate remote viewing. This was the technique of using actual map coordinates to find targets, directions to shoot for in our minds. It's what Ingo Swann had pioneered and taught us. But for Fern Gauvin and Dale Graff, a researcher who like Gauvin had attached himself to the unit after DIA took over, the best way to remote view was through more traditional and "acceptable" paranormal means. To them, that translated into channelers, trance mediums, and tarot card readers—a parade of Halloween charlatans. Gauvin and Graff had recruited a bona fide coven of witches to work alongside our highly trained and disciplined corps of soldiers. In one bold stroke, we were reduced from a legitimate scientific team who got the job done to a home for meaningless researchers and the politically challenged.

Because of this, many of our remote-viewing projects went to waste, hidden away for being too controversial. If what we uncovered could embarrass them in front of their superiors in any way, they'd immediately shelve it. We were way too hot to handle. Unlike Gauvin, Graff had always been polite and professorial to me, but I knew him for what he was, a man whose grasp exceeded his reach—a "civilian puke," as many veteran officers put it, officers who like me couldn't care less about politics and careerism. All we cared about was the mission. Always the mission.

It was Gauvin who initially brought the Higgins orders to me. I had been working an important project for the Drug Enforcement Agency zeroing in on Colombian cartel cocaine storage facilities when he tossed the file on my desk. His instructions were to "shotgun it to the top of the charts." This meant Higgins had the highest priority for the unit, and that no resources were to be spared finding him. How long Gauvin had sat on the orders was unclear, but I knew they'd been gone over more than once by others before they got to me. The original orders weren't to find Higgins; those would come later. First we were to determine if he was alive.

Gauvin circled me like a fly hovering above a single rotten raisin before giving me the orders. He was looking over my shoulder too, hoping to get a peek at what I was working on. Trying to weasel his way into my head.

"What's your guess, Ed?" he asked. "Is Higgins dead?"

I hesitated to answer, but Gauvin had a bad temper and was a large man, with hands and forearms like Popeye powering a vise grip developed over years of horseback riding. Usually horses were the only things he talked about, but not today. I couldn't be that lucky.

"I don't make guesses, Fern," I said. "I'll let your witches handle that."

Gauvin's face went beet red. "You mean Angela Dellafiore and Robin Dalgren, don't you, Ed?" he said, biting his lip.

"That's right, Fern."

We were both aware I knew their names, but he wanted to hear me say it, to bow to his authority. Not a chance.

"Who are you going to use on this job?" he asked now.

"Not sure yet, Fern. Maybe after I get a chance to look over the orders I should have gotten yesterday."

I knew the moment I saw the orders that Paul Smith and Mel Riley would be with me on this, but I wasn't about to tell Gauvin so he could screw it up. Smith and Reilly were the best remote viewers in the unit and this was one mission we couldn't mess around with. We were going to save a comrade, and that made talking to Fern Gauvin a liability.

The second he stormed out of my office I got Paul and Mel on the phone as well as Sergeant Lyn Buchanan and told them to report in. We barely slept that night poring over maps and satellite photos of southern Lebanon and the Bekaa Valley that had come in the packet with our orders. Sleep wasn't something I was getting much of anyway lately. My wife, Christine, and I were going at it on a daily basis over my freelance obsession with remote viewing what she called "the occult." I'd vanish into my study to look in on UFOs, life on other planets, and the like, solving age-old mysteries I'd only read about as a boy. It was as if someone had given me a time machine for Christmas with a telescope attached that could see anything. Sometimes I'd leave in the morning for my office and wouldn't return for days. She was right, of course, about my neglecting our family, but it was something I had to do, a challenge I had to meet. Our sons were the only glue holding our marriage together at this point, and it was my fault. I wanted Christine to keep up, to go where I was going with this, but she couldn't. I was wrong to ask.

Along with the satellite images in Higgins's dossier was a detailed intelligence report that tracked him up until his disappearance. He was in a station wagon behind two other UN observers when they noticed that his car was no longer behind them. By the time they doubled back to find him, Higgins was gone. According to the CIA and Israel's crack spy service Mossad, Higgins was kept only a few months by Hezbollah, probably at the home of Sheik Abdul Karim Obeid. The Mossad had kidnapped Obeid earlier, and many held them responsible for the same being done to Higgins. It was all insane, par for the course considering the realities of life in the Middle East. It was FUBAR to us—Fucked Up Beyond All Recognition.

The grabbing of Higgins sent shock waves through the American public and press and an unprecedented rescue effort was put into place. But those efforts were on hold as the terrorists moved the colonel every chance they got, shuttling him from house to house, from southern Lebanon to northern Lebanon and back again. The closest the CIA or Mossad could come to his position was in the vast Bekaa Valley, like looking for the proverbial needle in the haystack. Clearly it wasn't enough to go on. The commando unit assigned to the rescue mission was going to need better intel than that to locate Higgins. That's where we came in.

The long night I spent at home going over every bit of information finally ended. It was morning, and on my way out the door I glanced over at my sons, still sleeping in their beds. I couldn't help myself from thinking about Higgins's kids, waiting and hoping to see if their father would come home. Would they ever sleep peacefully again? I swore then and there that no one would interfere with this mission. No one.

We worked through the entire night remote viewing Higgins. The mood was somber, each of us understanding that this was a last-ditch effort and every second counted. Paul Smith wasn't used to this kind of intense pressure in the unit. He was a huge fellow, with a relaxed anything-goes kind of attitude. Nothing ever got to him, not events, not the work or people—a very different animal from me. Paul's peaceful demeanor made him an excellent viewer, enabling him to cut through bull directly to the target and lock in with an accuracy and consistency that even I found uncanny. It was a pleasure working with him. Tonight I was his monitor and he the remote viewer; I asked the questions, he gave the answers.

"What are you picking up?" I said to him.

"I'm not sure, but it feels like motion."

I noticed that Paul kept fidgeting in his chair as he spoke. He didn't seem conscious of it, but his agitation was obvious to me. "Why are you doing that?" I asked.

"Doing what?"

"There, you see? You did it again."

"Did what—*what*?"

"Rocking in your seat."

Paul looked down at his feet. "Holy shit, you're right. I am doing it."

"Is that what you're feeling, a rocking motion?"

"Yeah, but it's not even. The feeling is erratic, a bumpy ride."

"Anything else?"

"I'm getting odors of some sort. Something sweet, like perfume. *Bad* perfume."

"What do you feel around you?"

"Smoothness. Smooth and cool, maybe glass."

This went on for hours, nonstop. No dinner, no breaks, only time to hit the head and then back to work again. At the end, Paul was spot on as usual. After careful analysis of the data, it was obvious to both of us what he'd found.

"Higgins is sitting in the back of their car, bound, gagged, and blindfolded," I explained. "His face is pressed against the glass of a rolled-up window. The bad perfume you smelled isn't perfume at all. It's—"

"Chloroform," Paul interrupted.

"Yes. The gutless shits used it to overpower him."

"Makes sense. No way they'd go toe-to-toe with a marine lieutenant colonel."

"Not while he's awake," I added.

The marathon session was finally over. As we closed up shop for the night we were comforted in the knowledge that we'd accomplished something, that we were closer to solving this case. We knew Higgins was alive, that he was being tortured, and that the CIA intelligence reports placing him in the Bekaa Valley were right. We compiled our findings in a report and sent one copy to Fern Gauvin and the other draft to Jack Vorona at the Defense Intelligence Analysis Center. It was his job to tell us what to do next.

I couldn't sleep again that night. Waiting for Vorona to check in was killing me. I wanted to tell them all to go to hell and forward what we had directly to those handling the rescue mission. They would relay our intelligence to the commandos in the field and Higgins would be home with his family in time for breakfast. But I didn't. All our work would be tossed in the garbage if it weren't passed up the chain of command correctly, and only Vorona could make that happen. Only he had the authority. All I could do was wait. There was a meeting scheduled for us tomorrow. Just wait. Higgins would also have to wait. Bad luck for him.

I had to think of something to break my focus on this mission or I'd go crazy. Food always works for me.

Being a vegetarian, the very idea of German cuisine gets my stomach churning, but the Oktoberfest at Bolling Air Force Base was the highlight of my assignment whenever I was there. Located on the eastern side of the Potomac River with an incredible view of our Capitol, the base hosts an annual fête that features a hot dog eating contest, a log toss, and an arm-wrestling competition. But it was the way some of the normally straitlaced officials talked with their mouths full of schnitzel and sauerbraten that got me. It should have been the subject of an investigation. After washing down massive meals with thick chunks of German chocolate cake, it was time for a free game of bowling provided by the nearby Potomac Lanes Bowling Center—one of the many perks we got in the spy biz.

It was here on the sixth floor of the DIAC complex that Jack Vorona had his office. Though the Pentagon was officially his headquarters, DIAC was built in 1987 to consolidate Defense Intelligence Agency activities in Washington, where it houses the majority of employees and agents from the National Defense Intelligence College and the Defense Intelligence Operations Coordination Center. Like the air force, DIAC has its own game—and it isn't bowling. The huge facility enjoys a unique heating system. Classified documents kept here aren't only shredded; they're burned to a crisp. DIAC was heated by around-the-clock frying of top-secret papers, a bonfire of endless reams of confidential reports going up in smoke.

What fun.

. . .

Vorona hadn't arrived yet for our morning meeting—something about a call he had to take. He would be late, but he'd be here. Paul and Mel were with me, as was Lyn Buchanan. They had arrived earlier and were all excited to tell me something the second I walked in. But it didn't matter; a moment later I found out for myself anyway. In strolled Fern Gauvin and Angela Dellafiore. The bitch and his witch.

Angela wasn't what you'd call attractive, but she did have a certain air of mystery around her, an Italian charisma that seemed to scream "*piacere mio*"—my pleasure—as her final word on everything. With her jet-black hair and background as a top-drawer civilian Latin America analyst, it's no wonder she so easily hypnotized Gauvin and anyone else unlucky enough to enter her sphere of influence. This despite the fact that she went into trances, conjuring up helpful entities with names like "Maurice" and "George" to possess her body and provide data. It had all seemed like a joke in the beginning, but she and her ilk were taking over the program because of Gauvin. As much as I'd hoped that those at the higher echelons of the program would come to their senses and dump her, it never happened. Internecine rivalries, rampant incompetence, and operational failures contributed to the unit's slow decline. Gauvin and his broomstick pals were running us into the ground.

"Just what in the hell do you think you're doing, Fern?" I said. "This meeting is for viewers, no mediums allowed."

"I'm in charge, Angela is a member of the unit, and you're out of line, Major," he said.

"I'm in charge of operations," I told him. "And you should have informed me about what you're doing."

"Angela channeled Higgins and I served as monitor," he said with a smirk. "There—you've been informed."

My first impulse was to grab Gauvin by the short hairs and throw him out, but I thought better of it. Angela's channeling was bound to be judged useless and scrapped and then maybe she'd go back to her crystal ball. But as Gauvin had correctly pointed out, she was an official member of the unit no matter what I thought about her. I decided to let Angela stay. Who knew, by participating in an actual session maybe she'd catch on to how remote viewing really works. Maybe.

Vorona finally arrived and began going over all the data and analysis we laid out on his desk alongside the CIA maps and satellite photographs. He glanced up at me and said, "You look awful, Captain. When's the last time you got any sleep?"

"Not since I was seven, sir," I answered.

He smiled slightly and continued looking at our material. As he worked, I pictured him getting on the phone to command with our intel and off go the commandos to collect Higgins and blow his captors' brains all over the desert. This was how it would happen; it just had to be. This mission was a slam-dunk. Or so I thought.

Despite the accuracy and accessibility of our remote-viewing intel, all Vorona wanted was for me to go over it again and again as if none of it made any sense, like it wasn't sinking into that brilliant mind of his. Here was a man who regularly reported to the White House on the most complicated and arcane aspects of Soviet nuclear technology acting like a hapless child attempting to fit a round peg into a square hole. It was true he was no expert on remote viewing, but there was no way he couldn't absorb the information we'd presented.

After the third or fourth try repeating it all, I began getting suspicious. Vorona was just sitting there with this dour math-teacher-like expression while Gauvin was off in a corner muttering quietly with Angela. She was bouncing slightly on her toes, as if reveling in her ability to create total confusion. It was then that I realized Vorona wasn't even making an effort to understand the briefing. He wasn't missing what I was saying—he was resisting it.

Without warning, Gauvin walked to the middle of the room and plopped his finger down on one of the CIA satellite maps.

He was pointing at a barley field about a hundred miles from where our investigation told us Higgins was.

"We believe he's *here*," Gauvin said, looking over at Angela, who nodded and smiled like a tiger after the kill.

I began laughing. "Swell, that's just swell, Fern. He's in a barley field. Maybe he's helping the Muslims make beer."

Vorona sighed and buried his face in his hands.

"We have him, sir," I said, directing his eye to where we placed Higgins. "They're all waiting, sir, the commandos."

Vorona just stared at me.

I brought my voice down, didn't want him to think I was pushing too hard. "Sir. Colonel Higgins is in that village and he's alive. But he won't be for much longer if we delay any further, if you don't report what we have."

I was talking to myself. Vorona was like a stone; he'd stopped listening altogether. That's when it struck me—*He's not going to report our findings to anybody.*

As steadfast as Vorona had been in defending our unit against those who wanted us shut down, his fear of what might happen to his reputation had gotten the better of him. He could be discredited if his support of intel gathered by psychic spies ever got out. Vorona knew what had happened to Major General Albert Stubblebine, the former INSCOM commander who fell out of favor working with us. It pretty much cost him his career. Vorona, being the political animal he was, had picked up the ball when Stubblebine left but had yet to bounce it. He was not about to stick his neck out by launching a dangerous rescue mission based solely on information gathered by remote viewers. To him we were a scientific curiosity, an interesting fringe group he could play with but never stand behind. Facts delivered by us might threaten his job security. Officially we weren't even operational. We were a research project, like kindergartners figuring out how to build an ant farm.

Without even knowing it, Gauvin had given Jack Vorona the ammunition he needed to shoot down the Higgins mission.

By taking into consideration the junk data he and Angela entered into the record, Vorona had essentially muddied the waters of the project beyond saving. Since there were now two conclusions arrived at separately, all results became inconclusive. In the spy game, inconclusive intelligence means no intelligence at all. No need to take it any further than it was, no need to kick it upstairs so command could act on it. I was horrified.

"You won't allow that channeling crap to prevent us from rescuing Colonel Higgins, will you, sir?" I asked Vorona.

If looks could kill I would have been in a pine box after how Gauvin stared at me now. I had ridiculed not only his methods but also the man himself for using them. The carpet had been yanked out from under him in front of a superior at his crowning moment of glory. He wanted to put a knife in me.

Vorona seemed oblivious to what was transpiring between Gauvin and me. He rubbed his forehead and mumbled under his breath just loud enough for everyone to hear, "I don't know. I just don't know."

But I did. He was passing on the whole deal. All our work was for nothing, thanks to Fern and his working witch. All Paul and Mel and I could do was watch as Vorona gathered up the data and left.

Gauvin let loose on me the second he was out the door— "I'm gonna get you, Dames! I'm gonna get you." He shook as he screamed, a frothy bubble of spittle forming around the edges of his lips. I thought I'd seen it all when it came to stress—soldiers losing it in battle, the crazed paranoia of agents too long in the field. But they all had nothing on Fern Gauvin when it came to acting out anger. He was actually vibrating.

I could have lost control too, but I didn't. He and Angela had screwed everything to hell, but it was Higgins who would pay for it. That was the saddest part of this. They didn't seem to give a crap about what happened to him.

"I swear I'll get you, Dames, one way or another!"

"No one ever died from a threat, Fern," I shouted back as he and Angela headed for the door.

As she exited, Angela turned and sent me a sort of understanding expression, as if she could feel my pain over what had happened. It was her storefront-psychic "I know all, I tell all" bullshit, and I wasn't buying. This was the last mission she'd ever bury if I had anything to say about it, which I did.

As far as Gauvin was concerned, he might have made good on his threat to get me sooner or later in one of his hissy fits, so from then on I kept my Colt .45 Gold Cup Mark IV automatic stashed in my belt with a full clip just in case. This was how I had to handle it, to be on guard and careful. Things were getting really nuts at the unit, even more so than usual.

FUBAR.

DECEMBER 23, 1991. 1500 HOURS, ZULU TIME

The body of marine colonel William Richard Higgins was recovered dumped on a Beirut street. He was forty-five years old.

Two years before his death, I transferred out of the Psi Spy Unit into one that could actually have some impact on important missions. It wasn't my dustup with Gauvin that inspired the move; it was seeing a photo of a bound and gagged man dangling from a hastily assembled gallows in some filthy little room. The Organization of the Oppressed on Earth claimed the body was that of Higgins, but I knew it wasn't. It was torture that killed the colonel, not a lynching. He perished around the time we uncovered that he was still alive. CIA sources later confirmed this, stating that Higgins made an escape attempt and was tortured to death as a result. It was remote viewing that helped discover this, the same tool that helped me break the back of the Soviets, find Saddam Hussein's secret labs, and so much more. The same amazing tool that was in jeopardy now because of Gauvin, Graff, and their witches.

I had had enough.

Hard as it was for me, I decide to blow the whistle on the whole program. RV was falling into the wrong hands, dangerous hands. It was time for me to step from the shadows and tell the world what I knew about psychic warfare.

In an interview with the Seattle television station KIRO, I revealed the existence of PSI Tech and how we had provided United Nations envoy Major Karen Jansen with sketches of Iraqi biological weapons sites. I also entered into the record that since 1972 the military's remote-viewing operation had enjoyed the full political and financial support of the U.S. government. This wasn't something we were doing alone. The revelation lit off a controversy that spread like wildfire through the halls of power. It really hit the fan when Ted Koppel broke his "Psychic Spies" story on ABC's *Nightline.* The former CIA director Robert Gates explained how it was pressure from members of Congress that drove his agency's interest in the psychic program. Without it, they never would have gotten involved in the first place. Another guest on the show, a CIA technical adviser identified only as "Norm," spoke about the Psi Spy Unit's "eight-martini" results—mission results so accurate and mind-boggling that observers needed eight martinis to recover. Koppel looked like he could use a drink too as he listened to tales of government-sponsored psychics locating crashed Soviet bombers, state-of-the-art submarines being built, and plutonium caches in North Korea. They had never heard anything like it before in their lives. After the *Nightline* episode aired, America finally got the news that the X-Files were real.

The psi program was kept on life support a little longer with the backing of Senator Claiborne Pell and Representative Charles Rose, both of whom were convinced of remote viewing's effectiveness. But despite their help, there was nothing that could stop its eventual slide into oblivion. Plagued at the time by uneven management, poor team morale, and divisiveness, the Remote Viewing Unit's time had come.

Robert Gates, the current U.S. secretary of defense and the former CIA director.

The former Rhode Island senator Claiborne Pell (1918–2009), who together with the North Carolina representative Charlie Rose worked to protect the RV Unit from being closed down.

Like rats deserting a sinking ship, many top officials immediately ran for cover after we were exposed, most of them denying any involvement and demanding that something be done about this "frivolous waste of taxpayers' dollars." Those calling loudest for

Representative Charlie Rose.

action were the same members of Congress and heads of the Senate and House intelligence committees who were regularly briefed about our operations, the same people who routinely dropped by asking us to psychically dig up dirt on their enemies. Politicians were our biggest supporters and the most frightened by what we could do. When the veil was pulled on the Psi Spy Unit they publicly denied all knowledge of us while privately cursing me for having told the truth. Remote viewing had opened the door to a world with no secrets, and I had put a stop to them using it for personal gain. *Politics without secrets*—the very idea shook them to their cores. Truth to a corrupt politician is like kryptonite to Superman.

The Psi Spy Unit was finished and the former defense secretary Frank Carlucci was called in to clean up the mess. He closed down not only us, but a long list of other potentially embarrassing hip pocket organizations operating under the public's radar. We trashed two industrial-sized paper shredders dumping all the operational data gathered over the years. You could smell the belching smoke all the way to Washington, from one end of Pennsylvania Avenue to the other.

Frank Carlucci, the former defense secretary.

There was a price to pay for my outing the unit. Counterintelligence began closely monitoring me not long afterwards. I knew they were there—friends of mine had alerted me—and I could see them following me, hear the telltale clicking of their bugs on my telephone. I was being investigated by the Defense Intelligence Agency for having breached national security. It was a political ambush; they needed a fall guy for all the bad press, and I was their man. Problem was, they soon realized how hard it would be to prosecute a decorated intelligence officer, someone who once had the ear of U.S. presidents. I wasn't the easy target the blue suits believed me to be, and this wasn't the Twilight Zone anymore. I was a seasoned spymaster with a few aces up his sleeve.

The hand I held was simple enough. The technology used in remote viewing had never been classified, only the people directly involved and the results we achieved. The RV Unit itself was top secret, but how we did what we did was public record. I hadn't breached security or betrayed any trust. In a sense, I had faithfully returned to the American people what they paid for. What could the authorities nail me on after that? Court-martial a Legion of Merit holder for sitting in a room gathering information with his mind and a ballpoint pen?

Case dismissed.


During his imprisonment, William Higgins's official status with the United States government was "hostage," not "prisoner of war," and as such we hadn't insisted on treatment consistent with international law. Not that it would've mattered anyway, not with the kind of animals who were involved in his murder. Higgins was promoted to full colonel while in captivity.

In April 2003, after more than ten years of supporters attempting to have him recognized officially as a prisoner of war, Higgins was finally posthumously granted that status and awarded a Prisoner of War Medal. I'm sure it was a great comfort to his family.

American officials and UN personnel who served under Higgins in southern Lebanon verified his identity at the morgue of American University Hospital. The body, in a casket draped with the American flag for the fallen hero he was, took off after in an ambulance flanked by two government cars to the U.S. embassy. Then it was home. We had failed him. Everyone had failed him.

UN secretary-general Javier Perez de Cuellar later said of the hostage affair, "A dark chapter in the history of peacekeeping forces has been closed."

Thankfully, much the same could be said for the witches of remote viewing. And for me.

# 6

# SEEING THROUGH WALLS

To say the situation was awkward would be kind.

I was sitting in a run-down apartment I had rented in Philadelphia, waiting to interrogate an Afghan defector, and my interpreter was nowhere to be found. It was a failed squalid apartment, furnished with the kind of cheap rented furniture you wouldn't keep in your garage. The hideous flat wasn't my first choice to conduct business in or house Aarif and his family, but it was within the budget that Systems Exploitation Detachment would allow. Once we were done and he had been approved to remain permanently in the United States, more suitable living quarters would be found. Until then he had to wait, just like we were waiting for the damn interpreter to show up.

Aarif was as uncomfortable as I was in not being able to communicate, continuously crossing and uncrossing his legs as he chain-smoked what was left of a carton of Marlboro Reds I had brought for him. Looking much older than his thirty-eight years, he really enjoyed American cigarettes, motioning with his hands that they were smooth-tasting and the smell wasn't too offensive. No so for the revolting stink wafting in from outside. One of his neighbors apparently liked to keep his door propped open all night. Aarif smiled and pinched his nose and I did the same. It was quite a smell, like somebody microwaving a goat.

Mercifully, there was a knock at the door and in came my interpreter, Yazmin. The look I gave her for being late could be understood in any language. She apologized politely, made all the proper introductions in both English and Aarif's native Pashto language, and then pulled up a chair next to us. As we were about to get started, we were interrupted by the sound of muffled voices—women's voices—coming from inside the bathroom down the hall. Yazmin and I exchanged a look and she asked Aarif what the hell was going on. He smiled again and coolly launched into an explanation in Pashto that took a good five minutes to complete.

"Well?" I asked.

"It's nothing," Yazmin answered. "His wife and daughters are in there. It's a tradition where they come from."

"Locking women in bathrooms is a tradition?"

"No, no." She laughed. "It's a little hard to explain, but it has to do with respect for the husband when he's talking to someone important. That would be *you*."

Aarif motioned to me again with his hands that everything was all right and lit another cigarette. In all my years in deep cover at SED debriefing foreign émigrés and defectors, I had never heard of this locked bathroom thing. But Aarif was my first Muslim subject, so I gave him a pass and moved on.

Cool and confident, Yazmin began doing her job, laying out what I wanted in a straightforward way. I knew I could trust her; she was a real pro, former CIA. I knew that whatever questions

I asked would be translated word for word exactly the way I asked them. And Yazmin knew enough not to offer any suggestions or help to Aarif. There's always a chance in an interrogation that the mark will say whatever he thinks you want to hear. Defectors do that. They're funny that way.

In short order I learned that Aarif had been a medical doctor in Afghanistan before the Soviets invaded in 1979. He was a top graduate of the State Medical Institute in Nangarhar Province. Now, four years on, like so many of his fellow countrymen, he doubled as a guerrilla fighter struggling to kick the Russians' asses back where they belonged.

"Do you know my name means *knowledge* in English?" Aarif asked.

"Yes. I'm counting on that," I said.

Aarif nodded to Yazmin; he understood. The reason he was here today was to supply me with something very specific, only he didn't know exactly what yet. Always best to do that.

"Ask him about the incident he witnessed in the hills," I said to Yazmin.

"Which one?" Aarif replied, shifting in his chair, crossing his legs again. "There were so many."

"February 1982, the firefight with that Soviet squad dug in around the mountains outside Kabul."

Yazmin translated and Aarif acknowledged the question. His face grew more taut at this point. This obviously wasn't something he had been prepared to talk about.

"We were running back behind some big rocks," he said. "Then Ali stepped on a mine—it went off with a loud *bang*! But no one was hurt. Not even Ali."

"So the mine was a dud," I said.

Aarif listened to Yazmin and vehemently shook his head. "No!" he shouted. "No dud. It went off, but not like any mine I'd ever seen before. After the bang, a puff of green smoke came. A cloud of green smoke."

*Impossible.* What he was saying just couldn't be. I wondered if he truly comprehended the importance of what he had just described.

"Tell me more about the smoke," I said. "The green smoke."

Aarif fell into silence. He snuffed out his cigarette, twisting the orange nub of the filter into an empty dish.

"Later at night, many got sick," he continued. "We thought it was influenza, but it wasn't. Terrible headaches, then came coughing and high fever, vomiting and chills and chest pains. I tried first aid—I tried. Some felt better, they stood up, then they fell down like drunks. They fell and—"

Aarif dropped his head onto his lap and wept openly. Yazmin took his hand for a moment, and that seemed to help.

"They died where they fell," he said. "Dead. All dead."

Yazmin took his hand again.

A door outside slammed, wobbling the metal shade on our overhead lamp. I watched it shake and suddenly found myself staring, my eyes searching the room, trying to shape things in my mind. Eyes are supposed to shape things, process and paint a picture we can understand. What I saw wasn't in this room. I saw a green vapor that kills.

"Did anyone cough up blood?" I asked.

Yazmin looked unsure, like maybe she shouldn't ask that.

"Ask it," I said.

She did and Aarif nodded again. Yes, there was blood.

I slipped my pen into my jacket and closed my notebook. It's amazing how stories molded in desperation seem to ring true. I had no doubt in my mind that what he'd told me was the truth.

"We're done for now," I said.

As I rose from my chair, Aarif moved quickly to me, taking me by my shirt collar. Yazmin tried to intervene but I waved her off. He was a doctor after all. A very distraught doctor.

"Is poison, yes?" he asked in his best broken English.

"Affirmative," I answered. "Yes. They poisoned you."

He released my collar and slumped down against the wall, shaking his head in disbelief.

"This is why I come to America," he said. "For my wife, for my children."

I heard some commotion down the hallway and Aarif's wife and young daughters piled in, her with a big grin and the girls giggling. Aarif transformed the instant he saw them, smiling, embracing each with every ounce of his being.

Yazmin handled the introductions once more. I directed her to inform them that I would do everything in my power to help make sure they remained in the United States. They'd earned it. Aarif's wife hugged me so hard I could barely breathe.

"I guess somebody's happy to get out of the bathroom," I told Yazmin.

The wife smiled at me. "Oh, we could have left anytime," she said, in *perfect* English. "We just didn't want to be a bother."

Everyone laughed, a big whooping laugh at my expense. What the hell, I laughed too. I felt like a complete idiot. One of Aarif's daughters, who couldn't have been more than seven, unwrapped a bag and handed me a prayer rug she had made herself.

"For you," she said. "Thank you."

I held the carpet up. It was lovely, the colors bright and the craftsmanship top-notch. But the theme woven into it wasn't so pretty. It depicted children playing with toys on a battlefield, oblivious to all the carnage going on around them—a snapshot of how young lives see the tragedy of war. I couldn't bring myself to say that things were about to get even worse.

Her father had told me so.

What I learned in my session with Aarif was devastating, but not something I didn't already know. The green puff of smoke he saw and its deadly aftermath had happened before.

In the spring of 1979 people began dropping dead in the streets of Sverdlovsk. Located beyond the Ural Mountains, Sverdlovsk was the tenth-largest city in the Soviet Union, an industrial mecca where quaint tree-lined streets with cute shops and cottages and concrete high-rises belied its central role at the heart of Moscow's war machine. Guns and rockets and steel were all manufactured here, and it served as home to two army tank divisions and a hush-hush microbiological facility. We believed that inside this facility a host of lethal pathogens were being developed and tested. But that's all it was, a belief. Security maintained at the site was extremely tight. Even Boris Yeltsin, the local Communist Party boss, was refused entry. A very secret place.

*An explosion and a cloud of green smoke.*

This was what our Soviet agents picked up that April morning over Sverdlovsk. The explosion was big. Photographic evidence showed extensive damage and an eerie veil of green smoke dispersing in every direction. Then came the cover-up. Agents on the ground reported on the Soviet military's efforts to quell public panic over what they claimed to be nothing more than a case of tainted livestock. Leaflets warning the populace to refrain from eating meat were hurriedly distributed, buildings and trees and walls and anything else freestanding hosed down by high-pressure fire hoses, unpaved roads quickly covered over in fresh hot asphalt. Any stray animals caught up in the massive sweep were shot dead on sight. This went on 24/7 for days.

Quite an operation for a load of bad hamburger.

Then came the citizens stumbling half-conscious through the streets disoriented and crazed, collapsing dead on the sidewalks. Infection followed, spreading rapidly through the city and outlying communities. The coughing, vomiting of blood, the terrible headaches and killer fevers—every symptom Aarif's friends endured before dying like dogs in the lonely snowcapped mountains above Kabul.

Satellite and field intelligence combined with Aarif's testimony added up to one undeniable and horrifying conclusion: the Soviets had broken the Biological Weapons and Toxins Convention. Busted it into a million pieces.

In 1972, after the United States was roundly criticized for using poison gas and napalm in Vietnam, President Richard Nixon unilaterally ended our nation's offensive biological weapons program. An executive order was given for all pathogens and toxins to be destroyed, and all future development and acquisition prohibited. Other nations happily followed suit, leading to the eventual signing of the weapons convention. There were high hopes for the treaty at first, and for years all parties honored it. But in light of what we know today, it's clear that the agreement is a protocol that never was.

The possibility existed that Moscow was stockpiling forbidden bugs like parrot fever, Ebola, chikungunya virus, African equine encephalitis, and anthrax. We didn't have antidotes or vaccines for most of them, and if the Soviets had tinkered with their DNA in some new way, we were screwed. If they'd genetically manipulated these bad boys at the amino acid and peptide level, we would have no idea what variant they were using and so no viable defense against them. If they'd changed the genetic locks and we had no set of keys, whole populations were at risk. Catching the other guy looking the other way was the goal of biological warfare, and I suddenly felt a sucker punch coming on.

Despite their endorsement of the treaty, I suspected the Russians were attempting to weaponize these biological terrors for use against the West. Proving it, however, was another matter. The Soviet army's security apparatus was mind-blowing. All efforts by other covert agencies assigned to identify their activities had turned up nothing, blocked at every turn. This was why I came to SED, to do the impossible.

As a waterwalker, army intelligence gave me a lot more latitude than other operatives. It was I who chose to work at SED, not the other way around. My rising-star status meant I could pick any assignment I wanted, and I chose to go where the action was, where most of the resources to get the job done were allocated. The squeakiest threat gets the most grease. I picked one of the highest priorities in U.S. intelligence—biological warfare. SED was the place where I could meet this challenge head-on.

Being a waterwalker also meant open access to specialized personnel and programs only a privileged few knew anything about, tools that were mine to use however I saw fit. I began by approaching every leading chemist, microbiologist, weapons expert, and techno spy wonk I could get hold of, but none of them could get the job done. They gave me nothing but theories and suggestions, nothing tangible I could work with.

I tapped into every in-house espionage tool at my disposal—Imagery Intelligence (IMINT), Communications Intelligence (COMINT), Electronic Intelligence (ELINT), and all the Human Source Intelligence (HUMINT) I could muster—but they produced nothing of real value either. The assets I had were just not up to the task, wholly unqualified to think beyond their own levels of expertise. New ways of defending against biological attacks escaped them. Our people's level of preparedness for handling such weapons had always been far lower than for a nuclear threat. Even as our technology advanced, the ability to deal with or prevent a biological catastrophe shrank. Nuclear weapons require highly advanced technology, huge infrastructures, and rare materials that can be closely monitored and secured. Not so for biological weapons. They occur naturally, in plants, spores, bacteria, and viruses. They need no complex systems to produce and can be found in every corner of the planet. In the hands of the wrong people, anthrax and plague, as well as botulinum and ricin toxins, could be released in a short time, slaughtering an unsuspecting populace as they went about their daily lives.

This was what we were facing and my mission was stuck in the mud. The clock was ticking and I was getting nowhere. I had never come across such an expert job of hiding something you don't want anyone to find. My inability to make even the slightest headway infiltrating this Soviet weapons program was maddening. The Russians had thrown up an impenetrable wall of secrecy around it. What I needed now were people who could see through walls. What I needed now was a miracle.

I got one.

One morning, at a routine SED meeting, I was briefed about this quirky start-up unit staffed by a group of people who gathered intelligence with their minds—and only their minds. It sounded too good to be true. People who see through walls.

The man in charge of this unusual unit was Lieutenant Fred Atwater, or "Skip," as his friends knew him. Fair-haired and broad around the middle, Skip shared a lot in common with me. Like me, he was from California, had served for a time at SED, and found it quite natural to talk about such things as psychics, out-of-body experiences, and UFOs. His mother was inclined toward supernatural subjects and had encouraged a similar interest in her young son. I'd heard it said that Skip could take an out-of-body trip anytime he wanted, practically on demand. I'd have loved to find out more about that, but I had more pressing matters to discuss with him.

Atwater was an operations security officer assigned to the Sensitive Activity Vulnerability Estimate, or SAVE, team before it became SED. All cold war commanders were expected to take measures to protect their operational capabilities, so when a new threat was identified, the SAVE team would check in on various commands by challenging every aspect of their security. It was Atwater's job to hold their feet to the fire, making sure their defensive measures were up to snuff to meet those threats. I couldn't believe my luck meeting Skip. Here was a security specialist setting up an extraordinary unit to be trained as psychic spies for exclusive use on operational missions. If anyone could help me punch a few large holes in the Soviet bioprogram it was Skip Atwater and his psi spies. If they were real, of course.

• • •

At Fort Meade, in a small complex of buildings shaded from the Maryland sun, Atwater greeted me with all due military courtesy and then methodically related how and why his Remote Viewing Unit was created. Exploring his new office, as all new hires do, he had opened a safe and discovered three Department of Defense documents "mistakenly" left behind by his predecessor—left behind so Skip would mistakenly read them. Most people who knew him knew of his interest in clairvoyant experiences and his dabbling in the paranormal; it was no secret. These reports were right up his alley. The first two described the Soviet Union's research into psychic spying, and the third, written by Russell Targ and Hal Puthoff, discussed their remote-viewing research at Stanford Research Institute in Menlo Park, California. According to the reports, the Soviets were conducting parapsychology research at more than twenty separate institutions with an operating budget of over $21 million, all of it funded by the KGB. For Atwater, the defensive ace, this presented a serious potential security threat to the United States. It was as simple as they had something we didn't.

Much to his surprise, the top brass agreed. With hardly any argument, his proposal to match the Soviet psi program with an experimental one of our own was forwarded to the head of SED colonel Robert Keenan. From there it moved through the chain of command to the army assistant chief of staff for intelligence, Major General Edwin Thompson. Thompson and Atwater got along famously, and the general also shared his interest in the paranormal. He got a kick out of the idea of having an untried team of military psychics under his wing to play with. The project took off. Code-named Grill Flame, the Remote Viewing Unit was formalized and staffed by officers and a few civilians believed to possess varying degrees of legitimate psychic ability.

The psi spy team wasn't the first black unit Thompson created. He crafted similar wild-card operations with other select individuals like myself. I was once assigned to communicate with the former and now *deceased* Soviet premier Yuri Andropov. The thinking was, this guy kept a lot of secrets when he was alive, but could he do the same dead? Turns out the once-feared boss of the KGB was as unyielding in death as he was in life. He kept his mouth shut.

Some of the schemes rubber-stamped back then were unbelievable. I can't talk about most of them. Thompson felt there was nothing to explain when it came remote viewing or anything else dealing with the paranormal. All we needed to do was find practical uses for it. It was wild and crazy at SED, but sometimes you need wild and crazy people to get the job done. It's what brought me to Fort Meade.


Atwater was as happy to see me as I was to see him. Absolutely no one was making use of his Remote Viewing Unit.

He said he felt like the loneliest guy in army intelligence, like the old Maytag repairman in the TV ads sitting forlornly by the phone waiting for someone to call. It's true that few were informed about the unit's existence, but those that were either avoided or ignored it as just another crackpot creation from the boys at army intel. Many were simply afraid of the idea of remote viewing, afraid of even uttering the word "psychic."

Without any clientele, Atwater told me, it would be tough for him to continue justifying the unit. From a budgetary standpoint in the military, that meant eventual termination. He thanked me for coming, for putting him on the map, and hoped he could help. It was I who should have been thanking him. If his team could do half the things he claimed, they would be a godsend to me. I couldn't wait to work with them, to get answers to questions I wasn't even sure how to ask. I'd never spoken to a psi spy.

I tasked the Remote Viewing Unit with a mission we called "Project 8702." They got no information from me, as Atwater instructed, none of the physical intelligence I'd gathered from other sources, nothing to clue them in on what their target was. All they needed to know was that their mission was to identify the purpose of several buildings in a city located somewhere in the Soviet Union. They knew nothing about helping me penetrate the Russians' biological weapons program.

Each of Atwater's remote viewers worked independently, the sessions done blind, leaving them only to sense what was in their minds and report back to me. I took part in as many sessions as I could. After several days, the unit's preliminary findings began to filter in and I saw that a remarkable connection had taken place. Three had described something green, a billowing transparent mist like one produced by an aerosol spray. Another saw a dazzling emerald light, a translucent cloud rising in the air then descending and spreading like a stain over all it touched. The results they turned in were incredible; I was amazed by the unit's self-assurance and skill. These were no ditzy psychics coming up with preposterous stories. They hit the nail on head the first go-round, detailing the key element found at Sverdlovsk and in Aarif's account of his firefight with the Soviets.

The green cloud.

Not only had they seen it, they were able to relate its effects as if being in contact with it. The green cloud was debilitating to humans, beginning with a burning sensation on the skin, then a stinging feeling in the nose and a painful watering of the eyes—all the symptoms of anthrax infection.

Atwater then put them through their paces in an RV "movement exercise," relocating them with new instructions to perceive specific parts of the target. He explained that these could be in dimensions, moving ten feet closer or above or below the target, or directions, like going left and right, east and west. If the viewer had already provided precise data, it could be used to better position them in relation to the target. They'd already done that with the green cloud, I pointed out. I asked Atwater to follow up. I had to have more on the cloud.

The remote viewer on this day was a woman and a civilian. Atwater said she was one of the best and I took him at his word. He leaned forward in his chair when she was ready, and we began.

"Can you tell me more about the green cloud?" he asked.

I stopped him. "No," I whispered. "I want to know *how* the cloud formed first. What created it?"

"Scratch that," Atwater told the viewer. "Tell me where the cloud came from."

The viewer nodded, relaxed herself, and went into a trancelike state. I found it fascinating and a bit frightening. This wasn't a movie. This was real.

"There's a strong man, he's dressed in worker's clothes, like a maintenance outfit," she said, her eyes rolling back. "I feel air moving, blowing like a fan. The man is holding a metal mesh of some kind in his hand. He means to do something with it, something to do with the air, but he gets distracted. He puts it on a table. He's forgotten about it."

"What happens after, in the same area?"

"A suction sound," she said, becoming agitated. "Things getting hot in a machine, overheated. There's an explosion!"

"And?"

"A green cloud."

I looked at Skip and urged him to move on. I had gotten what I wanted. An explosion had produced this airborne toxic event.

"Go in the building," he said. "What do you see inside?"

The viewer thought for a moment. I could almost see her leaving the area where she was and heading somewhere else, all of it happening in her mind.

"I'm in a room, it's very large and well lit," she said. "There are different objects on a long table and handwritten papers about scientific stuff. Stuff to do with mixtures."

"Who's there with you?"

"There are people in the room. It's very antiseptic, like a room you'd find in a hospital. Very clean."

"What are the people like?" Atwater asked. "Take a closer look at the people."

"They're wearing visors and protective clothing from head to toe," she answered. "They find what they're working with revolting, they hate it. It's a man-made substance, a chemical of some sort, yellow and oozy. They don't want to be there, but they can't leave. They've been ordered to be there. They're afraid."

I couldn't help but think how a remote viewer has the edge on a conventional spy in a situation like this. Not only can they recount what they see, but they can gather intangible facts like what the target is feeling. I would never know someone was scared of something or wanted to run if I merely snuck into a facility and had a look around. And I admired the team's courage. For all intents and purposes, they *were* in a room filled with deadly chemicals, standing close by as an explosion occurred. It was real to them. Very brave people.

"There's something else," the viewer said.

"What?" I interrupted.

"What do you see?" Atwater said.

"I can smell it, hear them. Wait—there they are. Chickens and pigs, they have caged animals in the room."

Even a novice in this seedy business knew that the presence of animals in such a facility was consistent with biological warfare research. Now it was confirmed to my satisfaction regarding Sverdlovsk. Confirmed by an excited paranormal agent, but confirmed nonetheless.

Reports from the other members of Atwater's Remote Viewing Unit pretty much all told the same sad tale, from the explosion at Sverdlovsk to Aarif's encounter in the mountains.

Regardless of the fact that this detailed information came from a group of psychics, my assessment of the Soviet threat remained unshakable. An accident of some kind had taken place at the top-secret biological facility in Sverdlovsk, releasing a weaponized form of anthrax. This was what caused all the suffering and death among those who lived nearby, not tainted meat. And more than likely, devices to deliver the anthrax spores such as missile warheads, spray dispensers, and cluster munitions were also being developed there. Under the guise of being at war, Moscow was using the Afghan theater as a live-fire exercise to test out new biological weapons. Aarif and his freedom fighters had become nothing more than human guinea pigs for a much larger, more far-reaching military agenda. An agenda of biological death.

I later discovered that many top Soviet scientists had stopped publishing data about substances of organic origin in their popular scientific journals, which I scoured each day for leads. This Literature Intelligence (LITINT) could only mean that the KGB had shanghaied their research and taken it classified. With state security funds behind it now, it was only a matter of time before things went fully operational. These substances included gamma-aminobutyric acid, which occurs naturally in the human body to regulate the nervous system. When tweaked into a biological poison, however, it speeds up the heart until it seizes. All you would find in an autopsy was that the victim died of a heart attack. It was a brilliant weapon, and a loophole for the Soviets to break the weapons treaty. Agents of biological origin weren't covered by it. Very clever, those Russkies.

My intelligence estimate made the rounds at command level. Heads turned and voices were raised in heated discussion about my conclusions, but most were eventually convinced. The only thing left to do was report my findings to those who counted, the people who could make or break what I'd come up with.

I got my shoes shined, dressed up in my best civvy suit and silk tie, and made my way to the Old Executive Office Building near the White House. It was here that I'd be taking part in a briefing with several members of the National Security Council. I'd made sure to get all my ducks in a row ahead of time, going over and over my report to help me anticipate their questions. These NSC fellas don't fool around. You have to be ready for anything, one hundred percent. And you have to look good. They judge you on your appearance. No problem. I looked good.

The scene at the White House was straight out of the movie *Grumpy Old Men*. The staffers I had to persuade were older, highly experienced, and skeptical men. Luckily, I was there as part of a larger group of intelligence people, CIA, DIA, and NSA. You needed a program to tell who was who. One thing about me stood out, though: I was the youngest biological warfare briefing officer who'd ever attended a gathering like this.

I made the best of it when my turn came, calmly and concisely reporting my conclusions about the top-secret Soviet bioweapons program—the same program no one else in the intelligence community could crack. While others at the meeting handed out the same old-school stuff like "nuclear ICBM throw weights" and "megatonnage," I brought the specter of a biological holocaust to the table. In less than two years, I had uncovered proof that the Soviets were secretly developing a new generation of offensive biological warfare agents, horrors like cobra venom toxin and other poisons that leave no trace in their victims, as well as high-dose radiation weapons that would not only drop you like a fly, but kill in the most excruciating way possible—from the inside out.

You need to have rock-solid evidential support from several sources to get the NSC crowd's attention, to get these staid, stoic dinosaurs slouching behind their desks to stand up and shout, "Oh my God!"—which is exactly what happened when I closed out my report. My response to them was, "I'm sorry you won't be able to sleep tonight, but here's something else you should know."

When I was done, a few spit-shined aides grabbed my files off the desk and exited the room. From my window seat I could see a chopper outside on the White House lawn, its rotors spinning. It took off the moment my papers were handed to the pilot. Amazing. But this was only the beginning. Months after the briefing I learned that my intelligence work had become the focus of intense controversy and heated exchanges between Washington and Moscow. Accusations flew about the Soviets reneging on the weapons treaty and their continuing efforts to create bio-WMDs. The Russians denied everything, prompting President Ronald Reagan to change his policy on our weapons program. To Reagan, we had caught them red-handed and had no choice but to reinforce the U.S. defensive position in this arena. It was in our country's best interest not to let its guard down ever again. All bets were off. A different sort of biological weapons race was taking shape.

It wasn't until 1992, thirteen years later, when Boris Yeltsin rose to power as head of a new, kinder, more open Russian government, that the dirt finally came out in the wash. Yeltsin admitted to President George H. W. Bush that the United States' accusations regarding Soviet violations of the 1972 biological weapons convention were all true. The Sverdlovsk incident had been caused by the accidental release of an aerosol of anthrax pathogen at their military facility. On the day it happened, all the victims were clustered along a straight line downwind from the facility when a deadly green cloud descended on them.

The green cloud again. Exactly what Atwater's remote viewers saw. And they were right on the money as to the explosion at the facility. A worker who forgot to replace a simple filter in an exhaust system had caused the airborne leak of lethal anthrax spores. This was the maintenance man holding a wire mesh whom Skip's civilian psychic noted. The idiot who became distracted and forgot to do something he was supposed to do—protect people.

Yeltsin's personal connection to Sverdlovsk as the Communist Party chief in the region at the time added legitimacy to the story, which was later confirmed in a *Frontline* interview with Dr. Kanatjan Alibekov, former first deputy chief for Biopreparat, the civilian part of the Soviet biological weapons program. Alibekov said, for all the world to hear, that because of their illegal research, if the wind had been in the opposite direction that fateful day—toward Sverdlovsk as opposed to away from it—the body count could have hit hundreds of thousands, a self-inflicted massacre.

What astonished me and everybody else involved even more was what the Soviet leadership used as an excuse for skirting the biological arms convention. It wasn't the West their weapons were designed to neutralize—it was the Chinese. There wasn't enough metal ore in the Urals to construct enough bullets to stop a massive Chinese land invasion. It was their contention that no country would accept the threat of a well-trained, well-equipped million-man army swarming into their homeland unchecked. Only a font of virulent biological weapons could provide the security they sought, so in order to keep their borders intact the Soviets had lied about their program. It was a very convenient confession considering it came *after* I caught them. For my money, they were still lying. The fact that to this day no Western inspectors have been allowed to visit the Sverdlovsk facility bears me out. So much for a more open Russia.

The national security implications of my findings were characterized by top U.S. policymakers as "revolutionary." After that, I spent a lot of time on the road briefing staffers from all the national intelligence agencies, the secretary of defense, members of the National Security Council, and Congress on how I did it. As a result, assets were assigned to develop appropriate defense measures to deal with this new and highly disturbing Soviet capability. Congress also approved funds for the creation of the Maryland-based Biological Threat Analysis Center. With satellite offices across the country, the center would acquire and analyze intelligence on chemical and biological threats generated anywhere on earth. Getting caught with our pants down would not be allowed to happen again. A lot of folks have my team and me to thank for their jobs. We helped build an industry.

I received two Meritorious Service medals and a Legion of Merit for my efforts. More importantly, my work with the Psi Spy Unit demonstrated to those in charge that by applying this new and wondrous tool against a broad range of targets, "psychic intelligence" was dependable enough for any special ops where lives were on the line. I even coined a new abbreviation—PSIINT. Psychic espionage was no longer a joke, and money and resources were assigned to delve deeper into its development. Atwater and his psi spies had finally gotten the job security they needed, and me the sort of challenge I live for.

Exposing the Soviets did wonders for my career and my country. When I look back on it, the best years of my life were spent working with our scientists, meeting the RV Unit and operating undercover helping decent people like Aarif and his family. As usual, I wanted much more. Waterwalkers always do. I needed to be a part of this new mind-set at intelligence, this new openness to the paranormal. In the summer of 1983, I could think of nothing else.

When the legendary holdup man Willie Sutton was asked why he robbed banks, he very casually answered, "Because that's where the money is." Truer words were never spoken. If I were to become a psi spy I had to go where the psi spies lived. It was time to pay another call on Skip Atwater and his Remote Viewing Unit. It would be another visit like others I'd made since they helped me bust open the Soviets' weapons program. Only I wouldn't be assigning them a top-secret security mission on this pass. This time, *they* were the mission.

# ETHER WARS

It was late autumn 1983 when I made the trip from Maryland to Virginia for my rendezvous with altered states. A converted Greyhound bus would get me there, along with twenty other handpicked officers ordered like me to take a magical mystery tour of the dark side. Fort Meade was our launch point, our destination the Monroe Institute in Faber, Virginia, where we'd attend a six-day training course designed to sharpen our mental dexterity by reworking our brain waves.

That was my cover story. The real one is even stranger. The institute's unique paranormal curriculum is known worldwide as Gateway Voyage, but what isn't so widely known is that the U.S. Army had for years been clandestinely sending teams of intelligence officers there to make the trip as well. Interest in the institute began in 1977, when Skip Atwater and others associated with the Remote Viewing Unit began paying undercover visits to the institutes' founder, Robert Monroe. A pioneer of commercial radio in the 1950s, Monroe had no idea who were these nicely dressed young men in suits who were coming regularly to meet with him. He figured they were just another group of typical knowledge-seeking customers. Atwater failed to mention that he was there to pick Monroe's brain for information useful to the fledgling remote-viewing program.

Located southwest of Washington, D.C., in the serene Blue Ridge Mountains, the Monroe Institute is a nonprofit educational and research organization exploring human consciousness in not so ordinary ways. The core of the institute's work centers on the idea that our brains aren't mere gray matter, but also produce a frequency all their own. When that frequency is tuned just so, other stations along the universe's broadband can be picked up at will, even visited. To get there, the institute uses certain sounds that have dramatic effects on the mind.

Monroe had discovered that an audio frequency plugged into one ear of a subject, with a separate slightly higher frequency plugged into the other, could create a series of vibrations that triggered deeper states of awareness than meditation, out-of-body experiences, or lucid dreaming. He found that when these differing tones met, a separate third super-wave was generated, synchronizing the left and right hemispheres of the brain. While both typically share the mind's workload, Monroe's "Hemi-Sync" fine-tuned the coupling with startling results—results the army took note of.

With Hemi-Sync, when the left part of the brain handling our higher reasoning functions united with the creative and artistic right side, the pair had the potential to act as a runway for soaring flights of the mind. A psychic rocket could blast off, powered by that theoretical ninety percent of our brains we never use. Out-of-body joyrides were happening at Monroe—all you had to do was lie down in an isolated booth, relax, then tune in and take off. Electroencephalograms and other medical scanning devices later confirmed the dramatic brainwave changes.

Legend has it that Monroe established the institute after taking part in several sleep experiments in the early 1960s that produced a stream of chilling out-of-body experiences. The story goes that on one restless night, as he floated in the air free of his physical shell, Monroe was able to see himself from up high tossing and turning in the bed below him. The episode was as real as if he had something solid to catch at and grip. There were now two Bob Monroes, one anchored to the earth, the other speeding through outer space.

Like many of us, Monroe had read accounts of those who returned from close encounters with the grim reaper claiming OBEs as an integral part of their near-death events. Being giftedly curious, he simply wanted to find out if any of these zany stories were true—without actually dying, of course. The rest is history.

OBEs aren't anything new. The concept has been around and practiced for thousands of years, dating back to the monks of ancient China and India. Their wizened mystics called it "astral projection," a practice where, either awake or dreaming, certain adept individuals could cast off their earthly skin and propel their consciousness—astral body—into unknown spirit dimensions across time and space. A strikingly similar trajectory to remote viewing, only we go there mentally step by step, following a rigorous set of proven military protocols. We also hold on to our bodies as we go.

All new arrivals to the Monroe Institute are expected to check reality at the door. You can pick it up later when your brain lands.


The scene outside the base looked more like a high school field trip than a group of top military personnel departing on a professional development retreat. There wasn't one uniform in sight as we milled about waiting for the bus to arrive, myself included. The last thing I wanted was for anyone to suspect I was army intelligence. People got a little jumpy when they heard that, as if everyone I met was automatically a suspect. It wasn't really proper to ask too many questions in a military environment like this anyway. What you did or had done back in Washington was your business. Don't tell, don't ask.

We were a pretty casual bunch: jeans, tennis shoes, and a few die-hard supervisory types in their obsequious blue suits. And though we looked practically alike, all nice little cookie-cutter civilians, most were unaware that we were here for very different reasons. The army Intelligence and Security Command personnel were going strictly for Monroe's Gateway Voyage program, while the RV Unit was on track for something called Rapid Acquisitional Personal Training, a special seminar with exclusive consciousness-raising classes devised just for us.

What *nobody* knew was that I was still attached to SED, a benign mole if you will. INSCOM's commanding general himself, Albert Stubblebine, had instructed me to quietly vet and assess the best and brightest candidates at the institute as potential recruits for the remote-viewing program. As a personal favor to him, Stubblebine also wanted me to look in on his friend Bob Monroe. The old man was apparently having some difficulty sleeping and the general wanted me to find out why. I love a good mystery.

Captain Bill Ray introduced himself and the other members of the RV Unit before we boarded the bus. Ray was also a Californian like me, a smooth counterintelligence man straight out of central casting with his mustache and dark hair splashed with just the right amount of gray around the temples. A devoted pipe smoker with an equal devotion to beer and bad music, he insisted the hundred-mile drive from Fort Meade to the institute would be no problem for him, despite an agonizing back problem he had suffered years earlier in a parachute jump mishap. He was just happy to be there, he said. So was I.

Next was Charlene Cavanaugh, a pretty lady in her mid-thirties who worked as a civilian analyst at INSCOM, where she had impressed General Stubblebine enough with her psychic skills at dinner parties to be included in the unit. That she was a woman

Members of the Remote Viewing Unit.

Me.

and a civilian was a turnoff to many male military officers, and I was no exception, but it wasn't my place to judge. I had a mission to accomplish, and if those who helped happened to be wearing a skirt, so be it. I was an equal-opportunity spy.

Last was Captain Paul Smith, a balding heavyset man with thick glasses who looked more like the guy giving you a hard time at the DMV than a captain in army intelligence. Paul was a case study in contradiction, a devout Mormon who adored heavy metal music and spoke fluent Arabic. We'd be sitting next to each other on the bus and rooming together when we got to the institute. My feeling at the time was that we'd become good friends.

My comrades and I chatted as the bus pulled to the gate to collect us. It was clear they were all up to speed on our orders—at least what they'd been told were our orders. It was also clear that they were a bit wary of me. Someone must have spilled the beans about my being an SED spook, but I suspected they'd still have no idea what my mission was. Military secrets are the most fleeting, but they'd get nothing out of me.

The weather for our drive was classic southeastern autumn, the countryside lit with a dazzling display of changing leaf color and wildflowers blooming around a myriad of waterfalls and gorges. There's a good reason why they call these the Blue Ridge Mountains, the misty haze that rises off in the distance in late afternoon turning the hills a fortress of deep sapphire.

It was all picture perfect except for our driver, who kept hugging the right as he raced closer to the edge of the road. Below us was a sheer drop into one of those lovely gorges; there was nothing to prevent us from hitting bottom in a hurry should he slip up. The bus driver's terrible driving was causing some anxiety on board, but not with everyone. I could hear Captain Ray sitting in the back singing some godawful song that sounded sort of Irish, but I couldn't be sure. Not the way he was groaning it. Paul Smith hardly noticed anything either. He had a concerned look on his face that I chalked up to a bad case of nerves as we got closer to our destination. After we began talking, I learned he had something else on his mind.

"Did you hear the scuttlebutt about the RV Unit possibly being transferred from INSCOM to DIA?" Paul asked, just loud enough for me and no one else to pick up. "We'll be on pretty thin ice if that's allowed to happen."

I nodded. Yes, I'd heard.

"We would by law be forbidden to use anything we find in a session. We could wind up in prison."

I nodded again. He was right. The Defense Intelligence Agency by its charter had no business in field operations. They were a caboodle of techno wonks who ran statistics, made evaluations, and analyzed the results of intelligence gathered by others—everything we *didn't* do at the unit.

"We'd have to turn any intelligence we collect over to the operations people, and then hurry up and wait," Paul said. "Our boys could be dying out there and all we could do about it is write statistical evaluations. Can you imagine that?"

"Not in this life," I told him. "Worst-case scenario, I'll hand our work over to some friends under the table and let them take it from there."

Paul turned away from me, pretending not to hear what I had just said. We were spies who did the work of spies, a job we could now be arrested for if the transition to DIA actually took place. And if we got caught. From the looks of it, Paul didn't want to get caught. I dropped the subject.

The transfer to DIA posed serious problems, but something more immediate was getting to me. This bus driver of ours was a certifiable lunatic. His nasty tendency to squeeze the right was bad enough, but now he was doing it at over ninety miles per hour down busy Route 395 out of D.C. and just begging for trouble.

"Hey!" I shouted to him. "Try the center lane, maybe you won't bounce off the guardrails and get us all killed."

The driver looked at me, puzzled, like he didn't know what I was talking about. Like he'd done nothing wrong.

"Think of Goldilocks and the bowls of porridge," I explained. "One is too hot, one too cold, and the last one is *ahhh*—just right. Center lane, that's the road you want."

The driver finally scooted to the middle of the highway and I got a sustained burst of applause from my relieved associates. By coincidence, Center Lane also happened to be the RV Unit's code name. Center Lane was why we were here.

It was General Stubblebine who had made the Monroe connection possible, who thought Gateway worthy enough to truck his best people off to try it. Having participated in many Hemi-Sync sessions himself, he was enthralled by the process. Lying in a dark sensory-deprived stall with his mind floating in a sea of altered-state-inducing sounds was too seductive to resist.

A West Point graduate who rose through the ranks to lead troops at every echelon of army command, including a tour as head of army intelligence, Stubblebine believed Monroe's program fit right in with the other elements of his secret master plan to redesign the culture at INSCOM. The general's self-styled "Jedi Imperative" was to create a new breed of super-soldier with alternative techniques he was convinced would have vital military applications in the coming age of psychic warfare—odd offerings such as neurolinguistic programming, and cryptomental technologies like hyperspatial howitzers and photonic potential barrier modulators. My all-time favorite was fire walking. I got a real kick out of watching senior officers race tippy-toed over beds of smoldering hot coals to demonstrate their unwavering faith in personal power and Stubblebine's Star Wars imperative. It was beautiful.

All this eccentricity fell under the umbrella of "lateral thinking," looking at things from all angles, which the general was really good at. Albert Einstein once said, "You can't solve a problem from the same consciousness that created it," a quote we heard quite often around the office.

Getting money to fund his pet programs was something Stubblebine was also very good at. The RV Unit was an ad hoc organization until he came along, completely off the block chart. Borrowing officers from other jobs and getting money to operate from the outside were recurrent fiscal nightmares. Stubblebine solved the problem by doing an end run around the bean counters, explaining our participation at Monroe as an important professional development course. We weren't there just for the institute's weird out-of-body program, which he knew the stuffy government accountants would never agree to. We were there instead for Rapid Acquisitional Personal Training—RAPT for short. Some of us referred to it as being "rapted." The RV Unit was special and needed special training, Stubblebine argued, so cough up the money, fellas.

The fact was, Stubblebine used us and RAPT to disguise his true objective of getting as many warm INSCOM bodies as he could through the doors at Monroe. It was there that he would lay the groundwork to prepare his men for future conflict in what his top aide Colonel John Alexander tagged "the New Mental Battlefield." And he would use our unit's hard-won Human Use certifications to make it all happen. Human Use meant you were a lab rat who could be experimented on, but only with your permission. This wasn't the case in the 1950s and 1960s when servicemen were exposed to LSD and other powerful mind-control drugs without their knowledge. After the acid scandal, Human Use certification required volumes of informed consent paperwork before anyone had the right to touch you. These detailed forms and medical evaluations could take months to be approved, but not for Major General Albert Stubblebine III. By hooking up with our unit, he bypassed the entire bureaucratic minefield, clearing the way for his people to become psychic test dummies just like the rest of us. We were all Jedi knights now, serving in his grand quest to create the perfect soldier. Lucky us.

With Stubblebine's dogged support, the pencil pushers at army finance were finally convinced the RV Unit's operations were kosher, thereby justifying our existence as a bona fide military unit. If it weren't for him, I could never have approached Skip Atwater to join the team, or later study at the feet of the master,

Albert N. Stubblebine III, the retired army major general who as commanding general of United States Army Intelligence and Security Command (INSCOM) helped make the RV Unit possible. The general had an avid interest in parapsychology.

Ingo Swann. Because of Stubblebine, by year's end I was attached to the unit and we were fully funded and good to go. I became a psi spy.

For that, I am eternally grateful to him.

We were almost at Monroe now, another hundred feet or so left to negotiate along a rambling spiral path rising from the base of the Rockfish River Valley to the institute's entrance.

My feelings about arriving at the institute were mixed. On one hand, I had my mission to vet and assess new recruits for the RV Unit, as well as to investigate Bob Monroe's insomnia. But there was also an urge in me to find something here that would change my life. I was hungry to shake up my belief in my own knowledge and the knowledge of others, to undo life lessons I knew were wrong. I wanted the world to change for me, to have an unforgettable vision that turned it on its head. Anything less and I'd just try to have some fun. Having been ordered to this lovely place, I felt obliged now to enjoy it. For the first time

How I looked as an army captain
before I was assigned to the Remote
Viewing Unit.

since I couldn't remember when, I was able to relax, to take a
break from thinking into tomorrow, from planning all my days
in advance. I had been ordered to kick off my shoes and that was
exactly what I was going to do, despite being forced into it. No
Type A personality like myself relaxes easily, but it seemed worth
it. The Monroe assignment was my first vacation in years, one big
paranormal picnic. Maybe I'd find what I was looking for here.
Maybe more.

The road eventually ended on a remote hillside at a cluster of
modern buildings that comprised the institute. There to greet us
was the man himself, Bob Monroe. He was in his early sixties,
balding with a shock of white hair around the edges, and he spoke

with an easy southern drawl. The dark lines under his eyes were so deep they could have caught rain in a drizzle. He was not at all the satanic brainwashing brute as he had been described by some at headquarters, the straight-shooting, churchgoing crowd who liked their wars done clean, officers who found the spiritual aspects of his program not only an outrage against God but an affront to every military code of behavior.

Bob Monroe was no antichrist as far as I could tell. He was more the cigar-smoking, draw-poker-playing ex–advertising man I envisioned. At least I hoped so. The latter description would make it easier for me to stomach what was about to come. I was looking at lying naked in dark CHEC cubicles— Controlled Holistic Environmental Chambers—listening to hours of Hemi-Sync brain tapes followed by a group therapy session where we would all share our feelings. The thought of these tough guys hugging and weeping with enough high emotion to bring the house down terrified me, but that's what I faced. I had come to Monroe to make contact with mysterious sensory imagery, ethereal voices, and all-out OBEs, but they would take a backseat to my real mission here. Everything always did.

After a warm welcome and a couple of funny jokes, Monroe led the Remote Viewing Unit and me to our quarters. The sun was low on the horizon now as we went, and it was getting chilly.

Inside, the main building seemed more like a ski resort than a scientific outpost. Comfy and sumptuous, "the Center," as it's called, was replete with wall-to-wall white carpeting, cushy furniture, and wood paneling taken from locally grown stock that lined the countryside surrounding the institute. There were three stories and we entered at the top to an open balcony that wrapped around the entire upper level with sweeping views to those below us. Each floor had one thing in common—room after room of specially designed accommodations you couldn't find anywhere else. I'm not talking five-star; they were small yet comfortable, furnished with dressers, desks, and all the other necessities of life, except for one thing—they each included two CHEC cubicles. This was where we'd do our out-of-body business and sleep. Each CHEC came with a twin air mattress, blackout curtains, and built-in stereo speakers to pipe in the cheery wake-up Muzak we'd hear every morning before Bob steered us from one Hemi-Sync level, or Focus, to the next. These levels ranged from the Focus 3 state of relaxation tapes, to Focus 10 where the mind is awake while the body sleeps, to Focus 15 where all sense of time ceases to exit. After that it's up, tone by tone, layer by hallucinogenic layer, to the alternate realities waiting for us in Focus 21. Through it all would be Bob Monroe's resonant disembodied voice guiding us on our voyage, then gently bringing us home. Only home was never like this.

For the next six days our schedule would be reveille at 0700 hours, our CHEC workout, then lunch, then group therapy, then a chance to walk it all off on the institute's grassy fields. A hot, ostensibly home-cooked dinner came at sundown, and a few paranormal lectures and films concluded the day. It was strange, but I was glad to let someone else run the show for a while. Turning my watch over to others felt good.

As Paul and I prepared to settle into our room, Monroe turned to us and asked, "Which one of you is Captain Dames?"

*Shit*, I thought. Most of the unit was already suspicious of me; now this would settle the matter of my spying on them.

"I am," I answered.

Monroe grinned and handed me a copy of his book, *Journeys Out of the Body*.

"Thanks. Is that all, sir?" I said.

"Call me Bob—and no it isn't," Monroe answered, then whispered, "You were told about my 'sleeping problem,' yes?"

"Yes, I was told."

"We'll get to it in the morning, okay?"

"Sure. In the morning."

Just as Bob turned and walked off, a phalanx of INSCOM officers marched up from the other direction on the balcony toward Paul and me. They were not a happy group of campers to be sure; the angry expression on their faces could melt lead. No doubt about it, they were not too thrilled to be here. I knew from an earlier briefing that these guys reported directly to General Stubblebine, a cadre of hard-charging warriors who never in a million years dreamed when they got this job they'd also be signing up for out-of-body duty at Monroe's psychic hotel. Be all you can be—and more!

I felt like the top of my head would come off the next morning after completing my first Gateway session at Monroe. The weather was foggy and still, but everything around me appeared extreme, as if reflected in a funhouse mirror. Colors were crystalline, the sky bluer, the grass greener. Objects and surfaces seemed to momentarily ripple and breathe, the white plush carpeting under me moving like waves on the ocean. Every volume knob in my brain was turned up, sounds heightened to incredible levels. My own breathing was like that crushing train noise people say they hear as a tornado is about to hit. The reality of being in a small room on an air mattress had given way to a universe bubbling over with tastes and smells and textures I'd never sensed before. And though I didn't have the institute's advertised out-of-body experience, the "doors of perception" William Blake wrote of had opened to present things as they truly are—infinite. What I felt now was better than the best poetry or philosophy. The vision I'd hoped for the day I arrived at Monroe had actually happened.

And this was just day one.

Paul Smith looked none the worse for wear as he exited the CHEC cubicle next to mine. In fact, he was downright ecstatic. He hadn't had an OBE either, but talked about seeing radiant swirls of light while under the influence of the Hemi-Sync tapes, a warm tingle that flowed over his entire body like a shot of good brandy, and an overpowering urge to turn over on his mattress without moving at all. And if that weren't enough, in the middle of Focus 15 he suddenly returned to his childhood, to his great-grandfather's house in western Idaho. He could feel the vibrations of the old staircase he knew so well, hear the creak of the wood, taste the frozen cherries his grandma always made especially for him. The memory of it was clearer than any he'd ever had before. Paul had traveled back in time, exactly as we were taught to do in remote viewing.

He was home again, without ever leaving our room.

I asked Paul how as a Mormon he came to terms with such an un-Mormon-like experience. He straightened me out on that. For starters, much of what was done at the institute resonated with his faith, even traveling to other planets where alien beings might exist. The Church of Latter-day Saints maintains that all creatures are from God, all spiritual realms. How we make contact is irrelevant, out of body or not. He told me the early church leader Brigham Young himself preached the point that all of humanity was acquainted with otherworldly feelings, they just weren't aware of them. To Paul, God wasn't merely a myth created by our superstitious ancestors to account for things successfully explained now through science. If remote viewing had proved anything to him, it was that there was still plenty out there it couldn't explain. Remote viewing was real and worked, but the naysayers had no way of accounting for that, so they chose to denigrate and nullify it. Gateway was perfectly in line with Paul's beliefs, something I already knew anyway. Captain Smith was no hypocrite, not like so many other officers I knew who'd say anything to get what they want. He had a moral compass and

I respected that. He also loved the army as much as I did. That was enough for me.

Instead of taking our normally scheduled lunch that day, I gathered the RV Unit together in one of the institute's special "cool-down" rooms, a dark space dimly lit by soft red lights. As the operations officer, I was technically the monitor now, the man in charge. It was time they found out why we were here. I told them about Monroe's insomnia, leaning heavily on information provided to me by Skip Atwater and Bob Monroe. There had never been any formal briefing—Bob had approached me before breakfast to get me up to speed, and Atwater had mentioned some things General Stubblebine told him about the situation.

Monroe described a feeling akin to being "pinged," as in the sound of a sonar echo or a bullet striking metal. The sound was driving him crazy. He'd dial his phone and forget who he called, go to the store and forget what to buy, forget what people said then ask again and forget again. Most would call that the price of growing older, but not Bob Monroe. He was sure someone was watching him, accessing his mind, people he didn't know and was frightened of. They had come during one of his out-of-body excursions, confronting him in that netherworld between existence and whatever lies beyond. The encounter had made him unable to sleep right for weeks.

"Maybe he's having a nervous breakdown," Bill Ray said. "Things aren't exactly normal around here."

"I don't think so," I answered.

"He should listen to a few more of those tapes of his," Charlene said. "I slept like a baby last night."

Paul rubbed his hands together impatiently. "Listen, he needs to see a doctor, Ed," he said. "And we're not doctors. What's his sleeping problem got to do with us?"

"Everything," I said.

Now that I had their attention, I continued with the rest of the story, the juiciest part.

"During this OBE, Monroe also encountered a strange and beautiful woman. He's positive this woman is the one probing his mind. From what he could remember, her name was Inga Arnyet."

Eyebrows raised, more interest now.

"He got her name while out of his body?" Charlene asked.

"Yes," I answered. "I know, pretty amazing."

"*Cherchez la femme*," Ray chimed in. "Always a woman."

Charlene offered Bill an icy stare for his comment and he backed off. No more negative female stereotypes, thank you.

"We aren't going to take anything as a given here people, not what Monroe says or anybody else," I told them. "We've been ordered to find out why the old man's not sleeping."

"And how are we supposed to do that?" Smith asked.

They were all looking at me now. I answered slowly. "Remote viewing, Captain. Remote viewing."


As the unit got into position to begin, I decided to try something radically different, something that had never before been attempted on a remote-viewing mission. I was going to combine two RV systems into one that would ensure success.

Up to now, the accepted method for gaining knowledge of targets was ERV, or extended remote viewing. Based on traditional relaxation techniques similar to what Bob Monroe uses, the goal of ERV is to stem the tide of conscious thought almost to the point of sleep. Theoretically, in this power-nap state, a deeper connection with the psychic signal line is supposed to be made by cutting off all mental noise we create internally. Usable signals can then naturally enter awareness because the mind is clear and open. In practice, however, it doesn't always work out that way. More often than not, the endless voices and images we routinely generate in our minds are too strong to just simply eliminate. They continue obscuring and distorting important data. Results cannot be depended on as correct, a failing that doesn't cut the mustard if you're dealing with critical intelligence.

The altered-states approach is flawed in other ways. Remote viewers in ERV mode don't know whether they are viewing the target upside down or right side up. Precise orientation in space eludes them. Since the RV monitor doesn't know where the target is either, the whole project can go up in smoke. With ERV, an unsuccessful session turns into nothing more than a quaint psychic experiment the army couldn't care less about. They weren't paying us to experiment; they wanted tangible, verifiable intelligence. Thanks to the efforts of Ingo Swann, that's exactly what they got.

It was Swann who pioneered the more accurate CRV process, coordinate remote viewing. Here the viewer is given an abstract coordinate, wholly random numbers that act as a reference point, a psychic address that leads to the target. Through a series of steps Swann helped create, the CRV viewer is trained to access noise-free psychic signals by remaining fully conscious and awake. By staying in structure, CRV yields quality information more consistently and predictably than its half-asleep counter-part. If you ask a viewer to move 2.2 kilometers southwest, that's exactly what they'll do in their mind, and more. With CRV, the spatial orientation dilemma was finally solved. By merging the ERV method, which our unit was more familiar with, to the structured CRV techniques I had learned from Swann, past, present, and future events were now there for the viewing. All that remained was to get my team to do it. To see without being blinded by their minds.

The room was just right to begin, almost dark, barely lit by a single faint red light on the table in front of me. Starting with the ERV method, I told the unit to free and relax their minds, to suggest to themselves how at ease they were, no sensations in their bodies, all thoughts to go blank. I didn't want anyone speculating about anything, no bursts of psychic impressions clouded by mental noise. I wanted them to follow instructions with military discipline, to maintain the structure I was about to give in the exact sequence I gave it.

Because Monroe had provided us with the name Inga Arnyet, the unit had something to work with in the dreamy ERV state. They could hang their hats on that name as a starting point. As for me, the mysterious woman invading Bob's mind was the hook I'd hang a CRV search term on, and the target reference numbers. The search term that I used, which was for my eyes only, was "Bob Monroe/Inga Arnyet event." This was what we'd remote view, only the unit didn't know it. We would go back in time to when Bob first met this person, the same night he drifted out of body and sensed a human presence there with him. I gave the team the target reference numbers *3451/6723* and nothing more. They didn't like it right off.

"What the heck are those numbers?" Ray asked.

"Just relax and search for the target," I answered.

"We can't do our job if we don't know what we're looking for," Charlene said.

"It's not your job to know—your job is to work."

"This is Ingo's coordinate technique, isn't it, Ed?" Paul said with a sly grin.

I told him it was.

"We've used it before, but this sounds interesting."

I told him it would be.

"So what's next?"

"You were given the name Inga Arnyet, right?" I say.

Affirmative nods all around.

"So go find her."

"And the numbers?" Paul asked.

"Write them down and keep them in your head," I explained. "I'll be using them again later."

"Jesus, Ed," Ray said. "Just tell us what they mean."

"No. The rest you'll have to work blind. As monitor, I'll be asking the questions and moving you around. When you get a sense of something—anything—sketch it on the paper. Other than that, you're on your own from here on out."

Charlene threw back her hair and laughed. "C'mon, you can give us more, Captain," she said. "More is better."

I passed around pens and sheets of paper, scribbled the time and date on mine, crossed my legs, and looked at them.

"Begin."

The crew relaxed into the cozy chairs Bob had so generously provided for us and closed their eyes. The hits started coming almost immediately. They were somewhere else, moving back in time to remote view Monroe as he was many weeks ago. I wrote down everything they said.

"There's a man sleeping, but he's okay, comfortable really, nothing bothering him at all," Charlene said. She was slurring her words slightly, they all were. That's how I knew they were in the ERV zone. They sounded drunk.

"Not here. I sense a woman with him," Paul interrupted. "She's hovering over him, watching him."

"What does she look like?" I asked.

"Don't see her face. She seems pleasant enough, not outwardly threatening in any way. It's like she doesn't exist. Not in this world at least."

"What's she up to?"

"She's reading his mind," Charlene said. "Trying to access information, to expose secrets she thinks he has."

"Military secrets?"

"I don't know. What are you getting at?"

I had to be cautious here. I needed to steer them without waking them up, without shattering the moment. I couldn't suggest things or skew their minds in any way. They would lose focus, begin seeing what I wanted, not what they saw.

"Forget it," I said. "Just tell me what you see."

I looked over at Bill Ray. He'd been strangely quiet, no wise-cracks or running commentary, just silent, eyes closed.

"There's something about her, a peculiar air, a certain presence that I'm familiar with," Paul said.

"What else?"

"Her name is Inga Arnyet."

"Good. What else?"

Paul smiles. "Oh yeah. She's a spy."

I tried not to react to Paul's revelation, treating this bombshell like any other bit of information. I turned instead to Charlene. She'd become restless, agitated.

"Are you okay?" I asked.

"There are two others standing by the sleeping man, two men," she said. "They're with Inga. They work for her."

"Try to center on them, who are they?"

Paul was there with Charlene, as if he was sharing her vision. He saw what she saw.

"These men are not nice guys," he said. "But that isn't what makes me uneasy. It's their hands. They're soft, like they've never done a hard day's work. More spies, no doubt."

"Wait—something's wrong," Charlene said, trembling. "The sleeping man, he's tossing and turning, they're probing his mind, it's a focused attack, all three at the same time trying to impose themselves on him. They're hurting him."

"Why?

Paul made a fist with his hand. "They think he's important, a chief or boss or something. They know he runs an operation with a lot of people who do what he tells them."

"Yes," Charlene added. "They think he's the one."

Without any warning, Bill Ray all at once came to life. His tone was casual, no alarm in it. It was as if everything that had transpired since we sat down together had never happened to him. He had been out somewhere else the whole time.

"Spires reaching for the sky, round yet pointed like an onion, so quirky and colorful," he said. "They're at the end of a huge square near a hotel of some kind with a river running through it."

For all his zoning out, Ray had just hit the nail on the head. He was onto a place I knew like the back of my hand. I wanted them all with him now.

"Everyone, look at those spires, rise five hundred feet above them, and get a fix on what you see."

It took a few minutes, but the unit switched gears to join up with Ray in the middle of the square he had spoken of.

"I see another building, regal but frightening, a source of fear for so many innocent people," Charlene said.

Ray massaged his bad back with his hand. "She's right," he said. "Lots of poor souls went through there, I can almost hear their screams. Been going on like this for centuries."

"Is it still in operation?"

"Yes," Paul said, "and our spies are walking toward it. Oh, and by the way, they're speaking *Russian*."

Charlene and Ray opened their eyes and started fidgeting in their chairs. They'd disconnected. This session was over. Just as well, I didn't want anyone burning out anyway. They had done well, and there was so much left to do.

"Let's call it a day," I told them. "We'll pick it up again tonight, after dinner."

"What are we supposed to do until then?" Ray asked.

"I don't know, take a walk down by the lake. I hear there's a rowboat and canoe down there. Very romantic."

Charlene rolled her eyes and left.

"Are they showing those funny cartoons today?" Ray said.

He was talking about the enlightening animations the institute presented in the late afternoon, the ones that tested and honed perceptual ability. Sometimes they were funny.

"I think so," Paul answered. "Let's do it, I could use a good laugh. What about you, Ed?"

"I'll be along later. Got some work to do."

"So what else is new?" Ray said.

"'Bye," I said.


I took my notes from the Monroe session and stepped out onto the institute's long porch to go over them. The expansive lawn stretched out before me as if it had no end, vanishing into a deep valley that rose steeply to the rolling hills beyond, rich with southern maples and open fields.

I had to put it all together in my mind. Prioritize. The rest of the RV Unit was at lunch or by the lake or watching cartoons, it didn't matter. I knew where to find them. I could see people hiking off in the distance along a broad gravel road where small groups of cows were grazing. It was those unhappy army officers we met earlier walking off knots of nervous tension. I envied them. Mine were just beginning.

Russians.

When Paul had said the ghostly spy trio spoke Russian, it all fell into place for me—that along with Ray's nearly exact description of what I believed to be St. Basil's Cathedral in Red Square. The church cemented my feeling that Moscow had a hand in all this. But I couldn't let on that those I suspected of probing Bob Monroe's mind were a team of Soviet psi spies, a team just like ours. I still wasn't completely sure, and even if I were I couldn't tell them. This was on a need-to-know basis, and they didn't need to know. Not yet.

My suspicions came from top-secret reports stating how the Soviets were moving fast into paranormal research. There was more than ample intelligence confirming this, solid evidence that their experiments in psi's military potential were advancing at an astonishing rate. Unlike us, the Russian scientists could depend on the hefty financial backing of their army, secret police, and other governmental agencies to foot the bill. With a growing "psi gap" looming like black storm clouds on the horizon, the old pros of cold war spycraft like Stubblebine had made it plain to all concerned what the dire consequences would be for lagging behind. Our country's security was at stake if we fell asleep at the wheel on these new psychic technologies. In no time the Reds might get their hands on classified documents, learn naval and troop movements and the whereabouts of our most covert military installations.

I was also privy to information that the gang in Moscow was experimenting with something called "psychotronics." In stark contrast to remote viewing, which gains knowledge about targets, they were instituting a remote-influencing program, transmitting commands *into* their targeted victims. Working on the human subconscious, psychotronics could be used not only to demoralize or disable our armed forces, but also to kill them outright from a distance. This went for our political and military leadership as well. Call it remote killing. No one was safe. How could you be safe from an enemy you couldn't see?

The pressure was on and a consensus finally reached. The Soviets would not be permitted to cross the finish line before us in the psychic arms race. Remote viewing quickly jumped to the intelligence front burner, and me along with it.

Monroe's sleepless mystery was unraveling. Paul Smith was right on the money when he said these were Russian spies we were engaging. But why? I rifled through my notes looking for the answer. I found it. It was something Charlene said, something about Monroe being "the one." Then it came to me. If Soviet intelligence had even cursory knowledge about our psi spy program like we did of theirs, who better than Bob Monroe to be at the head of it? It was known that INSCOM was sending officers there to train under him, so maybe they had found out. After that it wouldn't be much of a stretch to assume he was in command of the program. Just look at all the military types coming and going at his place, hanging on his every word. The Russians had psychically probed Bob Monroe in the mistaken belief that he was in charge of the entire RV operation. Nothing could be further from the truth. He was in charge of nothing. All they had accomplished was a vicious mental attack against a vulnerable old man while he slept. What a victory.

Monroe's troubles were only the tip of the iceberg, an isolated symptom of a hidden, more serious threat. What the rest of the unit didn't know, and I was not at liberty to tell them, was that we were in reality part of an elite group of skilled soldiers fighting a war in the ether, the hypothetical material supposed to occupy all of space beyond the heavens. We weren't only about uncovering targets. We had a specific though yet unknown foe against whom we were going on the offensive. Our adversaries: the secret Soviet psi spy team known only in black ops circles in whispers as "Extrasensors." We were the first ever to have encountered them.

And we'd meet up again tonight.


Much like everything else provided to institute clientele, dinner had the feel of being home-cooked, something you knew had been developed over time and perfected. Only local chefs needed apply here. The Faber, Virginia, townspeople prided themselves on inventive and tasty creations, and the visitors to Monroe generally ate it up. I know I did.

Before dining with my RV mates, I decided to remain behind in my room to go over the intelligence I had received from my contacts at SED, which was composed of satellite reconnaissance photographs and several clandestine phone calls to me. I learned that what we had remote viewed was true. The towering spires Ray saw and sketched matched up exactly with the vividly colored onion-shaped steeples of St. Basil's Cathedral in the heart of Moscow's Red Square. The other massive building they sensed as a source of terror for so many was none other than KGB headquarters itself. Since the time of Catherine the Great, this edifice of pain had served as the center of Russian secret operations, where literally hundreds of thousands who passed through its gates were imprisoned, interrogated, and killed. Dictator Joseph Stalin lived large when it came to torture chambers, ordering that another wing be built to accommodate all the new guests he was sending over. It was here in the murderous shadow of Uncle Joe that I'd turn the tables on Inga Arnyet and her friends.

In this morning's RV session, Paul had mentioned that he saw our Extrasensor trio moving quickly toward the KGB building. This was obviously where they were stationed, smack in the middle of the Soviet intel machine. Our mission was to remote view where they were going, not so much to follow them but to direct our attention to where their bodies were, to RV their current location. They were the targets now, the prey to be hunted down in the ether. The Bob Monroe blunder had revealed their existence, and I was determined now to flush them out.

I gave the unit the same set of target reference numbers as before so there would be no confusion about returning them to the exact spot we left off this morning. The search term I changed to "Inga Arnyet/Extrasensors" to include the mysterious lady spy's cohorts. I wanted them all together when we made the hit.

It didn't take long to enter the zone, the soft red light, the darkened room, the silence of the place once again working its magic perfectly. It was Charlene who kicked off the action first, drifting into the ether immediately, connecting with the target in less time than it took for me to give her the CRV coordinates. She'd become one hell of an asset, a surprisingly top-notch remote viewer, especially in a pinch.

"It's freezing cold outside, but where I am is warm," she said. "This is an office of some kind, not that many people. Some are on the telephone, some doing paperwork, others chatting with each other. About what, I don't know."

"Yes, it's administrative stuff, none of the folks we saw before," Paul added.

"One of the guys is looking at photographs," Ray said.

That's what I wanted, what we were snooping around for. "Move in closer on the man with the pictures," I told them.

They did as I asked. Paul had this one.

"I can't quite make it out, but he's looking at photographs of a ship, a large steel-plated vessel of some sort," he said. "Hold on—it's one of *ours*. This clown's got pictures of one of our navy ships. From the look of it, they're satellite images."

It made sense. This was exactly how I did it. Remote view a target, nail its location, and then confirm what I'd found with other intelligence sources, satellite recon being one of them. This Soviet officer was more than likely an analyst inspecting information gathered by the Extrasensors.

Ray was sketching something on his pad. I crossed the room and peered over his shoulder at what he was drawing. It was a black box, with a single bright ray of light coming from it.

"Explain what you're seeing," I said.

"It isn't very big, mounted on the wall above him," he said. "There's a light coming from it, like a spotlight, only smaller. I don't like it—it makes me feel itchy."

"These boxes are in every room," Charlene said.

"Pay them no mind," I said. "Move forward in time, locate the people we saw this morning. Focus on the people."

There was no reason for the unit to get all wound up by the black boxes. I already knew what they were, and there was nothing to be concerned about. They were Faraday cages, named after Michael Faraday, the brilliant nineteenth-century English scientist who invented them. Still made basically the same way as in Faraday's time, with some modern improvements, the cages are constructed out of an enclosure lined by a highly conductive wire mesh. The mesh behaves as a shield, blocking electromagnetic waves by redistributing them, watering them down enough to cancel out their radio frequency signature. It does this to all forms of RF energy, like radio and television waves, keeping them from exiting the box. If a shoplifter lined a shopping bag with aluminum foil he could walk out of the targeted store with no problem after stealing what he wanted, bypassing the retailer's alarm system. The foil acts as a Faraday cage. It's the weapon of choice for thieves to rip off RFID-tagged items. Kids, don't try this at home.

More to the point, the Faraday cage can prevent someone from electronically eavesdropping on you. Just step into the box and talk. I first penetrated a Faraday cage when the RV Unit helped me expose the Soviet bioweapons program. Believing they were safe within their electric cloak, the Russians never knew that the inner workings of their defense council had been breached. The equivalent to our National Security Council, the Soviet Defense Council met in highly controlled environments, but we got in anyway. We had no problem targeting their briefings and downloading invaluable intelligence about future military operations. No amount of fancy electric bars around their birdcages could keep a remote viewer out. They meant nothing because we weren't using technology to get in. The Russian briefings existed as patterns of information, ideas outside of time and space. We didn't connect physically to them; we mentally tuned in the pattern as it sat stored in the collective mind. The unconscious could give a hoot about stupid black boxes. It connects to the event, much like reading a book. Turn to the page you want and copy what you need. There was no way they could stop us then—or now.

"I see her, I see Inga!" Ray shouted. "She's alone, in one of the rooms, just her. She's got this weird expression."

"It's like she's meditating," Charlene said. "She's sitting in a chair, breathing slowly, measuring each breath as if in a trance. Her eyes are closed, even though the room is dark. Just this weak lamp on the table in front of her."

"Sounds familiar," Paul said. "Just like us."

"I sense the other two, the men. They're in separate rooms too," Charlene added. "Also in a trancelike state."

She was spot-on again, and so was Paul. Inga and her people were doing precisely the same as us under the same ERV setup, right down to the dim lights. But there was one important difference. They were isolated, working alone. This told me they weren't military. There were no protocols here, no standards to work with. The Russians were using clairvoyants to do their remote viewing.

*Witches.*

We knew the Soviet military intelligence service GRU was combing the country for psychics, shamans, witch doctors, and anyone else with even a shred of credibility to fill the ranks of their RV program, but what we didn't realize was that they were searching exclusively for them. Reports that GRU had used drugs on regular military personnel to chemically induce altered states and then remote viewing must have been true. They didn't have the training program we did, no Ingo Swann showing them the way. After a host of their army "volunteers" died as a result of these experiments, the Russians moved in on those who didn't need drugs to travel without moving. They got themselves a troop of superior natural psychics to do the job. If Inga and her crew were any indicator, we were up against some of the best paranormal experts the Evil Empire could produce. They had no choice but to use them, but I did. My team was properly trained. They could do it all when called upon and in any way we wanted. I had an idea.

When the Extrasensors were pinging Bob Monroe, they did it as a unit, one concentrated effort directed at their subject. Though they picked the wrong target, their combined efforts did the trick as they got inside his head and freely prodded around in there. We'd do the same thing.

"I want all of you to converge on the image of Inga Arnyet. Circle her, close in on her, get under her skin and tell me what she's doing."

"Like a pack of wolves on the hunt," Ray said.

"No," I replied. "More dangerous."

I could almost see them mentally moving in their minds, trying to join up in the ether, to work as one thought, one remote viewer. Ray sipped coffee, Charlene took a deep breath, and Paul shook his head to clear his mind. Whatever it took to slip into another universe. They were magnificent.

"She's rubbing her face, uncomfortable," Paul said.

"Like looking around for flies she can't swat," Ray said.

Charlene swung her arm over her legs and sat forward. "In her mind, she's baffled by what she feels. Worried she won't be able to work, to do her job. Concerned about her family, I sense it. A daughter. She's beginning to sweat."

"We're scaring the shit out of her," Paul said.

Ray cupped his hand and hollered into them like a microphone: "How do *you* like it now, honey?"

"Cut it out," I said. "This isn't the opposing team in a football game. She's our enemy. Stay on her and don't let up for anything. No one breaks the circle, am I clear?"

They gave me the thumbs-up, all in their own way.

"Difficulty breathing, panic, no window to open," Charlene said. "She's looking everywhere now, under the desk, on the walls, at the box on the wall. She can't understand."

It was Paul's turn to sit up now, his back straight as a plank, eyes wide shut. "Banging, fists pounding on the door. *Boom-boom.* Like pistol shots. Someone wants in that room."

"The door opened. There they are, the others," Charlene reported. "They're shaky too, confused, looking for her to explain what's happening to them. Why they feel the way they do. They're looking around now too. Searching."

"The two men, they've lost their nerve," Ray said. "They've become ineffective, and they know it."

"Inga, she just jumped out of her chair," Paul said. "Wait— wait. She's found what she's looking for. They all have. They're looking up, they're looking at *us!*"

Charlene snapped out of her dream state and grabbed me by the arm hard. "They're looking at us looking at them."

Ray jumped out of his chair now. "We've been made," he announced. "Our cover's blown."

"Shut down. Shut it all down," was my final order. "Disconnect, drop out, stop feeling, but shut it down now."

Each began to deflate, like a tire after you stick a nail in it, a slow drawn-out leak. The mental impressions they'd called into existence didn't fade away easily, but they did eventually go. The psychic cat-and-mouse game was over for now.

"But how?" Paul asked. "How could they know we were watching them when we weren't even there? Unless—"

"Unless they're remote viewers like us," Charlene said.

They stared at me, waiting for me to say something.

"We'll discuss it later," I told them.

"Why not now?" Ray asked. "Now's a good time for me."

"Me too," Paul agreed.

"Same here," said Charlene.

I smiled. "It's nice to see you all operating like a team for a change, but this isn't a democracy, remember? You have your orders, so please follow them. We'll discuss it later."

They weren't happy, but that was okay. No soldier ever is. But they did as they were told. My psychic spy vs. psychic spy tale would have to wait. This was the United States Army, not *Mad* magazine. Generally speaking, of course.


I was back on the institute's long porch, again holding session notes in my hand. The weather was turning nasty, a cold wind blowing in from the north, from Washington, no doubt. Winter was on its way, heralding an end to the fall season. The caretaker out back was stoking a fire to burn the leaves he had raked and I breathed in the toasty smoke. My favorite part of autumn. I liked the cold breeze too, the crisp clarity it brought to thoughts. I needed that right now. Clarity.

*We were compromised.*

The remote-viewing program was no longer a secret to the Russians, if it ever was at all. It was true that we had exposed the Extrasensors through Bob Monroe, learning how they used remote viewing to spy on U.S decision-makers. While they had been wrong about Monroe being our leader, they had demonstrated their phenomenal skill at targeting individuals and getting inside their minds. It could be a commanding general one day, the president of the United States another. But we could do the same to them as well, and find new ways to thwart their efforts too, so things were even Steven on that account. But we were still compromised. The Soviet psi spies could track us back through the ether to Fort Meade or anywhere else. We were endangering not only ourselves but the entire military. They knew where we lived. But measures were in the works to limit the risk, ways that Ingo Swann and others in the program could slow them down some. Knowing this made my decision easier. The last thing I wanted was to close up the unit.

I stepped down off the porch and walked toward the caretaker and his fire, clutching my RV notes tightly to me. I made some conversation, waiting for him to turn away and rake some more leaves. When he did, I tossed my notes into the flames. I watched as they ignited and crisped, sending a light wisp of bluish smoke into the sky. It was done.

I had reached the conclusion that reporting to my superiors on what had happened would be counterproductive. There were enough people at command just dying for a good reason to permanently shut down the RV program, and I wasn't about to hand it to them on a silver platter. This was no time to throw the baby out with the bathwater. Remote viewing may have been a far-fetched fantasy to them, but I knew its real value. The Bob Monroe episode proved that. That's why my notes were burning; I couldn't let some jerk pull the plug on us. There was still so much to learn from RV. No one would ever find out what had happened. Not even the unit.

I warmed my hands over the fire and chewed the fat some more with the caretaker, a local man in his sixties with a few stories to tell of his own about the characters that had crossed his path at the institute over the years. We'd make the list, I was sure.

We both stopped as a couple of huge Green Berets walked past us. The biggest one was really pissed off, even his hand gestures marked by struggle and anger. I was almost embarrassed for him.

"I'm sick of it here," he shouted. "When the fuck do we get out of this damn mind trap?"

This mind trap was my office.

The drive back to Fort Meade was pretty much uneventful, no rampaging bus driver veering to the edge of the highway. As we headed into Washington, both Paul and I noticed a signpost warning about an approaching road repair situation up ahead. It read CENTER LANE CLOSED.

We laughed, wondering if this was a sign of things to come. Considering that our unit shared that name and we too could be closed down if our transfer from the army to DIA went through, it came to us as a joke. But that didn't last long.

"Maybe we ought to remote view it," I said.

"No, we'll be the first to know," Paul answered.

Back at the fort, before I could even unpack my toothbrush, Skip Atwater called me into his office—something important, he said, something that couldn't wait. Thoughts of him having me brought up on charges for not reporting what had happened at Monroe invaded my mind. My mouth was so dry it felt like the entire 3rd Armored Cavalry Regiment was marching through it with General Patton himself riding point. As I opened the door, three men wearing what looked like identical drab blue suits were there waiting for me, along with a very serious-looking Skip Atwater. *Oh shit*, I thought. *This is it.*

As it turned out, the men were from the Secret Service and were here regarding something that crossed their desks that concerned them very much. I had almost forgotten, but several months earlier I had contributed some disturbing information to a Scientific National Intelligence Estimate on paranormal research and development behind the Iron Curtain, and the Secret Service was on the distribution list. My SNIE, as it was called, contained classified material detailing several out-of-the ordinary subjects, including remote influencing, remote viewing, and target selection and acquisition protocols. All of it focused on psychic phenomena.

"Is it true you can stop a goat's heart just by looking at it?" one of the agents asked.

"I've heard it was done," I answered.

"Then you can also do that to important people, right?"

"Possibly."

Another agent finally said what was really on their minds. "Can the Russians hurt President Reagan?" he asked flatly.

"No way, boys," I said with all due authority. "They can look in on every secret he has in his mind, but they can't physically harm him in any way. Nobody can."

"Fair enough," the lead guy said, and off they went without another word.

It was their job to protect the person of the president, not what was in his head. According to some, there wasn't much there to begin with anyway.

When the agents were gone, Skip joked that we should all start wearing Ronald Reagan masks when we remote viewed; maybe the Soviets would think it was Ronnie himself looking back at them. I managed a controlled laugh. If he only knew how close he was. They were indeed looking back at us.

Skip then asked me to sit down, but I declined, citing a slight cold I had picked up sleeping in the CHEC room at Monroe. I was headed for bed, but he had one more thing to tell me.

"Just wanted to let you know that the move to DIA is going down in a few weeks," he said. "The whole thing was approved from up high. No more Center Lane. Sorry, Ed."

All I saw was that sign on Route 395.

"It's okay," I said. "You know, FUBAR all the way. We'll make it through."

"Not me, I'm glad I won't be around to see it. I just put in for retirement and named you as the man to replace me."

For some reason, I still couldn't get the CENTER LANE CLOSED sign out of my mind. Skip had just informed me that I was going to take over the RV Unit, a dream I had never even imagined, and all I would say to him was:

"Wow, thanks a lot, Skip."

"Don't thank me yet," he added. "I hear they're going to recruit tarot readers and spoon benders to work in the unit. Glad I won't be around to see it, yes sir."

"Witches," I mumbled under my breath.

"How's that?" Skip asked.

"Nothing," I answered. "Nothing at all."

As a footnote to all this, it was a good twenty years later that I happened to run into one very distinguished, well-dressed Russian gentleman named Ivan Sokalav at a remote-viewing conference here in the states. After a few vodka martinis, and much to our mutual surprise, we discovered that we were once arch-enemies. Sokalav was the operations officer for the civilian-run Soviet Extrasensor program while I was in charge of ops for the RV Unit after Atwater's retirement. We also learned that both of us had elected not tell a soul that we ran afoul of each other one day while carousing out in the ether. The fear of having our units shut down had motivated us to the same conclusion. What's more, when the KGB discovered what he was doing, they had officially closed down his unit as a weird liability they were unwilling to support a moment longer. That was exactly what had happened to us when General Stubblebine stepped down from INSCOM, leaving us in the hands of Lieutenant General Harry Soyster, the

Harry Edward Soyster, a retired U.S. Army lieutenant general, served as director of the Defense Intelligence Agency, where he made life miserable for the RV Unit.

director of DIA and a notoriously rabid remote-viewing hater. It was Soyster who wasted no time slamming the doors once I revealed the existence of the unit to the press. He couldn't hold his water another minute.

We had a good laugh, my Soviet counterpart and I, sipping martinis and talking about it all that day, a day I never wanted to end. But like all good things, it had to pass. But remote viewing didn't. It was just beginning to grab the public's imagination, still producing undeniable results on a host of cases I took on for a growing list of private clients. Something Ingo Swann would call a genuine "eight-martini result."

Or was it ten?

I'll have to ask Ivan next time I "see" him.

# POWS NO MORE

"Don't move the tank, I'm here—don't kill me!"

I shouted as loud as I could, but nothing. No one heard. I yelled it again and again so hard I thought I'd burst a lung, but still nothing. Only the deafening boom of 105 mm canon shells and the rumbling sound of diesel tank engines preparing to move out. All I could do was wonder how it feels to be crushed.

It was night and pissing rain and I was belly up on the ground stuck in waist-deep mud between two M-60 Patton tanks. I had made the mistake of riding on the fender of one when the thing suddenly lurched forward, hurling me into the mushy earth and sandwiching me in. A still very wet-behind-the-ears lieutenant at the time, I was stationed in Germany and had pulled duty as range safety officer for night gunnery practice. Low-ranking juniors like me did that when our name came up on the rotating duty roster. Then—the miracle. A voice:

"What the fuck are you doing down there, Lieutenant?"

I looked heavenward to the friendly face peering down at me.

At first I thought it was an angel talking, but the voice belonged to a young sergeant who just happened to have glanced down and seen me there squirming like a fish out of water half submerged in the muck. Hoisting me up by my field jacket, he dragged me into his nice warm and dry tank cabin. All that was missing was a cup of hot coffee.

I'd be missing too if it weren't for him.

Because of one alert sergeant who sensed another human being's peril and trusted his instincts, I'm alive today to tell the tale. In his own way, he personified the soldier's sworn pledge to a stricken comrade—"Leave no man behind."

Ironically, this code of honor was made famous during the Vietnam War, the concept being that whether you fall or are captured in combat, your brothers in arms will stop at nothing to bring you home. But it was also in Vietnam where so many veterans' families and others maintain that the reverse came true. That we knowingly left behind our own to rot.

And worse.

It was H. Ross Perot, the Texas computer billionaire, philanthropist, and two-time independent U.S. presidential candidate, who more than anyone else brought the tragic and often shady issue of America's abandoned POWs to the front lines of public awareness. With his characteristic in-your-face style, Perot for years single-handedly used his vast financial resources on behalf of these cast-off servicemen to pound away at the lies and roadblocks erected in the name of "national security." No politician or fat-cat government official escaped his celebrated wrath. After subsidizing one rescue mission himself and watching others crash and burn, the diminutive Perot reportedly stared down the six-foot-four assistant secretary of defense Richard Armitage by confronting him with solid evidence exposing his campaign of deception about POWs left behind in Southeast Asia. Getting nowhere with that, he took his case to then Vice President George Bush, where "Poppy" unceremoniously showed him the White House door. One thing about Perot, he was as convinced of his own moral rightness as he was loath to accept the possibility of being wrong. He also carried a grudge like nobody's business.

It didn't take long for Perot's labors to "mysteriously" leak to the press, forcing Armitage to allegedly bow out of his appointment as secretary of defense, where he had been considered a shoo-in under his buddy and now president George Bush. The big guy had taken one for the team. What a rock-hard hero.

By the mid-1980s, it was Ross Perot that every Joe Six-Pack with a POW/MIA YOU ARE NOT FORGOTTEN bumper sticker on his pickup turned to for justice. And for a time it seemed that was exactly what they'd get. Perot succeeded where so many before him had failed. His high-pressure tactics eventually led to the opening of a congressional hearing to determine once and for all if any POWs remained in Vietnam so long after the war had ended.

This was where the Remote Viewing Unit stepped in.

Under the hot lights of the media, the political elites in the Senate and House pushed the elites in the military to start producing some results. All intelligence agencies were put on notice that not a single stone go unturned in their search for the missing POWs. That meant every acronym in the playbook would take the field—CIA, NSA, NIC, NSC, and of course the DIA, which was where my unit and I served.

The mountain of paperwork on our transfer from army intelligence to the Defense Intelligence Agency barely had time to gather dust before the call came for us to bring our unique skills to the POW effort. I was ordered through channels to meet with Brigadier General James Shufelt to discuss what role the RV Unit would play in the upcoming investigation. Shufelt, the ex–deputy commander of INSCOM, who like us had moved to DIA, got the unenviable job as point man to deal with veterans' groups, Congress, and the relentless H. Ross Perot. He also had to answer to his superior, Lieutenant General Harry Soyster, a rigid man who wanted nothing better than to kick our remote-viewing keisters into the ether. "Anywhere but DIA" was his slogan regarding the RV Unit.

I was already familiar with Shufelt, as was everyone else in the unit, since he had recently married one of our own, Charlene Cavanaugh. I liked him. He wasn't afraid to call bullshit what it was, a quality he shared with his new bride. Charlene had shown me through her work that my animus toward women in the military wasn't only wrong, but was getting in the way of missions. She was one of the best remote viewers on the team, with abilities at her disposal few others possessed, abilities that could make or break an operation. Being a DIA general's wife was a plus too. We needed all the friends we could get as Soyster sharpened his knives to stick us.

As a senior DIA officer and chairman of the hastily assembled National Foreign Intelligence Board Interagency Committee on Vietnam MIA's/POW's, it now fell on Shufelt to evaluate any evidence regarding unaccounted for U.S. military personnel in Southeast Asia and provide a summary of DIA's conclusions. To do that, he needed to review all archived and current case files, the handling of those files, and sniff out any hint of impropriety or cover-up. The main focus, however, would be on the credibility of the live-sighting reports that overwhelmed his in-box the moment Congress launched its televised hearings. Suddenly it seemed like everyone in the Far East had spotted a POW at one time or another. Some wanted their fifteen minutes of fame for helping, others the money celebrity naturally brings. Most of their stories amounted to nothing.

Shufelt's command also included the sweeping mandate to go anywhere his investigation took him. It didn't matter whose toes he stepped on or how many sacred cows he gored along the way, he could do no wrong as long as DIA remained within its charter. We were responsible for the analysis of information provided by all branches of the military intelligence community. *Analysis*. Actually going out into the field to collect that information was strictly forbidden. The RV Unit was essentially banned from doing the very job we were trained for because we were now DIA. Only in the military.

But Shufelt didn't care. To him it was about the mission, as it is with all authentic warriors. He would get results and didn't give a rat's ass about crossing departmental lines. When you're under the gun like he was, you do whatever it takes, the rules be damned. Us old army grunts call that "taking the initiative." So with a nod and wink, General Shufelt stealthily tasked the RV team and me to do everything we could to *collect* intelligence on the POW question—to act like the bastard unit Harry Soyster insisted we were and operate without restraint outside the DIA's official charter. Beyond that, our mission was one of not getting caught.

As Shufelt began presenting his case to Congress with the whole country watching, the Remote Viewing Unit went to work. The plan was to move in twelve-hour shifts, seven days a week, until we found something. Not wanting to overlook even the most seemingly insignificant clues, we decided to split the team into two details: the altered states ERV group led by Gene "Kincaid," and me at the helm of the Ingo Swann–taught CRV troops. Kincaid, a warrant officer whose real name was Gene Lessman, was a Special Forces human intelligence expert with two brutal tours of duty in Vietnam under his belt. A big badass man, Lessman loved his Irish heritage enough to use his mother's maiden name as a tribute to family members still living in the old country. To me, he was the best damn soldier I ever had the privilege of serving with. The enemy shot so much meat off this guy that when he returned from Vietnam he was immediately ordered to retire. Instead of riding an easy desk job to oblivion, Lessman chose instead to bring his wealth of combat and Special Ops experience to us rather than watching it all go to waste. Being of use to his country meant more to him than his own failing health. We were fortunate to get him. I almost felt bad dumping Gene in the hands of the phony witches taking up space in the ERV group, but it was either him or me—and it had to be him. He was a lot more tolerant than I was.

Here was what we were up against:

In January 1973, a diplomatic effort dubbed "Operation Homecoming" led to the return of more than five hundred American prisoners of war held by North Vietnam. Three C-141A "Hanoi Taxi" transports flew the lucky soldiers first to Saigon and then home to freedom. After that, still more were released in dribs and drabs until the spigot eventually went dry. Reported sightings of POWs continued well into the next decade and beyond. Many contended the men had become bargaining chips for a Communist government bent on using them to gain political recognition and an open checkbook for war reparations. Simply put, the North Vietnamese were holding our boys hostage for ransom. Blackmail. But there were those in our government and powerful business circles who adamantly denied this, wanting closer ties with the new Communist government. They dared anyone including Ross Perot to prove them wrong. This was why Shufelt employed every asset he had, including us. Depending on information from others would be sketchy; he could count on being stonewalled at every turn. No problem. Seeing through walls was our specialty.

The first element of our assignment was to remote view whether the POWs even existed and, if they did, where the Communists were keeping them. Knowing what I did about the enemy from my undercover days, their disregard for human life and zero code of military conduct, the prognosis wasn't very good.

We had our own buildings now at Fort Meade, away from the regular action at the sprawling base. They were two single-story shacks with the purposely nondescript addresses of 2560 and 2561 Llewellyn Street. If you didn't know where they were, you'd never find them. And you shouldn't try.

Isolated in an open lot, secluded by a sparse chain of trees, the only thing connecting the RV Unit's "headquarters" to the rest of humanity was a small stream that drained at its end into a park and lake. Built more than forty years ago, the cottages once housed an army mess hall and bakery school. Now it was our turn to do some cooking here.

My team included all the usual suspects: Bill Ray, Paul Smith, the newly married Charlene Cavanaugh, and a not-so-newcomer by the name of Mel Riley. A master sergeant whose wife and son lived on base, Riley was in fact the army's first official remote viewer, having been recruited at the start when targets located in the United States were used to test RV's effectiveness and find those with the talent to make it happen. Mel was a star in the program and soon signed up when it materialized as project "Gondola Wish," fielding demands for psychic spycraft from every corner of American intelligence. He later returned to his duties as a crack intel photo interpreter, participating also in covert cold war missions, including flights inside the risky Berlin Corridor over East Germany. After that, it was back to the RV Unit and me snatching him up for my team.

Convincing Mel to go with us didn't take much effort. Since he was a kid growing up in Racine, Wisconsin, he had had a penchant for the paranormal, experiencing visions of being part of a working Native American village from another time. Bilocation came as natural to him as falling off a log, the sense of being home and in that village at the same time. When Riley learned of Ingo Swann's breakthrough in coordinate remote viewing, he said the hell with all that altered states crap and eagerly joined us. He could have the best of both worlds with CRV, the new technique and protocols improving the accuracy of an RV session, producing more precise results more often. Riley was trained to be accurate. In his line of work, any incorrect analysis of an aerial image could lead to bombing the wrong targets and a tremendous loss of innocent life. That was something Mel wouldn't tolerate. He expected much from himself and the same from others. When the thin blond Irishman with the piercing electric eyes wanted in, he got in. He fit our little group to a tee.

I had the perfect crew now, a remote-viewing dream team. Each member brought to the table traits unique to them. Charlene was good at identifying people, locating them, and describing in great detail their mental states. Paul Smith, with his superior education, could better than anyone put into words the formless images of the unconscious we sensed in remote viewing. Then there was Captain Bill Ray, a superb counterintelligence man with a deep pool of intel experience to draw from. Finally there was Mel Riley, who, in addition to being a gifted natural psychic and top-notch image interpreter, was an excellent sketch artist and mapmaker.

We were ready for anything, and Shufelt gave it to us.

The general kicked off our mission with a kind of controlled experiment, apparently to test us out. Supplying both Lessman and me with two sets of photographs, one depicting a group of buildings in Vietnam where it was determined POWs had been held, and another where there was certain proof none were. We were to RV the targets in the pictures and tell him which was which. Only Lessman and I knew what Shufelt had in mind, and we didn't care much for it. Testing us wasn't part of the deal. We had nothing to prove to anybody about the accuracy of remote viewing. But we had to swim in the same ocean every soldier does and follow orders. Shufelt may have felt his trial balloon had merit, but as far as I was concerned it fell flat as a pancake. I decided right then and there to give him a hell of lot more than he'd bargained for. I'd begin at eight the next morning.

• • •

It wasn't easy rousting the unit to work on a beautiful day. Paul was off writing articles on military life for some magazine, and Bill Ray was paging through a book of Irish pub songs. Mel as usual was sitting Buddha-like under a tree doing Indian bead-work, while Charlene moved at her normal lightning pace, taking over two hours to get dressed. But I somehow managed to gather them up and hustle them to 2560 Llewellyn Street.

This was our operations office, where we did the bulk of our remote viewing on base. The hub of our administrative arm was next door at 2561, complete with a makeshift foyer, a fridge, the perennial coffee pot and mugs lined up neat and straight on the counter, commanding officers' offices, and a string of cubicles opening to a conference room at the end of the hall. Our secretary was a gawky, furtive woman who'd blush every time somebody said something dirty. Some of the guys liked to invade her cubicle and deliver nippy one-liners just to see her turn red. For us, it was home, be it ever so humble.

Once things settled down, I removed two envelopes with Shufelt's Vietnam photographs in them. The envelopes were sealed; only I knew what was in them. The team would get a set of target reference numbers for each and that was all. They had no clue about the photographs, knew nothing about our mission to locate POWs or General Shufelt's involvement. They understood the routine—focus on the numbers, tell me what you sense, then sketch what you see.

Our journey back in time began as all voyages do, with that first noble step. I asked them the definitive RV question:

"Tell me what you see."

The answers came immediately. The unit flashed directly to the target tuning in without even the slightest hesitation images of buildings they knew nothing about. And though I'd seen them do it a thousand times before, I still marveled at the human capacity to manufacture awe. It was a humbling experience to watch.

"A structure, not very big, not built so well," Bill Ray said. "Not a building I'd pay big rent to live in."

"I sense people around the buildings, a surge of faces. The streets are bustling with bicycles and carts and cars," Paul added. "But it's all ghostlike, as if they're not real."

"Yes, I can't describe their faces, it's a mass of flesh, traces moving, moving," Charlene said. "So many people."

"Stay on the buildings for now," I told them.

"There's more than one; I see two separate buildings in two different locations," Riley said, quickly sketching what he saw on a sheet of paper.

"These building are different," Paul said.

"How?"

"I'm not sure."

Charlene closed her eyes like she does when she's hot on the trail of something. "It's not that they're different, they just mean different things to different people."

"What people?"

"The ones using them, or should I say—*it*. One of the buildings is empty, but not empty like nobody's there, but empty as a target. I'm getting nothing from it," she explained. "The other is alive, extremely important."

"Important how?"

"The ones in it, they have a purpose in mind. It's where they work, a place of business. But not ordinary business."

"I don't understand."

Charlene crossed her legs now, eyes still shut tight. "They're engaged in something with others in the building, people sitting in a room."

"The ones they're doing business with?"

"No. It's not like that."

"These others, what's the building to them?"

She paused, face muscles tensing.

"A trap."

The team heard her, the words sinking in, but no one moved. It was apparent to all of them that Charlene was right. And she was. Two buildings. Only one was significant to me. The one the POWs were in.

"Forget the other building," I said. "Stay on this site, tell me more about this spot. Give me a landmark."

"There's lettering on it, a sign or billboard," Mel said, holding up the sketch he made. "Looks like Chinese, but it isn't. I—I just can't recognize the writing."

"You're right, it isn't Chinese," I said.

Now I knew why Mel Riley was considered one of the best in the business. He had dropped us right into Vietnam with one stroke of his pen. I wanted to tell them the sign was written in Vietnamese, but I couldn't. I couldn't front-load them with information or it'd ruin everything—distract them, cut them off from unknown facts.

"Direct your attention inside the building. Go inside."

Ten minutes passed as they went deeper. Ten minutes that seemed like a lifetime to me. Then they were back again.

"I'm in a small room, dark, dingy. I can taste the dust in my mouth. It's filthy," Paul said. "Smells exotic, the odor of ethnic food coming from a window overlooking the street. But no light, the window is blacked out, covered with a heavy curtain. Otherwise there's nothing in the room, no windows, nothing on the walls or on the floor."

"No, there's something on the floor," Ray said. "Men. Charlene's 'others.' Their backs are to the wall, their heads down. They want to look up, but they can't."

"Who's stopping them?"

"The other guys. They have guns."

Charlene lifted her head, her hands clutching the armrest on her chair, nails digging into the leather. "The men on the floor, they're frightfully thin. It's hard for me to even look at them. They're all just skin and bones, and hungry."

"How many are there?"

"There's twelve of them," Riley answered. "But they're not like the men with the weapons. They stand out."

"What do you mean?"

"The men on the floor are white, actually two are black. The men with the guns are Asian."

The team looked at one another and nodded. They agreed. Normally I'd halt the session now because they thought they knew something, their minds had drawn a conclusion, blocking any fresh future data. But I made an exception here because they were correct—and we were running out of time.

"They're so hungry, why doesn't someone give them something to eat?" Charlene pleaded. "They've been sitting there for days, up against that stinking wall. Why are they there, why doesn't someone give them something to eat?"

We all looked at her now. This is what you call being connected. Charlene was so high *I* was starting to see things.

"The bastards with guns, they're pointing them at the boys on the floor now," she continued. "And some other men have entered the room—large men, not little like the armed ones. They're also white, or white-looking. They're asking questions, screaming questions. They want some information. They have heavy accents, but they're speaking in English."

Riley finished scribbling furiously in his notepad. He smiled that eureka smile as in, *Yeah, I got it.* "They're definitely speaking English, and the heavy accent is Russian. I'm sure of it. They're *Russians.*"

Russians. In Vietnam interrogating American soldiers. The effect Mel's revelation had on me was profound, almost intimate, like those Soviet shits were here in the room with me breathing the same air, moving with me, seeing what I saw.

"No—no, don't do that," Charlene said suddenly, her expression raw, like someone about to fall off the edge.

"They're beating him!"

I looked over at Mel Riley for more on this.

"They pistol-whipped one of our guys on the floor, Captain," he said. "He won't play ball, won't answer their fool questions. None of them will."

"Somebody do something!" Charlene shouted, covering her face with her hands as if that would help blot out the dark images she'd seen. But how could it? They were in her mind.

"They're beating him to death!"

Everything stopped.

The unit was too lost in thought to connect with anything outside the session, but I heard a sound coming from behind the mirror on the wall opposite us. It was a two-way mirror, so people could observe us without disturbing the rhythm of our work. I knew who was watching. It was General Shufelt come to check on our progress. By now he knew the RV Unit had passed his test with flying colors. Given nothing more than a simple photograph, we had found what he was looking for. And we had uncovered more than the building his POWs were being held in, something Shufelt's sources already knew. We had established exactly how many there were and that they were still alive. Alive at the time the photographs were taken. My team had salvaged the aura of these trapped and tormented men, the psychic residue of their sweat and blood and pain. It was all there for Shufelt to see, written on his new bride's face. The scant act of simply raising her head revealed pouchy wet eyes and shadowy lines running across her forehead and cheeks. It was plain as day. Charlene looked older now.

We tried to pick up where we had left off afterwards, to pinpoint the precise location of the POWs using Mel's landmarks. I could later confirm them with other intelligence assets I had. But as time dragged on it became evident that RV burnout was setting in. It wasn't so much how they all appeared, but what they were saying. The clarity of the moment was still there, but it was ending, the flow becoming disassociated, memory traces growing vague, a breakdown of effortless functions like suddenly forgetting how to stand up. We'd all had enough today. Thirteen hours of enough.

"We knock off here," I told them. "Everyone go home."

No one said a thing. They just left.


I needed to walk. I crossed from the private comfort of Llewellyn Street through the empty lot, zigzagging like a happy little boy between rows of trees just for the fun of it. I'd try anything to deflate the pressure I felt, the stiffness in my neck. I needed to get a quiet civilized meal off base, some little café with tablecloths and icy pats of butter lounging on tiny saucers. A few cold ones would be nice too.

I passed some barracks, imagining everyone asleep inside, a huge mass of bodies in heavy rest discharging one loud nasal sigh. The notion made me tired, as did the emptiness of everything. All the fort's shops were closed, movie theaters dark. A solitary soldier on guard duty walked by me, his trusty German shepherd watchdog at his side. There's something reassuring about shepherds, the fierce head, sturdy frame, always present and alert, able to hear sounds beyond our hearing, to sense subtle changes in the stream of information around them. Natural remote viewers, German shepherds.

I kept walking. I needed to analyze things coldly, methodically, break them down piece by piece and scrutinize. I needed to go home. I walked back to Llewellyn Street.

A friend had taped Shufelt testifying before Congress and I put up a pot of coffee to help me get through it. I knew pretty much ahead of time what to expect, and that wasn't very much. George Washington himself compared Congress to a mug in which "coffee not only cooled, but turned bitter and cold." Facts have a way of dying at congressional hearings.

It was difficult to watch a good man like Shufelt be grilled the way he was by these corrupt officials, most of them greedy liars whose sole interest was their coffers and those who filled them to the brim. They were merciless, clobbering the general with questions he had no way of answering, topped off by insinuations that the intelligence community was in some way responsible for creating the POW crisis and then covering it up. If there were people at DIA covering up, General Shufelt certainly wasn't one of them. Those who might be hiding data were doubtless doing it at the behest of their masters in the Senate and House who danced like hypnotized puppets to the tune of special interest money.

It came out during the hearings that while the Vietnamese had never raised the issue directly with us, the U.S. government had reportedly made every effort to bargain live POWs or their remains in exchange for war reparations and foreign aid cash. The brilliant minds behind this plan believed that if the North Vietnamese negotiators bit, this would be an admission they had POWs and we could get on with getting them out. But the Communists never took the bait, at least not officially. Though they had no intention of turning over any POWs, they so desperately needed the dollars normalization would bring that they pocketed payoffs whenever possible, taking gullible U.S. searchers on a vain merry chase through the jungles. Still, that didn't stop the corporations and money whores from wanting to get their beaks wet by dunking them in the vast markets an open Vietnam had to offer. It's been well documented that major U.S. industrialists armed and financed every enemy of ours, from Adolf Hitler to Ho Chi Minh and Saddam Hussein. Business is business, after all.

Some on the committee wondered aloud if it was the American way to call its young men to war, abandon them after it was over, and then coldly close the books so financial assistance could be doled out to those very people responsible for making them missing soldiers in the first place. Clearly it wasn't, but hats off for asking anyway, Mr. Congressman.

Another even more contemptible claim surfaced that drug money was at the heart of the POW question, and that the intelligence community was pulling the strings. Witnesses asserted a link between the lucrative heroin and cocaine trade to the CIA and their covert operatives in Southeast Asia. They backed it up with a separate government commission report pointing to the possibility of American military deserters and civilian contractors in Laos and Vietnam having been involved in drug trafficking. Several stated that drugs were the principal explanation for why our POWs *didn't* come home.

Outrageous as it seems, these individuals insisted that not only did the CIA murder drug-dealing defectors at the close of the war, but also unwilling POWs who might become a financial liability and major embarrassment should they come home alive. With folks like Perot offering huge rewards, defectors who enjoyed their freewheeling lifestyles and growing bank accounts could poke their heads above the fray at any time with a few good POW stories and get a free ride home. This would not be allowed to happen. As for the POWs, a wrong word, a veiled truth exposed, a few big names dropped that the public would recognize, and there went the whole apple cart.

The argument here was that shadowy and powerful insiders with a stake in the hundreds of millions of dollars exchanging hands over drugs would stop at nothing to protect their profits and position in society. If any of this got out and was proved, the trail could lead all the way to the very top.

That meant the leadership of intelligence organizations; the State Department, the National Security Council, and the Pentagon might be involved—not exactly a group of nobodies. Anyone who attempted to bring them to light would surely be fair game to a rigorous campaign of lies, character assassination, and intimidation designed to shut them up. Perhaps even murder.

To these people, executing expendable GIs was a small price to pay for protecting the very foundation of our social order. The supreme irony was the allegation that men of good conscience also dipped into the drug money pool to fund covert missions to rescue the POWs, missions that were ultimately sabotaged by the very agents contracted to get the job done.

It was the stuff a conspiracy theorist's dreams are made of. Was any of it true? Time would tell. What intrigued me more was the testimony regarding POW information dating back nearly half a century. Information I could use right now.

Thousands of American soldiers who served their country bravely were abandoned to Soviet torture after World War II and the Korean conflict. Those who investigated these charges speculated the atrocity was allowed to occur for two reasons: first, because Soviet operatives had burrowed deep into our own government, gaining positions of power and influence to control it; and second, because the misguided knee-jerkers running U.S. policy had deluded themselves into believing their own fairy tales. They believed that leaving our men behind would contribute to a better world by achieving a harmonious relationship with the brutal Soviet Union. All we had to do was look the other way. According to witness after witness, many did just that.

Some of the hottest testimony came from a top-ranking Soviet defector who confessed his willing participation in the violence against our people. This general stated that the capture for use as guinea pigs of American citizens, both soldiers and civilians, became official Soviet policy as far back as the early 1950s. The purpose was to make them lab specimens for training military doctors and for conducting experiments with mind-control drugs, chemical and biological warfare agents, and radiation. The ghastly experiments took place undercover in such war zones as Korea and Vietnam, and inside the Soviet Union itself, where the most sensitive operations were carried out. Tens of thousands of American POWs and hapless civilians were imprisoned, then carted off to Russia for this purpose.

Mind-control drugs became the centerpiece of the Soviets' long-range strategy against the West, especially the United States. We dabbled in that arena as well, I'm sorry to say. But where our hands were dirty, theirs were foul.

What grabbed me here was that Soviet operatives were choreographing the capture, detainment, and torture of our boys in Vietnam. They had a long unbroken history of doing it. Those voices we picked up during our remote-viewing session—the ones peppering our guys with questions, ordering them beaten by their captors—could now be positively identified as Russian. This confirmed that the men we saw were POWs, and that our targets were possibly still alive. We had to act fast.

The Taoist philosopher Lao-tzu once said, "There is no difference between the quick and the dead, they are one channel of vitality." I could feel this vitality growing over me, gaining breadth and range, finding new outlets, new means. Death was close to me now, inhabiting the same world as me. It was breathing down my neck.

I awoke from an unholy teeth-grinding sleep. I had spent the entire night in dreams crammed with nightmarish figures assaulting me in great tremors and waves. It was good to be awake. I had never appreciated being alive more than this moment.

I walked past my sons' bedroom to check on them before leaving for Llewellyn Street, where the unit was setting up for today's all-important RV session. My kids were still fast asleep and I wanted to be close to them. I felt almost devout watching them this way, sleeping, as if I were part of a spiritual system, something akin to standing in a grand spired cathedral with marble pillars reaching skyward and beams of mystical light angling through Gothic stained glass windows. Watching my sons was the nearest I came to God these days.

Time to get going. General Shufelt would be stopping by after the session today to collect a formal report on the status of our unit's intelligence concerning the missing POWs. We had to be ready.

The sun was out as I crossed to our operations center. Inside was another story. A uniformly gray room greeted me with no colors or life of any sort, nothing to distract us. The unit was all together—Paul, Charlene, Ray, and Mel Riley—and they looked primed and as raring to go as I'd ever seen them. What they were remote viewing was no longer a mystery to them. There was no way to escape the publicity surrounding the congressional hearings, and after what they had seen in session, everyone understood this was no Christmas party we were looking in on. We had found twelve missing POWs. We had done it. This was our baby now. Once we had the target, we had chain of custody to the flow of information. Nothing would get lost with us as so many photographs, maps, and other data kept in the CIA and NSA archives had before. Reports from agents on the ground would often get swallowed up over time and then DIA people like me would have to sort through it all. Not this time. We were fully operational thanks to General Shufelt, we collected our own information, and no one but him would ever get their hands on it. More was on the way.

"Ladies and gentlemen, lock back onto the same reference numbers and move forward in time," I told them. "Think of it as a slide rule. Moving to the right brings us to the future. Our target is someplace else now. Move with them."

"*Move* is right," Bill Ray said. "They're on the move, being shifted from one place to another."

"They're tied up, in terrible shape, dirty and torn," Charlene said. "They're being treated like animals."

"Not relevant," I interrupted. "Just tell me where they are, we need to know where they are, not how they look."

Charlene didn't like it, but she refocused on what I was saying, letting go of her emotions just enough to stay with the men and forget their physical condition. Location, location.

"They're in a van or truck, driving someplace isolated," she said. "Far from the city, from the buildings we saw."

"Good. More."

"This is tough," Paul said. "It's a kind of shell game, they're here one day and gone the next. The time frame is tight, I'm not sure how often or where they're being moved."

"That's right, they're going all the time," said Ray. "How can we find them if they're always in transit?"

I could see we were hitting a wall on this. The sensory data they were getting showing the changing position of the POWs was good, I could work with that, but I had to do something about pinning down actual locations. It was now or never.

"Connect the dots. Where are they now, then the next place and the next," I explained. "Don't assume anything. Shift into the future, keeping sliding that slide rule."

"Wet—I'm getting the sense of wet things that smell like trees after a storm," Mel said, beginning to sketch something on his pad. "It's hot and humid, the rain never lets up. We're in the jungle—*they're* in the jungle."

"Jungles are big places," I said. "Pin it down."

"That's where I am too, a rain forest, beautiful but with a sense of terror," Paul added. "I'm trying. Wait. They've stopped. I hear Russian being spoken again. Those men with guns, the Asians, they're pulling on the tied-up men."

"Pulling them toward what?

"One of them resists, I can sense his youth, his boldness," Charlene said, closing her eyes, the signal of her diving deeper into the vision. "They hit him—he's bleeding! They threw him in first, like a sack of garbage."

"Threw him in where, Charlene? Where?"

She shook her head. She couldn't see right now.

"A cage, filled with the smell of feces," Paul said. "Rotten food infested with insects. They want to break them, not bones, but their spirit. And fear, the fear that any one of these so-called human beings can kill you on a whim."

Paul sat back in his chair and wiped the sweat off his face. He was getting closer; I could see it with my own eyes. He wasn't really here anymore. He was bilocating—he was *there*.

"Darkness. It's all darkness. A trench, dug into the earth, I sense it clearly, a cavelike structure with slats covering it," he continued. "The slats are made of bamboo."

"Slide forward again, where are they now?"

"Same place, in the trench with the slats. The asshole Russians have stopped moving them around."

"There are other structures around, on stilts, raised above the hole in the ground," Mel said. "This is a camp, a prison camp. Guards. Men in a hole. It makes sense."

"Darkness, pitch black. I can't see my hands in front of my face. Tunnels, snakelike. Around the camp," Paul said.

"They've thrown them all in there," Charlene said.

That was it. I had an up-to-date snapshot now of a clandestine prison camp. The North Vietnamese Army had built a jungle jail with the sole purpose of hiding American POWs who weren't even supposed to exist. I'd heard of these places before, at the close of the war, primitive mountainous country seemingly intended by nature to protect people from the elements, now used to shield the detection and movement of imprisoned men. It was the fashionable way regimes in this part of the world always treated the people they wanted to disappear, small mobile camps of up to twenty-five prisoners continuously on the move, held in caves, bamboo huts, or underground tunnels, chained in the dark in the rain. About thirty percent kept there never made it out.

"I can get a landmark off this, sketch the geometry of the place," Riley volunteered.

"Go for it."

This was what Mel Riley was best at, why I was so lucky to have him on board. Not only could he find targets, but he could show you where they were on paper. I read an account of how he once found a shipment of Chinese Silkworm missiles headed for Iran on a ship and stopped them cold in the water. The case was legendary. If anyone could draw accurate details of this jungle site as it appeared today, it was Mel Riley. He'd give me the marker I needed to compare with archived CIA records to confirm. With that in hand, our boys would be POWs no more.

"Okay, I want to move forward in time again," I told them. "You've seen the men underground, now locate them today. Time is our creation, let it pass like a warm wind."

Something was happening. It had happened. It would happen. There was a story, a stream of consciousness and possibility. The unit was tapping into that story, slicing through time and space in a sequence, all simultaneous somehow with the present. The future was coming into being now. Charlene was the first to get there.

"Listen everybody," she said suddenly and with more upbeat energy, a slight buzz in her throat, her pitch higher. "They're being moved again, all twelve of them. One by one, they're pulling them out of that filthy hole."

"Yeah, they're leaving," Bill Ray said with a broad grin. "The guards are smiling. Maybe it's over."

Charlene took a quick breath; she could barely speak she was so excited. "Food. I can sense them getting food. One of the guards must be giving them something to eat. Wonderful!"

"It was still raining, though," Paul said.

I look at him. "*Was?*" I asked.

He corrected himself, inching slowly through his sentence to get to the point. "I mean, it will rain, by that I should say— Jesus! What is wrong with me? *It's raining.* It's still raining where they are."

Not good. Paul's difficult passage from past tense to present unnerved me. It had the sound of something to overcome, an obstacle, a restriction on his remote viewing forward. As if there was something out there he didn't want to see.

"Look at that," Charlene said, still bubbling, forgetting she was the only one seeing it. "Cloth, soft cloth, and dry. Hands reaching for it. I believe the guards gave them towels to dry themselves off. They're even patting our boys on the back and smiling at them. It's helping. They're relieved."

"What about the Russians?" I asked. "What are they doing?"

"They're not smiling," Paul said.

"Why not?"

"They know something our guys don't."

A hush fell over the room.

"They're turning their backs, shaking their heads," Paul continued. "I hear the sound of engines turning over, two vehicles. Jeeps. The Russians have gotten into jeeps and are driving off the same way they came in."

Bill Ray laughed. "Good riddance to them."

"Yes, they're leaving. It's good," Charlene insisted.

"No. Something's not right," Paul said.

"What isn't?"

Paul cupped his face in his hands. He was white as a ghost. "One of the guards is leading them down a path a short way from the huts. They're following him, they have no reason not to. He's still smiling. Two more guards are behind them."

"So what's the problem?" I asked.

"They're checking their weapons. Oh my God—"

Paul stopped. He said nothing.

We all waited for him to pick up again, but still nothing. Then his expression changed; he wasn't only pale white, he was stunned, like the shock of a vile fact had been jarred loose.

"What's happening, Paul?"

Silence.

"I asked you a question, soldier."

Paul sat up in his chair, his knuckles turning red as he clenched his hands. "White-hot flashes. Bursts of bright white like lightning. Only it isn't lightning."

"Then what is it?"

"I know—we all do. It's the blast of a gun barrel, machine-gun barrels. The flash of gunfire. The guards are shooting. They won't stop for anything. They're reloading. They're shooting!"

Paul stopped again. And again we waited.

"Talk to me, Paul."

He turned to me now, his head cranking incrementally like the second hand on a watch. He drew a tortured breath.

"They're gone," he said finally.

"Who's gone?"

"Our guys. They're gone."

Charlene stood up. "He's right. I don't sense them anymore. What's going on here, what's going on?"

"I'm not getting them either," Mel said.

Charlene began sobbing softly to herself.

"Son of a bitch!" Ray howled.

I stared at Paul, asked him if he was sure. He nodded. His mouth was open slightly, trembling slightly, clinging to the breath of presence. He'd come back to this world, feeling the full weight of it over his body. He struggled up from his chair, taking a few strides before reaching the door. From there he looked at us and whispered, "They're gone."

He left the room.

I followed him, outside into the light, wondering where he was going and if he was okay. He didn't go far, just next door to our offices at 2561. I was right behind him as he walked in, barely standing on his own two feet. Gene Lessman was there, and together we both watched as Paul practically fell onto the sofa in the foyer. *Collapse* is a better word for it.

"What's wrong with him?" Lessman asked me.

"We completed our mission."

"Yeah, we did too. We found some of our boys in a prison camp near the Laotian border. How about your team?"

"Fine, yeah."

"We're trying to nail down the exact spot," he said.

"Don't bother."

"Why not?"

"They're gone."

Lessman looked down at the floor. Shook his head.

I watched as Paul drifted immediately into a deep sleep. I'd never seen this happen to him before, a total crash. Lesser men would have cried their eyes out, but not Paul Smith. He just needed to lie down. What he saw had taken its toll on him, on all of us. But it was good that he had viewed the tragedy in his mind and wasn't physically there for the slaughter of our comrades. The nightmare images would fade over time this way. If he had been there, they would remain with him for as long as he lived.

It was night when General Shufelt dropped in at Llewellyn Street, one of the foggiest nights I can ever remember seeing. A hoary mist rolled out of the hollows in the woods like a living thing, unearthly and stern, blotting out the sky and stars and any trace of human kindness.

Shufelt had come for his POW report, and I was anything but ready to give it to him. He was so late I figured he wouldn't show, so I dressed more informally, trading my sports jacket for for a pullover sweater that I accidentally put on backwards. When I heard him at the door, I had to decide whether to take it off and put it on again or deal with the discomfort of it riding my neck for however long he planned on staying. Maybe he wouldn't notice.

"Good evening, General," I said, letting him in.

Shufelt stared at me puzzled and then figured out what's bothering him.

"Your sweater's on backwards, Captain."

"Apologies, sir." I sank about three inches in my shoes.

Shufelt walked in, a gliding walk that reminded me more of an astronaut floating weightless in space than a man carrying the stink of the world we call "Congress" on his shoulders. He had testified again on the Hill today, as he had every day for the last two weeks, and was still around to talk about it. Ross Perot himself was there too, so it must have been fun.

"Can I get you some coffee, sir?"

He didn't answer.

"You know," Shufelt said in a low monotone, "I saw what I thought was a dead squirrel in the drive outside. Turned out to be a strip of curled burlap, but I still walked past it feeling sorry for the damned thing."

"I understand, sir."

"Do you have something for me?

"Yes, sir."

"I don't have much time."

I stepped to my desk and pull the POW file on the RV Unit's most recent sessions. A set of CIA satellite images were included along with our findings, images confirming the location where we believed the POWs were before being killed. Information regarding their Russian interrogators was also included. I thought that to be quite important, but I was wrong. The general skimmed through the dossier in less time than it took for me to clip it closed. His expression never changed as he read, a straight-on, businesslike poker face.

"Is that all?" he asked.

"Yes, sir. Unfortunately, that's all there is."

"Damn shame."

"Yes, General."

Hooking the file under his arm, Shufelt headed for the door, then stopped and turned to me.

"Well done, Captain," he said. "Thank your team for me."

"I will, sir."

"And—oh yes."

I snapped to attention.

"See about that sweater, will you?"

With that he stepped back into the night, a sad silhouette vanishing into the eeriest fog I'd ever seen.

I watched Shufelt the next morning on one of the networks that deemed it worthy enough to televise in place of some asinine game show. There he was, the same deadpan poker face he had displayed for me the night before. Little wonder why he had been picked for an intelligence command. The general was good.

He told them nothing. Though they hurled one accusation after another, blaming him personally and DIA for covering up or obscuring the truth about the POWs, Shufelt never flinched. He said nothing about our findings, nothing about the CIA confirmation, nothing about how and why the men we uncovered were killed. In fact, I'm sure he never told the POW families, Ross Perot, or even his commanding officers what we had found out—perhaps with the exception of Jack Vorona, who was in charge of the RV program at the time. If you weren't read on to the list of people who needed to know about us, you would never even know we existed. Brigadier General James Shufelt wasn't the kind to kiss and tell.

What did come out in the hearings was a steady stream of claims and counterclaims about the missing POWs, and on occasion even the evidence to back them up. But overall, it would be the passage of time that revealed what truths could be told. In one of its clipped TV magazine stories, CBS News's *60 Minutes* produced what it said were mountains of eyewitness statements, official documents, and even admissions from the president on down the line to intelligence experts in the Pentagon and National Security Council stating that the United States had intentionally abandoned its POWs in Southeast Asia in 1973 and sabotaged the efforts of more than half a dozen rescue attempts with high probabilities of success. The corker came with the assertion that our government had ordered its covert operatives to eliminate live

POWs on sight. To terminate them with "extreme prejudice." To murder them.

Jobs were lost at CNN over this allegation. The cable news giant was forced to fire two of its top correspondents and retract reports it had made about "Operation Tailwind" on the program *NewsStand*, which merged CNN resources and content with those of *Time* magazine. The report claimed that deadly Sarin gas, a chemical nerve agent classified as a weapon of mass destruction, was used by U.S. black ops teams to do the dirty work of offing deserters and POWs. The gas was supposedly discovered at known POW prison camp sites along Vietnam's border with Laos.

Just where we said the POWs were being held.

The RV Unit had exposed twelve men; twelve we know were butchered by North Vietnamese army regulars, not rogue CIA assassins. But for me to say the murder of our troops by our own people never happened would be a lie. I only know what we uncovered. The rest of it was way out of my pay grade. I just don't know.

As to the Russians being involved as interrogators and human experimenters, few people seemed surprised by the revelation. No one would put a few vicious POW camps past the people who brought you Stalin and the Berlin Wall and who helped the North Vietnamese infiltrate every U.S. and South Vietnamese military intelligence and political network there was. They were quite able to plan, execute, and bury their tracks on something simple like clandestine killer prison camps. Again, I only knew what my unit knew, and that meant Russians were at the site we remote viewed. On that account, I'm sure.

Russian Federation president Boris Yeltsin himself confirmed it, telling the American press that old Soviet archives revealed the transfer of American GIs to the territory of the former Soviet Union, where most were kept hidden away in labor camps. What they did to them there he wouldn't say. Not enough "complete data" was his reason.

Rather than leap through this window of opportunity to recover our boys on a rare confession provided by the leader of the "Evil Empire," true to form our government downplayed Yeltsin's comments as hollow. Is it any wonder why people hold our Congress in contempt? And there was more.

In 1985 the Associated Press published a story under the sterile headline "Army General Is Found Dead in Apparent Virginia Suicide":

A 52-year-old Army brigadier general was found dead of gunshot wounds at his home Monday in this Washington suburb in what police and Army officials called an apparent suicide. A Fairfax County police spokesman, Warren Carmichael, said that the officer, Brig. Gen. Bobby C. Robinson, was believed to have died early Monday morning. Maj. John Barnum, an Army spokesman, said Monday that General Robinson's death "was apparently a self-inflicted wound," but added that there had been no coroner's report. General Robinson served as deputy executive director for chemical and nuclear matters with the Army's Materiel Command in Alexandria, Va., Major Barnum said. The command is responsible for managing Army depots and overseeing the logistics of moving weapons and supplies.

I spoke with General Robinson just weeks before his "apparent suicide" over some leaking poison gas canisters discovered under his watch at Dugway Proving Grounds in Utah and Kwajalein Atoll in the Marshall Islands. Both served at one time or another as biological and chemical weapons offensive systems test sites, as well as nuclear ballistic missile locations. He was all set to retire when I brought him the bad news. What I didn't know was that he had even more urgent issues on his plate, life-and-death issues.

Robinson was alleged to have been involved in planting Sarin gas munitions in Southeast Asia so the Soviets would be blamed.

In this tortured bit of logic, he and others would motivate Congress to get off its ass and increase chemical warfare spending. On June 7, 1998, the CNN producer April Oliver and the correspondent Peter Arnett reported the results of an eight-month investigation into allegations that Sarin was used by U.S. forces during a secret mission into Laos in 1970, and that this covert mission was in reality a cover story for employing the deadly nerve agent to kill U.S. defectors and POWs. John Singlaub, the highly decorated retired major general was quoted in the piece providing a simple motive for the killings. POWs and defectors could compromise military secrets. End of story.

Citing eyewitness testimony, the CNN correspondents revealed that caches of Sarin were shipped to Laos when this horror went down and that the drop was made near known POW camps. While the report, which aired on CNN and in *Time* magazine, was hotly denied by high-ranking brass who questioned the unnamed officer serving as the source of the controversy, no one denied that Sarin was indeed in Laos at the time in question—Sarin that General Robinson had supposedly been responsible for transporting to the area.

The troubled general killed himself shortly after the matter came to the attention of military investigators.

Coincidence?

I don't know. All I remember about the incident was how General Robinson's eyes flashed crazy when I told him he had a new problem to deal with. The Soviets appeared to have developed a new generation of biochemical weapons. Now it was his job to spearhead the development of U.S. defenses in light of this new threat. It was as if I had dropped the final straw on a back about to break. Local police still doubt the army's conclusion about his suicide. So do I. No coroner's report was ever filed.

In the intelligence arena, where I've spent the better part of my life, there are secrets and then there are *secrets*.

In remote viewing we have a world without them, but like anything else, some manage to surface while others never will. That's the way it works. Should these secrets ever see daylight, they would change the way we view history forever. There are those who like their history just the way it is. Talk about it out of turn, say things you shouldn't be saying, and you might get a face full of Sarin gas to quiet you down. Or you might get the sudden urge to kill yourself.

The secrets the Remote Viewing Unit uncovered about our missing POWs have never been released to the general public.

Until now.

# TARGET: THE ARK OF THE COVENANT

We saw the end of the world.

The way the people who lived it did.

It was a place of unspeakable horror, a firestorm of blood and pain, the wholesale butchering of old and young, rich and poor, the ruin of homes and businesses and places of worship. An orgy of destruction aimed at people of faith.

We watched the downfall of a sacred city condemned to death by one of history's most ruthless regimes. An empire backed by a military machine unmatched for its brutal killing efficiency. It happened nearly two thousand years ago. It was autumn.

This was no nightmare, no Armageddon prophecy fulfilled. The appalling vision was all in a day's work, the result of my wanting the RV Unit to unwind a little, to get distracted and have some fun. Needless to say, it didn't work out that way.

My laid-back session involved a topical search—an open exploration of a target you're not sure really exists. The subject here is usually an ancient legend or myth, something you wouldn't normally think about. The idea is to offer a diversion to someone totally worn out by the monotony of what they're doing. It's well known in experimental psychology that novelty acts as a stimulus to snap you out of your doldrums. The minute a dolphin wakes up it moves immediately to investigate anything new in its environment. It can't help itself, something unexpected has disturbed its routine and it wants to check it out—*needs* to check it out. It's the same with remote viewing. After working the same class of targets day in and day out, the mind falls into an ennui, an oppressive boredom punctuated by ho-hums about everything. It doesn't matter how exciting the target might be, if you know it's going to be related to the last one you looked at, the effort becomes a real struggle. The RV Unit needed a time out in the worst way. Our last mission was a mind-bender.

We had just dropped a dime on the infamous international terrorist Ilich Ramírez Sánchez, better known to the world as Carlos the Jackal. Because we worked so closely with counterintelligence sources on the Jackal and the sensitive nature of that work, I can't reveal much more about the case except to say we helped reveal Mr. Sánchez's central role in the kidnapping of U.S. brigadier general James Dozier and steer authorities to his rescue. It took months of RV drudgework to track him down, session after grueling session, going over this, confirming that, and then back to the drawing board. After the Jackal was convicted of murder in Paris, the unit was ready for some rest and relaxation. They'd earned it, something fresh and different to cure the remote-viewing blues. Luckily I had no shortage of ideas about having fun. A target you could relax to.

I gave two of my best remote viewers an objective so removed from everyday thought that the very act of looking for it would temporarily take their minds off the missions we were sweating bullets over. That was my plan. Charlene Shufelt and Mel Riley needed a break and I was going to give it them one way or another. The target I chose was perfect, an authentic legend you could really sink your teeth into.

I picked the Ark of the Covenant.

What I knew about the ark wasn't very much. My family wasn't exactly the conventional churchgoing type, and Bible studies weren't included in the ROTC officers' training curriculum. Like a lot of people, the first I heard of it was when the director Steven Spielberg released his highly popular adventure film *Raiders of the Lost Ark* in 1981. It seemed entertaining enough, an object of great power revered by the Jewish people, which after being ark-napped by a gang of Nazi thugs incinerates its evil captors with the aid of some ferocious heavenly spirits charged with guarding it. Only later did I learn the ark's significance as a holy relic and source of one of mankind's greatest unsolved mysteries.

The Old Testament states that the ark was built on Moses' command at the foot of Mount Sinai around 1250 BC to hold the two stone tablets inscribed with the Ten Commandments. Similar to a simple wooden chest, it measured roughly four by two and a half feet, overlaid inside and out with the purest gold. At its corners were four golden rings through which passed two rods to carry it. The bars were to remain always in the rings, even when the ark was placed in its special chamber inside Solomon's Temple in Jerusalem, its home. Seated on the lid were the sculpted figures of two kneeling gold cherubim facing each other with wings spread so that both sides of the mystical chest were completely covered. Only the highest-ranking priests could go near the ark; to do otherwise meant certain death. It was the focal point of God's presence on earth, a direct line to heaven with an unlisted number.

For two hundred years the ark brought victory after victory as the clergymen of Israel going into battle held it aloft, crushing their enemies before them. Described as a "light and a fire," it could inflict severe burns, halt the flow of rivers, and lay waste to cities and armies, an unstoppable force that acted variously as a focused particle-beam weapon, poisonous biological agent, tactical nuclear device, and divine flamethrower roasting anyone and anything that got in the way. This included priests careless enough to disobey the strict rules about handling it. Some insist that there was a chain attached to the priests' ankles in case an error in judgment required them to be pulled clear of the ark. If there was anything left to pull, that is.

The whodunit aspects of the ark legend began with its disappearance after the destruction of the Second Temple at the hands of the Romans brought in by a violent Jewish revolt, an uprising against Rome's rule in the Holy Land. Once they were on the march, you can bet the empire's legions didn't miss the opportunity to sack the immense riches laid at their feet. It was a wild free-for-all of looting and murder. And so the ark vanished from history.

Modern-day Indiana Joneses and professional archaeologists have crisscrossed the planet ever since hunting for the sacred relic, though its existence has never been proved. I had no grand illusion of proving anything historic today as I prepared the unit for our remote-viewing session. I'd settle for my original goal of giving them a relaxing exercise they could enjoy. I wasn't expecting anyone to find the long-lost ark. But it wouldn't be bad if we did.

As always, the crew got nothing from me, only the assigned target reference numbers and instruction that this would be a topical search, a mystery that needed solving. I told them to go into the collective mind; find out what it was saying about the target, past, present, and future. Knock yourselves out.

"Okay," Charlene said. "I just hope you came up with something better this time than 'who's buried in Elvis's grave?' or 'what's Madonna's kidney look like?'"

"I like to offer a broad range of targets," I said.

Mel Riley smiled. "I sure enjoyed the last one; that was really something."

The last one was when I tasked the unit to locate Excalibur, the fabled sword King Arthur yanked from the stone, setting him on the throne of Britain. It was Mel who nailed it, sketching a slanted line during the session, sensing an object vaguely red and crumbly. We later understood this to be the genuine sword, hidden in a lake somewhere in Britain, all chipped and oxidized rusty red from having been submerged in cold brackish water for centuries. Nice job on Mel's part.

We didn't get much of a chance to enjoy the discovery because something urgent came up. Now it was happening again. One minute I was looking at my team, preparing to ease into a training session, and the next everything suddenly changed. All the color emptied out of Charlene's face. She clasped her hands together, back straight, breathing dementedly. I asked her if she was okay, but she didn't seem to hear me.

"Hold on," she said.

"What? What is it?"

"Something made of a metal, shiny, smooth and cool, chestnut-colored. Bronze. A door, so immense you couldn't open it with a full squad of men. But it is opening."

"How?"

"It's opening by itself."

I hunkered down, following wherever she took us.

"Things can't open by themselves," I said. "How is it opening?"

Again Charlene didn't hear me, her attention drawn to I didn't know what, but the change in her demeanor was dramatic.

"A voice," she said. "A voice like a thousand trumpets. Coming from above—from everywhere—all at the same time. It's saying something. It's saying, 'We're leaving.'"

Charlene grimaced, covered her ears. "The voice. It's so loud, almost deafening!"

Mel got into the act now. He too was pale and agitated. He sounded shaky. Just like that, my plan for them to relax had gone down the tubes. I didn't like what was happening here. But at the same time, I was spellbound by it.

"There's a group of men," he said. "Can't recognize what they're wearing, but it seems like a uniform of sorts. They're officials, standing alone in a huge courtyard, an inner court. Clouds overhead, but not earthly clouds, too massive and moving too fast. It's surreal. One of the men drops to his knees. He's praying. These men are priests."

"What kind of priests?"

"I don't know what religion."

"Are they Christian?"

"No. But they're from another time, that I know."

"What's beyond the courtyard?" I asked.

Mel stared at the floor. A long, drawn-out look.

"It's all part of one structure," he continued. "A beautiful building erected on a summit surrounded by four prominent towers and white rock walls. There's a multiarched crosswalk emerging from one of the towers. Places to wash before entering the main structure, stones on the ground at the entranceway with a grape leaf design. A lot of people have passed through here at one time or another."

"Can you sketch it for me?"

Mel picked up his pen and did an incredible thumbnail of what could only be the biblical Second Temple in Jerusalem. I recognized it from drawings I dug up when I had decided on this practice target. It was the Jerusalem of two millennia past, the city where the Ark of the Covenant was kept.

Mel loosened the top button on his shirt. "Fires, raging inside the structure, on the streets. I'm hot, I can feel it," he said, dabbing at the sweat on his forehead. "I smell burning flesh, it's terrible."

"People running in panic in the area surrounding the structure," Charlene said. "It's as if the whole city is a battleground.

A replica of the Ark of the Covenant in the Royal Arch Room of the George Washington Masonic National Memorial.

Bodies stacked up like firewood on the steps of the building, some with swords still gripped in their hands. Fighters of some sort. Dead fighters."

"Who's doing this to them?"

"Soldiers, some wearing chain mail armor, others wearing leather. They're killing everyone in sight; men, women, and children, it doesn't matter to them. Stealing whatever they can get their hands on. Some are drinking—they're drunk."

"One of the priests, an old man with a long white beard dressed all in white, is talking to one of the soldiers," Mel said. "The old man looks like Moses to me, like from one of those statues in Rome. The soldier is an officer, better dressed than the rest. He's the commander. He has a red tunic on, arrogant and sneering at the old man."

"They're doing business," Charlene said, astonished. "In the middle of all this, they're talking business. Bargaining like they do in bazaars over a carpet."

How she knew this was beyond me. But the picture she was painting spoke to a deal. I know that if I was watching everything I held dear being destroyed and there was something I could do about it, I was going to do it. I'd make a deal with the devil to save my family. What Charlene saw made sense. My best guess in this scenario was a high priest negotiating with the man responsible for razing his temple. What he had to offer I wasn't sure yet. The officer was grinning because he knew he had the upper hand, the leverage to get whatever he wanted. It reminded me of how Hitler danced a jig after accepting France's surrender outside the same railroad car Germany signed off on the 1918 armistice ending World War I. The pompous bully beating up on the nerd with glasses. I hate bullies.

"The old man is nodding, as if they've agreed on something," Charlene said. "He's leading them somewhere."

"Where is he taking them?" I asked, hoping it was to the ark. "Go forward, try to sense where they're going and why."

Charlene thought it over, traveled once more through time, moving forward a few moments, not a few hundred centuries.

"I don't know what they said, but I have an image in my mind, blurry and yet bright. Gold. What I see is gold, and lots of it. Bowls and plates and platters, horns and jewelry, candelabras all made from gold. Fine clothing and spices, silver, exotic things."

"They're walking down stairs made of stone," Mel said. "It's a secret place; only the old man knows where it is. He's taking the officer to someplace underground. There're so much gold here I can see it shining in front of me."

"Is it a cave?"

"Yes, like a cave or tunnel under the structure. The old man in white has led them to a treasure trove hidden under the building. Wall-to-wall treasure. There must be tons of it."

I couldn't help myself, I had to take this to another level, ask specific questions, get specific information even if it meant leading them.

"Do you see a box, a large chest about four feet long by two feet?" I asked.

"Yes, I do. How did you know?" Mel said. "Two small golden figures on top with wings."

"Like angels?"

"Yeah, they look like angels," Mel answered. "With their wings swept over the top of the chest, as if protecting it."

"Are they taking that too?"

"What do you mean?"

"The soldiers," I said. "Are they stealing the box?"

"I don't know. Wait. Yes, they are. No—I'm not sure. The image is fading, something blocking me from seeing it."

"What's blocking you?"

Mel struggled to get this picture more in focus, trying to reconcile two realities happening at once.

"You won't believe this," he said finally. "It's like a giant hand covering a camera lens. I can't see the chest anymore through the hand. I've lost it."

"What is this?" Charlene said. She saw it too. "It's not human, it can't be."

A hand. I knew this symbol well, a dream symbol common in societies around the world. It's known as the hamsa in Islam, hamesh in Hebrew, and for the Hindus it's humsa—an ancient symbol used to bless and protect against misfortune, a paranormal defense from evil. I shuddered at the thought of some all-powerful hand barring us from seeing the ark just as we finally had it in our sights. But was it doing it for our own good? Either way, it was frightening.

"Wait, it's moving off," Charlene said.

"The hand is gone now," Mel agreed. "I'm somewhere else."

"What's happening now?" I asked.

"I smell that stench again, burning bodies," Charlene said. "The dead and dying. I can't take this anymore."

"All right," I said. "Let move forward in time. Follow the money. Where's all that gold now?"

I waited. Charlene and Mel needed to shake off the demise of a city before they could move on. They were lost now in a vast and strange place, set adrift in a remote mindscape of violence and menacing shadows. This wouldn't be easy, but I wanted to see it through to the end. They had had the ark and lost it. It would be a crime against history for us not to try again.

Charlene stepped in first. "Water," she said. "All around me. I'm by the sea, on the shoreline, waves lapping at my feet. The water is warm, lovely. It's the dead of night, no lights. I sense I have a job to do here, I work here."

"Me too," Mel said. "I feel the same thing. And I'm glad to be here, to be alive. I can see off in the distance the flames rising from the city. The whole place is on fire, like looking into hell. I'm very happy to be near water."

"What else is there around you?"

"I see the soldiers again," Charlene said. "They're making their way down to the beach. Silently, sneaking in from a rear gate outside the city under cover of night. No torches, nothing to light their way, they're coming in complete secret. Hundreds of them."

"Where are they going?"

"Where we work, of course," Mel said, with a slight smile. "There are carts and horses and several ships docked in the harbor. People like me loading what they've stolen. They're not asking us, they're ordering us, jabbing us with swords."

"Yes. I'm lugging heavy baskets filled with silk and grain into the ship's holds and onto the carts," Charlene said. "There's no end to it, so much to take. So heavy it hurts my back."

"The air is calm, no wind. Great night to pull a heist," Mel said. "These guys know what they're doing. It isn't the first time they've looted a place. Real professionals."

"Something's happening," Charlene said.

"Everybody's stopping," Mel said.

"Why did they stop?"

"It's happening on the beach, men approaching dressed like the priests we saw before," Charlene answered. "The old man with the long beard is at the front. He looks terrible. He's watching them load cases of gold and silver objects onto it. His eyes are red, he's weeping. They're all crying."

Mel saw more now. "There's smoke coming from the metal vessels the priests are carrying," he said. "They're swinging small containers with incense in them as they walk to the biggest ship. This is a religious procession of some kind."

"The gold isn't just jewelry," Charlene added. "These are the items the old man bargained for. The deal they made."

"What about the chest?" I asked. "With the angels?"

"I don't know," Charlene said. "I assume it's on the ship."

"Don't assume anything." I looked over at Mel. He shook his head, disappointed.

"Sorry, boss, not getting it," he said.

"Charlene?"

"Nope. Still nothing," she answered.

I paused. I knew I was pushing them, but the ark—I had to know where the ark was. I thought quickly, had to be creative, couldn't let this moment be lost in time. We might never have an opportunity like it again.

"Advance in time, wherever it takes you, don't look back for any reason," I told them. "The golden box is your target. Find the golden box."

I turned to Charlene. She shrugged. She had nothing. But Mel did.

"I'm not exactly sure where I am in time here," he said, "but it's hot and dry, sandy, dusty gritty, dry riverbeds all around. Lots of erosion at the location, canyons, it's a remote place, nothing around. Just cliffs and gulches."

"Any caves?"

"Yeah, now that you mention it. I see a cave, or is it an abandoned mine? It's not at ground level or at the top, kind of somewhere in between. It's a fairly large dark space, and cool. I see the chest object, I see it."

"The same golden box?"

"I'm not sure. There's nothing to indicate gold on it. It's just plain wood, not fancy. I sense that at one time something enclosed it, drapes, like a four-poster bed with drapes hung on each side."

"No gold cover?"

"Could have been gold at one time, but discolored now. Nothing valuable jumps out at me. Not in good state of preservation. If you saw it today it wouldn't be recognizable as the box we viewed before. You'd be hard pressed to say they were one and the same."

"Where is it?"

"It's not easily accessible from above or below."

"Where—*where*?"

Charlene and Mel both looked at me now, taken aback by my outburst. I knew I was acting obsessed. I *was* obsessed.

"Just a guess, Captain," Mel said. "But if I had to put my finger on it, I'd say in the desert, in the Middle East."

"Why the Mideast?"

"Well, it isn't Arizona. It's the Mideast, I don't why."

"Are you in Israel?"

"Maybe, or along the border with Jordan."

"And."

Mel wrung his hands, thinking, thinking. He wanted to give me what I wanted, but it was that wall again. RV burnout. They were both shot, no more to give. If I pushed them anymore it could affect their performance on our next mission, and I couldn't have that. I had to drop this now. I hate to admit defeat, but it was finished, there was nothing more to be gained here. Mel and

Charlene got up from their chairs and walked out without saying a word. They had no idea what I was looking for, but the emotional impact of what they saw was something they'd never forget. I heard Mel muttering to himself as he went.

The fun session was over.

Nobody was laughing.

Time moves in strange ways if you follow along closely. A collection of sound scraps, tatters of images, whirling specks of faces and places and things. Sometimes the act of remembering it all becomes a refuge, a place of serenity. Other times it can drive you mad.

I was at home in Sacramento, recovering from an intimate party friends had thrown me the night before on the occasion of my sixtieth birthday. They apparently thought being sixty was something special, but for me it just meant more aches and pains. But I was thankful for one thing: a fading memory. As you grow older your mind becomes more selective, allowing you to pick and choose what you want to remember. I've got a wide selection.

At the borders of my living room were elemental things: an exposed radiator, some old army blankets I couldn't bear to part with when I retired, an ironing board leaning unfolded against the window, a couple of posters and items fans had sent me over the years. My favorite was the yellowing photos of the old army RV Unit, disbanded and shut down now. I was noticing things more than usual on this day. Maybe it had something to do with turning sixty, I don't know. It was raining. I had a small fire going, hot tea brewing on the stove, and the radio playing. All the comforts of clean California living, circa 2009.

I couldn't get too comfortable, though. I needed to get dressed and head down to the airport Holiday Inn where my Matrix Intelligence Agency team would be waiting for me. The crew was getting ready to leave after flying into town to assist me on a case, a Bangladeshi girl from the Detroit area named Tangena Hussain who'd gone missing. When I heard about her, I posted a set of target references numbers on my MIA website under Project Goldeneye and my MIA investigators joined me a week later. The case grabbed us, as all missing and child abduction cases do. We never turn our backs on children.

Tangena's story revolved around the boyfriend of the little girl's mother, Jamrul Hussain (no relation to Tangena). Police said he'd told them he'd left the three-year-old inside his locked car when he went inside a service station convenience store. When he came out, as he explained to detectives, the girl was gone. Jamrul claimed that Tangena was abducted, even though there wasn't a shred of evidence to prove that anyone had broken into the vehicle.

An Amber Alert was issued early for Tangena, who had reportedly last been seen wearing a long-sleeved T-shirt, brown with some kind of cartoon character on it, white nylon cargo pants, and gold sandals. The very next day, Jamrul Hussain was arrested on unrelated charges of misconduct and kidnapping involving a Dearborn, Michigan, girl that allegedly occurred later. Mr. Jamrul was apparently a very busy man.

Having remote viewed Tangena myself, I had come up with the sad conclusion that she was dead—the same tragic end I saw for Christina White years earlier. And as with Christina's case, my team and had I followed the exact same methods in an attempt to recover her remains. Once I knew she had passed, I contacted the Detroit Police Department, volunteering information I had gathered about her body being in a specific area along Interstate 94 and French Road on the city's east side. I got lucky on this one. Detroit police commander Paul Welles advised me that he'd cooperate in any way he could. I never seek out police help, but when it comes like that I take it.

I forwarded a Google map of the area where I strongly believed the body was hidden and flew immediately to Detroit. Welles generously offered to help me search the area, but I decided to go it alone. It involved climbing down into a tight drainage ditch and I didn't want anyone getting hurt on my account. As usual, the press found out about me and mobbed the area. No problem there—any publicity you can get when a child vanishes is good publicity. The case soon after appeared on the television program *America's Most Wanted*.

While we didn't find Tangena, the MIA information helped the police in their continuing hunt to pick up the crud responsible for her abduction. I can't comment further on an ongoing police investigation except to say that my unit and I won't quit until we have something. I never quit.

They say it doesn't rain much in California, but what they don't tell you is that when it starts it doesn't stop. I heard on the radio that the airport was temporarily canceling or delaying all domestic and international flights out of Sacramento. As much as I hated saying it, the downpour was on my side. It was like a sign from God. My crew would have to stay a little longer, and that's just perfect for what I had in mind. I wanted them to go over a cold case, a case so frozen they'd probably laugh themselves silly if I told them what it was—which I wouldn't. Instead I'd tell them it was a practice target, a topical search I wanted them to RV before they left. It wouldn't take long to do, not as long as it had taken for me to revisit the case, which was going on thirty years now.

I wanted them to find the Ark of the Covenant.

Because of our work on the Hussain disappearance, the team would be well oiled and ready. The search for Tangena had been complex, two days of solid remote viewing, but it was over for the moment. My desire to find the ark, however, wasn't. I'd never been able to get it out of my mind. Hopefully with the help of my MIA unit we could finally close the book on it.

Much had happened since the army RV Unit and I tracked the whereabouts of the ark back in 1981. Many books had been published on the topic, many theories floated by people who claimed to have a lock on its location. Little wonder considering the financial windfall waiting for those who brought it in. The books sold like hotcakes and Steven Spielberg could tell you from firsthand experience that reigniting interest in history's most hunted artifact means gold at the box office. The Ark of the Covenant was good for business.

One theory asserts that the ancient chest resides today at St. Mary of Zion Church in the town of Axum in Ethiopia, the place where the African nation's emperors have been crowned. It supposedly rests in a secret compartment next to the chapel, guarded by a handpicked priest who maintains his vigil over the holy relic from the age of seven until the day he dies. That's what I call job security.

The story goes that the ark was smuggled out of Jerusalem and into Ethiopia by King Menelik I, the reputed son of the Queen of Sheba and Israel's renowned leader King Solomon. The problem with this tale is, no one has ever been allowed into the chapel to see the ark except the chosen priest, and there is absolutely no record of this legend in Ethiopian history until the end of the thirteenth century. It just doesn't hold up.

In Israel, some experts say the ark was too valuable to keep around and was melted down for its gold by those who plundered it. Others speculate that the Vatican absconded with it after the Romans sacked Jerusalem and it later landed in the hands of the Catholic Church. The pope and Vatican authorities hotly deny the charge, stating for the record that there is no evidence in their archives that the treasure was in Rome from the medieval period onward. Go argue with the pope.

Many Jews feel that when it comes to the ark, all roads lead back to Jerusalem. It never left. On June 7, 1967, Israeli troops recaptured the Old City in the Six-Day War and the Western Wall of the destroyed Second Temple was in Jewish hands again— hands eager to start digging. Archaeologists burrowed deep into the exposed parts of the wall buried for two thousand years where they believed at the end of a gate they would find a secret room where the ark was located. Not all of the digging was done legally, and a subterranean brawl broke out between Palestinians bent on protecting their revered Al-Aqsa Mosque built over the ruins of the temple site and Jews sworn to return the ark to its rightful owners. Israeli police permanently sealed the passage to the Temple Mount and that was that. If the ark is there, it will have to wait to be uncovered until the volatile politics of the region simmer down. Nobody has that kind of time.

Perhaps the best recent theory, the approach that most interested me, is the one that follows the money. In this scenario, floated by Dr. Sean Kingsley, an archaeologist and historian, the Ark of the Covenant is no longer the centerpiece of the search, but rather other items filched by the Roman emperor Vespasian and his erstwhile son Titus. This prize includes the seven-branched golden candelabrum or Menorah, one of the oldest symbols of the Jewish people, a set of silver trumpets to herald the arrival of the messiah, and a host of other priceless biblical objects. The timeline for this notion follows the ark's turbulent history across more than five hundred years and the rule of four different civilizations, from the Vatican, to the Vandal palace of Carthage, to Constantinople's Hippodrome, and finally the desert wilderness of Judaea, where according to Kingsley's narrative the jewels of the Second Temple dwell today. The new home is said to be a Christian monastery. Go figure.

As for the ark, no one is making any claims in this hypothesis as to where it might be, but no one is denying the chance that it too is hidden in the same place. The location: the labyrinth of caves and tunnels beneath an isolated Greek Orthodox monastery called St. Theodosius.

The monastery's original claim to fame was as the place where the three wise men purportedly slept after visiting the infant Jesus. More to the point, it was Modestus, patriarch of the Orthodox

Church in Jerusalem at the time, who found himself in charge of the precious temple spoils as the Persian army invaded the Holy Land. Without anywhere to go with them, he supposedly carried them all away from the Church of the Holy Sepulchre, hiding them in the caverns under St. Theodosius. Modestus didn't know that the Muslim hordes would soon overrun the monastery as well. The Persians slaughtered everyone they could get their swords on and flattened the church. It was later rebuilt under the auspices of the Greeks, but its underground caves remained as they were before the slaughter. This is where the money trail ends and the mystery begins.

Maybe the Second Temple riches are there, maybe not. But one thing is for sure in all this, one solid piece of evidence no one can deny. The triumphal marble Arch of Titus near the Forum in Rome commemorating the capture and sack of Jerusalem

The Arch of Titus in Rome, depicting the triumphal procession of Roman legions carrying off the treasures of the Second Temple in Jerusalem.

clearly shows the seven-pronged golden Menorah and twin silver trumpets of the Jews being paraded down its narrow streets. The money pinched from all that gold helped to build the huge Roman Coliseum and fund their savage games at the Circus Maximus. This is a fact, a fact set in stone for all to see forever. St. Theodosius is another matter. What we remote viewed decades ago closely resembled it, so this was where we'd kick off our search today. It was beneath this monastery seven miles north of Bethlehem in Israel's disputed West Bank that I believed we'd find the lost Ark of the Covenant. My Matrix Intelligence team would handle the heavy lifting on this one. Only they didn't know it yet.

It was still raining cats and dogs outside when I pulled into the parking lot of the Holiday Inn. A strong wind was blowing leaves off the trees and down the streets in sweeping gusts. I raised my collar and hustled into the lobby, where it wasn't exactly crowded, and the bellman raced up to me, his face red, curiously excited about some firemen who had removed a burning sofa from an apartment across from the hotel. I was the only customer he'd seen all day, so I guess the sofa incident loomed large in his life at the moment. Despite being the seat of state government in California, Sacramento sure feels like a small town sometimes. It was pathetic and endearing at the same time.

I stepped into the conference room, where my agency people were patiently hanging around in anticipation of my arrival. I'm hardly ever late, but this storm was a real whopper and California drivers are notorious for not knowing how to handle the wheel when the sky is crying. They don't understand rain.

Not everyone from MIA could make it up here for the Tangena Hussain investigation. But those who did were among the best remote viewers I've trained, all of whom worked the Christina White disappearance and a dozen other missing children cases. There was Brent Miller, Alex DiChiara, and Dawn Stoltz, each of them exhausted and eager to hop on a plane for home. They were aware that the storm was going to delay their flights, so there was plenty of time to shoot the breeze and discuss some matters. When I innocently offered them the opportunity to run through a topical search for practice, they jumped at it. It didn't matter what the search was for, as long as they got to work with me. This was one dedicated bunch.

The conference room would serve for the session, though I could hear the occasional commotion in the hotel's hallway. Mostly we were on our own and it was quiet. I gave them the target reference numbers without letting them know it was the ark we'd be looking for. The numbers were a link to the information Mel Riley provided so long ago on Llewellyn Street. The key here was the sandy desert location, the remoteness of the place, the cliffs and gulches he sensed. The details pictured the ark situated in what appeared to be an abandoned mine, a place difficult to get to if you didn't know where to look—like the secret caverns under a monastery.

The search term I used was "Ark of the Covenant/now."

We began.

"Tell me what you see," I said.

They smiled; the words were familiar and comforting, like hearing the name of a loved one when you're far from home.

"It's a desolate place, wherever I am," Brent said. "Sandy and rocky, a flinty smell. A desert, but not like any desert I've ever seen before. It smells ancient, if that makes any sense."

"Go on."

"It's sunrise, and there's a road—no, a path is more accurate. Extending over high rocky ridges."

"I sense something like that," Dawn said. "It's a wild region, deep ravines. If you make a misstep it's the last thing you'll ever do. I'm on the brink of some very scary chasms and precipices."

"It's a barren place, but something spiritual about it," said Alex, a strange comment coming from a former wrestler. "It's like the scenery in the movie *The Ten Commandments* and I'm expecting Charlton Heston to come walking by with his rod in his hands."

"You're saying this is Bible country."

"Yeah, I guess so. There's a great plain below me, and as I climb higher I can catch a glimpse of a sea through breaks in the cliffs. It sparkles blue, beautiful really. Maybe Heston will part the waters with his stick. He is Moses after all. He'll always be Moses to me."

Alex didn't know it, but what he was seeing was more than likely the Dead Sea and the plains of Jordan. We were definitely on track here. But we needed to move on to where the ark might be. The storm could let up any minute now and I'd have to call the session. I couldn't let that happen.

"Take the path you're on and follow it to the end," I told them. "Slide into the future."

"Horses, I feel a horse under me," Dawn said. "I'm part of a group of men wearing tunics with crosses on them. I know the outfit, saw it in a history book once. Crusaders, it has to be. They're Crusaders heading somewhere up ahead."

This was very good. Dawn had moved back in time instead of forward to when the Crusaders controlled segments of this land. St. Theodosius is built on the remnants of an old Crusader building. We were getting closer.

"Whoa, I almost got knocked over!" Alex shouted.

"By what?" I asked.

"Not Crusaders. They were more like Arabs, an Arab army sweeping down like locusts from the north into this valley. Man, these guys are on a mission."

Again, right on the mark, this time sensing what he believed to be Arabs but who were in reality Persians as they invaded, wiping out churches and anything else in their path as they attempted to take back the Holy Land.

"There's a building up on one of the hills," Brent said. "Dilapidated, in disrepair, but oddly wonderful in its own way.

It's a church, a beautiful old church, but nearly deserted. Doesn't look like any visitors are welcome. There used to be monks living here, hundreds of them, but not anymore. Just a handful maybe, and some elderly nuns. I know their mode of dress, the long black coats, the beards and hats. It's Greek. It must belong to the Orthodox Church."

Bingo. As usual, Brent had hit the nail on the head. We were at the gates of St. Theodosius in present time. This was exactly where I wanted to be. Time to find what we came for. What I came for. But I had to move slowly, step by step.

"There's a staircase, not ordinary stairs, made from stone," Brent continued. "The stone is wet and slippery. I can even tell you how many there are, eighteen steps in total. It leads to an underground chamber. I'm walking, one leg in front of the other, walking with caution, don't want to fall."

"Keep moving down the stairs, and watch yourself."

That got a rise out of them, some nervous laughter. I thought they were beginning to understand that we weren't doing this for fun. There was something serious going on here. But I kept a straight face, nothing to reveal what I was thinking. It was what they were thinking that was important. What was in their minds.

"I sense a cave, it's dark here but the walls are so white they pick up whatever light there is," said Dawn.

"It's a burial cave," Alex said. "Like the catacombs under Rome. I saw them once, I still got family in Italy."

"A burial chamber, someone is buried here, a revered monk, one of them, maybe the man who founded the place. There are alcoves inside the cave too, more dead people. Their bones are packed tight in there. Skulls, lots of skulls."

"They didn't go easy," Alex said. "All kind of cuts and holes in them. Like someone murdered them. Vicious."

"They have crosses in their eye sockets," Dawn said, her complexion going slightly greenish now. "I'm scared."

"Just keep working it," I said. "Don't be afraid."

"There's a door, a secret door, more stairs to go down," Brent said. "No one's been down this passageway in a very long time. I'm not even sure anyone knows it's here. The door just kind of opened for me."

"Just—kind of opened?"

"Yeah, I see it too," Alex said. "A figure leading us. Don't ask me what it is. A shrouded figure like a monk, but not a monk. Maybe not human. What the fuck's going on here?"

Dawn was starting to tremble. She said nothing, but I know she saw it too. I didn't want to say what I thought it was.

"This ravine goes down deep into the cavern, maybe a hundred feet or so," Brent said. "The walls are solid rock. Even still, I feel like I'm stepping out into space, an unimaginable void. This is the gateway. There's danger here, I feel it all around me. Something powerful hiding in there."

I could see the blood pulsing through a vein on Dawn's forehead. I needed to keep my eye on her.

"Go closer, go deeper into the cave," I told them.

"There's something in there too big for the room," Alex said. "A thing that can't be contained in a chamber like this. It's too strong. Like putting a V8 engine in a VW."

"Gold," Dawn finally said, her lips quivering. "I see gold and silver. Musical instruments. Two horns—no, they're trumpets. A candleholder is right next to them."

"That holds seven candles?"

"No, it holds oil in them, one of those old oil lamps or something. Very old. It's gorgeous."

That was it. The temple artifacts said to be hidden in the monastery. I couldn't believe it. There they were. But this was all too easy, as if we were being led here for some purpose. Too easy. It made me uncomfortable.

"Is there a box inside there too?" I asked.

"What kind of box?" Alex asked.

"That's for you to find out."

"The figure is pointing at an object in the corner, just sitting there among all the jewels and gold," Brent said. "Who is this guy?"

"It's a ghost," Dawn said, moving her hands into her pockets and then out onto her lap and then into her pockets again as if she didn't know what to do with them. "It's a spirit, I'm telling you. We shouldn't be here."

"Forget the ghost," I said. "Examine the chest."

"We shouldn't be here," Dawn said again, this time in an anxious whisper. "We really shouldn't be here." She began scratching her arms violently. Her world had been stripped of everything she knew and all she saw was this faint ghostlike monk. She was beginning to lose it.

"I'm trying to make out the chest," Brent said. "There a white light coming off it now, heat."

"Like an oven," Alex added.

"It's not made out of gold, no precious metals or stones on it at all," Brent explained. "It's simple wood, decaying and discolored, not in good shape at all."

Exactly what Mel Riley saw, a box in a run-down state of preservation. I could barely contain myself now.

"How big is it? Give me the dimensions."

"I'm getting the sense of a small crib here, maybe four feet by two. Like a child's crib."

"The spirit, it's doing something," Dawn interrupted. "It's so hot in here, is anyone else hot? I can't breathe."

Dawn threw her arms up in front of her face.

"A hand, a black hand, but translucent," she said. "Filled with stars, swirling and brilliant stars. I can't feel my legs, my eyes are burning. The hand is blocking me, almost as if it's absorbing me into it."

I looked over at Dawn. She stood up slowly from her chair, her expression dead, her skin a sick milky white.

"I understand now," she said.

She was tracing something with her finger in the air.

"It's all clear to me now."

She began wobbling—

"Moonlight is moonlight, so many stars," she said. "Blame it on the fog."

"Dawn!" I shouted, taking hold of her and sitting her down again. I moved closer to her, could feel that she was icy cold.

*Where is she?* The shock of riding the currents of time had been too much, wandering from one reality to another, independent of the logic of hours and minutes, months and years. I knew now better than I ever had that we're all made of time. It's the force that defines our existence.

"Where are you, Dawn?" I whispered to her.

She exhaled suddenly, stirring slightly. She was coming back, but coming from *where?* "Are you all right?" I asked.

"It was so beautiful," she said.

"Welcome home," I said.

She nodded. "So beautiful."

An announcement came over the hotel's loudspeaker. The storm had let up enough for flights out of the airport to resume. Dawn got up slowly, Alex right there with an arm under her shoulder to steady her. She was okay. She was going to be fine. All was as it should be, the sequence of time restored to what we understand, the arrangement we all agree on so we can stay sane. I stepped to the window; there was a soft mist outside, rolling low toward the mountains, no amoebic murk, just a gentle ordinary fog, like the one Dawn had described. The one she saw before she went out.

They could all go home now. It was done.

"What were we looking for?" Brent asked.

"You know I can't tell you that," I said. "It was a practice run. You guys took it down a weird road, that's all. It was really just supposed to be fun."

I knew they didn't believe a word I was saying, and they knew I'd explain it later. But for now I just couldn't.

They moved silently to the door, no one talking, no one looking at each other. Alex stopped and turned to me.

"Some fun, boss," he said.

It was raining again when I got home. The team was gone, their flights probably departed now. No one called telling me any different. It was the kind of day when you forget words and drop things and wonder why you came into a room. You rack your brains and then sooner or later you remember. Whatever it was gets communicated somehow.

I couldn't begin to explain what the shrouded figure the team had viewed was, and part of me didn't really want to know. We had found the Ark of the Covenant hidden underground in the caverns of a monastery near Bethlehem called St. Theodosius.

*I know where the Ark of the Covenant is.*

Just thinking it makes me shiver.

I'd already spoken with several contacts of mine to see if I could get into the monastery to confirm, but they all agreed it would never happen. The monks in charge wouldn't even allow tourists inside most of the time, not to mention credentialed archaeologists and researchers. I wouldn't have a prayer.

The Israeli government wouldn't be much of any help either. The Palestinians in charge of the Temple Mount don't exactly have a great record when it comes to dealing with them. In Nazareth, Muslim zealots have been trying to construct a large mosque that would dwarf the Christian Basilica of the Annunciation, and following repeated attacks by mobs against the Jewish holy site of Joseph's Tomb in Nablus, the place was sacked and burned and later converted into a mosque. Rachel's Tomb at the Jerusalem-Bethlehem border has come under continued Palestinian sniper attack, and most of the world is familiar with the images in 2002 of Palestinian Tanzim militia from Yasser Arafat's Fatah movement taking over the Church of the Nativity in Bethlehem for weeks at gunpoint. Now that

St. Theodosius is within their new political leader Hamas's territory, nobody wants to touch the area or even get near it. If any treasure were to be found at the monastery it would constitute another proof that the Second Temple existed, something the Arab world denies. Even worse, something told me that should I get in there and uncover the ark, someone in the "community" would be more than happy to ship it off to Christie's or Sotheby's for piles of cold hard cash. That's just the way it is in the Middle East, and everywhere else on planet Earth. Money talks and mankind's legacy walks.

The oddest thing about my discovery was that I wasn't even sure I wanted anyone to know about it. Why burst the bubble on a legend so intriguing and wonderful? It would be like telling a child there's no Santa Claus, and who wants to do that? I wasn't the only one who felt this way. In the Bible, the prophet Jeremiah says with no doubts that "the Ark of the Covenant of the Lord shall not come to mind, nor shall they remember it, nor shall they miss it, nor shall it be made again" (Jeremiah 3:16). He should have told Steven Spielberg.

Funny as it may seem, it was Spielberg who probably got it right on what the final disposition of the ark should be. At the end of *Raiders* he has the holy relic being hidden in the bowels of a government warehouse where it will be lost and forgotten like all things under the control of bureaucrats. What better place for the ark to vanish than in their hands? Nobody will ever find it.

Perhaps this is what's meant to be. Maybe we're not ready to possess the ark. Maybe the distorted cruel parts of our souls disqualify us from having a direct line to God, or the universal spirit, or whatever's in fashion at the moment to call powers we don't understand. But then there's remote viewing. A connection to the universe anyone can make.

Maybe we are ready.

# A NEW AND YOUNGER
# WORLD

A classroom somewhere in China. Twenty-five kids, seven- to twelve-year-olds, all neatly dressed in their cute school uniforms. They watch in hushed wonderment as their teacher removes something from his desk. The teacher, mid-thirties, typically unassuming in his simple polo shirt and blue sweater, holds a color photograph up to them. The image is of a *missile*—a U.S. intercontinental ballistic missile. The kind we'd unload on China in a war.

Grinning and confident, the teacher asks the children if they can see the missile. The answer is a spirited yes. Then he asks if they see one specific area of the rocket, a shiny section near its solid propellant boosters—the same spot where the massive engine is encased in a reflective coating to protect the flexible alloy skin beneath it.

Again the children shout, "*Hao!*"—yes.

Very good.

Now he tells them to focus on the rocket's coating and start a small fire there using their minds. They've done this before, so no problem. It's like a big game to them, they're eager to do it. The kids shut their eyes and concentrate on the target together, as if they were one person, one mind.

More than eight thousand miles away, a U.S. ICBM test fails miserably. Just as it hits boost phase, still under its own power and closest to its launch point, the state-of-the-art nuclear missile blows itself to smithereens. More tests follow, with the same disastrous result, leaving the scientists and military personnel involved scratching their heads. When told by intelligence sources that a secret program in China using schoolchildren against military targets may be responsible for bringing their prized rocket down, the scientists laugh and go back to business as usual. Remote influencing doesn't exist, they say. No one can destroy a missile using only their mind. No one can start a blaze by simply willing it to be. It isn't scientific, so it can't be true. Remote influencing isn't real. It must be something else.

This incident never happened, by the way. But it will.


Looking back on the fall of the Shah of Iran in 1979, the U.S. secretary of defense and ex–CIA director Robert Gates said his agency dropped the ball predicting the calamity because in government, "We have the will *not* to believe." Despite the dire political signals and intelligence red flags, the CIA fell short by choosing not to believe their own eyes and instincts. In truth, they went out of their way not to believe. To do so would have been to admit that everything they knew was wrong, that every conclusion they had reached using traditional intelligence-gathering methods was mistaken. It was impossible for the Shah to be overthrown and that was that. All their past experience and knowledge told them so, and they had so much of both. Any evidence to the contrary was questionable. It was better to stick to what you knew than what you saw. Dogma before intuition.

The CIA isn't the only professional clique that likes to bury its head in the sand when faced with things unknown. It makes things easier for the best-trained experts and academics too. The world is a much friendlier place when you reject out of hand what you can't understand or explain. People can't start fires with only their minds, pull a beetle through a sealed bell jar without harming it, or make a pocket-sized radio receiver disappear. But I don't have the luxury of not seeing. Having participated in similar experiments, I bear witness to the fact that they actually took place. I was there and saw it all. It's not something you forget.

We face the same irrational resistance in remote viewing, always have. Since the beginning, RV has been wrongly associated with all that New Age biocentrism mumbo-jumbo that we're the be-all and end-all in the universe peddled by a long list of shaman quacks. It was an uphill battle all the way, but we clawed our way to at least a grudging acknowledgment from our harshest critics by proving that what we said was true. Those critics over the years have included legions of closed-minded cranks like fundamentalist army officers who cast us as satan's servants, skeptical scientists determined to sink us without even reading our data, and paranoid government officials threatened by the idea that somebody could sneak a peek at their dirty deeds without using a camera or listening device. Even our own colleagues in the intelligence community refused to step up to the plate in our defense, insisting we weren't worth a plugged nickel when compared to their proud record. As if sitting on the sidelines warming your rear as Ayatollah Khomeini rose to power was something to boast about.

The culprit behind this militant rejection of remote viewing is cultural. We in the West live and die on the precepts of the scientific method. Our modern civilization with all its technological gizmos and high standard of living was built on its blueprint for searching out answers to cause-and-effect relationships in nature. Put simply, the method involves observing some unknown aspect of the universe, inventing a tentative description of it called a hypothesis, using the hypothesis to make predictions, testing those predictions by experimenting, and then repeating it all over again until no discrepancies exist between your theory and what you observed. The key to success along this route is having an opening somewhere in your idea that allows someone else to prove you wrong. There has to be enough wiggle room so that another theory or discovery has the chance to knock yours off its feet. Scientists make predictions based on their experiments all the time, but others disprove them if given the opportunity. That's how it works. In science, things either are or aren't. There's rarely any middle ground. But there is another way of looking at the universe even if you can't see it.

In China, people live in a reality beyond the West's yes-or-no scientific method. They prefer to see the world as a series of interlocking parts rather than a supposedly logical either/or model. What they and the Russians practice and teach in their schools is based on a system and philosophy known as dialectical materialism. There are two sides to every story.

In contrast to the scientific method, dialectics requires a defocusing on the duality of things in favor of a fusion of opposites that might end up by rejecting both, or by getting to the truth via a pathway that uncovers a hidden relationship between them. In dialectics, you have to drop the idea of things being apart and distinct. To understand the parts requires an understanding of how they work within the whole system. This is what remote viewing is all about, joining the parts to get a picture of the whole. But you need to have the parts.

The "blind men and the elephant" story is a great illustration of this. A group of blind men are asked to touch an elephant to learn what it's like. Each feels a different part—one its leg, another the trunk, and so on. When the men compare notes on what they've found, they discover that no one knows for sure what an elephant really looks like. The moral to this story is that reality may be seen differently depending on who's doing the seeing. But put the pieces of the puzzle together and a true picture emerges. It could be an elephant, a person you're looking for, or the precise location of a critical target. This is why the Chinese are so far ahead of us in remote viewing. They have the will to believe in what they sense—the very core of psi spying.

Most people know about remote viewing as a military intelligence tool, but not how it came about. It was the U.S. Navy that, faced with the bugbear of tracking Soviet nuclear submarines, initiated the first full-scale research into the phenomenon. The program was an act of desperation. We could follow the Russians' nuclear missiles when they were mobile on railroads, or hunt them down with satellites if they were hidden on land, but mount one inside a submarine and all bets were off. When these armed Soviet subs called "boomers" hit the scene, we became insanely vulnerable to a surprise attack. You can't stop something you can't see. Necessity being the mother of invention, the navy went looking for someone to give birth to a new way of seeing. The search was kept in-house.

The Rand Corporation (the name stands for "Research and Development"), a nonprofit think tank working mainly with U.S. armed forces to formulate solutions to problems applying operations research and systems analysis, was approached to study the situation in the late 1960s. They harvested ideas from a wide range of interdisciplinary sources, such as the Monte Carlo method, which uses random samplings of information repeated over and over again like a slot machine to work out results, and game theory, which mathematically calculates how a person's success in strategic confrontations often depends on the choices of others. What could be more of a strategic confrontation than taking on a Soviet nuclear sub?

Both methods are intended to predict how an opponent would likely behave in a given situation, and which side is more likely to win. The Russians might decide it was better to preserve their boomers than to try to shoot down the attack force coming for them, especially if they knew their chances of inflicting heavy losses on the attacker were small. Insights like these were supposed to help the military understand how they could achieve the best outcome, but it didn't turn out that way. They soon discovered it would take more than a bunch of theories to find the Soviet armada. They needed a preemptive first-strike capability, and Rand couldn't answer the mail on that using standard science alone.

What came next got the RV ball rolling. Despairing over their failure to deliver, Rand stepped as far out of the box as they ever have, turning to professional psychics to help find the boomers. Joining with naval intelligence operatives, they hit every Madame X, crystal ball reader, and storefront psychic in the United States for help, paying them handsomely to see what they could come up with. Luckily for our national security, one of those professional psychics was Ingo Swann. In short order, he and other "natural psychics" gave the navy the proof of concept they were hoping for. It was in the Russian city of Semipalatinsk in what is now Kazakhstan that people like Swann provided the drawings of a cluster of buildings and a huge construction crane using nothing more than the map coordinates given to them. Not bad considering that aside from suspicions that the site was important, nothing solid was actually known about it. We had nothing.

The location proved to be very important. It was an underground storage facility for Soviet missiles. Satellite recon later verified the psychics' conclusions, and more jaw-dropping results were to come on Kamchatka, a 750-mile-long peninsula lying between the Pacific Ocean to the east and Sea of Okhotsk to the west. Along the coast of the peninsula is the nearly seven-mile-deep Kuril-Kamchatka Trench, where psychics again hit one out of the

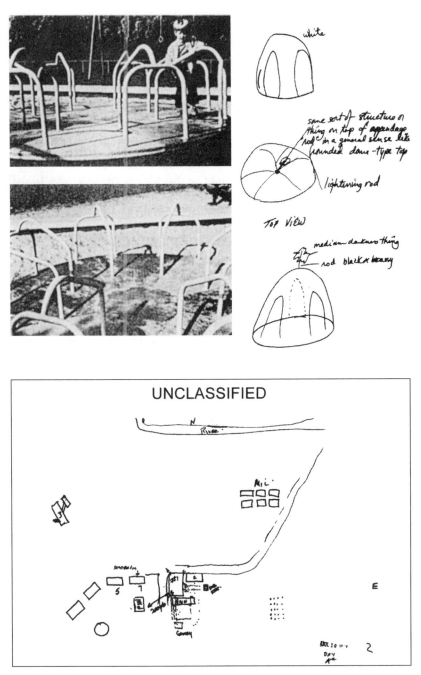

white

some sort of structure or thing on top of appendage rod in a general sense like rounded dome-type top

lightning rod

TOP VIEW

medium darkness thing

rod black or brassy

UNCLASSIFIED

N
River

Mil

smoodim

E

DAY

Remote-viewing sketches of merry-go-round with photos of the actual target.

park by uncovering Soviet subs being built underwater. Armed with this intelligence, the navy could blow the boomers out of the water before they left port. Once this and other test cases were confirmed, the CIA took over the project in 1970 and began funding more research through the Stanford Research Institute in Menlo Park, California. Now working under the code name SCANATE, for "Scanning by Coordinate," the technique of sensing targets from long distances that Swann helped pioneer became known as coordinate remote viewing. Suddenly there were a lot of new believers in military intelligence.

They finally got it.

Still, there were those who could barely say the words "remote viewing" without getting all worked up. It wasn't so much their objection to the "unscientific methodology" behind the system as it was emotional. One influential group described the process as "demonic" without ever denying the accuracy of its findings. When the RV team's first commander, Lieutenant Colonel Jachim, read on the head of the Presidential Foreign Intelligence Agency Board to the existence of the Remote Viewing Unit, the man's face went a whiter shade of pale, and with trembling hands pointing at the secret briefing book, he said, "Man should not know this until he dies." PFIAB monitored the overall performance of the U.S. intelligence community, and the man trembling was a Nobel laureate in chemistry. Not exactly a comforting thought, his being responsible for keeping the president up to date on our enemies. Colonel Jachim had pulled the anchor out from everything this guy thought he knew about science. And he did it by informing him that the mind can travel faster than light and be anywhere in space and time in the mere blink of an eye.

He was not a happy camper after that.

The remote-viewing program and its psi spies went through a series of incarnations and code names over the next twenty-five years, strange names like Gondola Wish, Grill Flame, Sun Streak, and Star Gate. But the missions we were tasked with by everyone from the CIA and NSC to the White House and Joint Chiefs

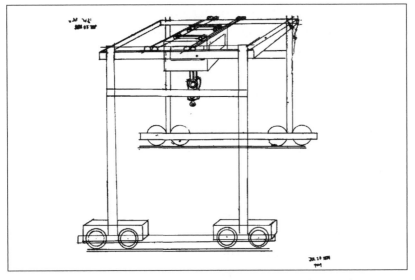

An RV sketch of a cluster of buildings, which later turned out to be a Soviet nuclear weapons testing site in the city of Semipalatinsk.

A declassified RV sketch of a construction crane and full rendering of the Semipalatinsk target site.

of Staff were not so strange. I was not a player yet in the unit when these missions were executed, but they included uncovering the CIA mole and double agent Aldrich Ames, the location and condition of Americans held during the Iran hostage crisis, the hunt for renegade U.S. customs agent Charles Jordan, and many others. In spite of cracking these all-important cases and the long list I was involved in, the unit suffered the same fate as all things ignorantly perceived as expendable—we were shut down.

But remote viewing marched on into the public arena. Today RV is practiced by the likes of for-profit corporations, Wall Street stockbrokers, lottery winner hopefuls, and, worst of all, the witches and charlatans who call themselves "teachers," camp followers who know there's money to be made in RV and no shortage of folks willing to pay for it. I make a living teaching remote viewing as well, but unlike those with no real-world experience, my bona fides are out there for anyone to check. And to the players who claim similar expertise, I challenge them to match my degree of knowledge after having worked more than twenty years in the field of remote viewing looking for missing children, diagnosing illnesses, and accurately predicting natural disasters. I've stuck my neck out for this new science, taking punches on radio and television and in the press. Now I challenge them and the skeptics to disregard my most recent accomplishment, the creation of RV Geofix. With this new innovative mind tool I can locate any target on Earth. That's what I said—any target on Earth.

Without my revealing the proprietary details of Geofix at this time, those familiar with associative remote viewing should understand the principles behind it. RV has always been about concentrating on "seeing" or "viewing" a scene or event taking place at a far-off location at any point in the past, present, or future. And though the results are highly accurate, relying solely on descriptive information about a target is often not enough to actually locate it. Mistakes were made.

The Geofix method employs a technique known as associative remote viewing. In ARV, a group of target photos is chosen, each having a different outcome associated with it. When the viewer's perception matches one of the blind targets, the outcome associated with that target is known to be correct. ARV targets can be linked with virtually anything, including events ranging from stock market advances and declines to earth changes and missing persons. This discovery took me more than four years to accomplish. Now Geofix can locate any target 100 percent of the time and to within sixty feet. Not too shabby.

I've been a one-man show for a long time, vilified and criticized for my work in remote viewing, but I suspect that with the advent of Geofix the skeptics and "professionals" will grow quiet, knowing I'm the only one in RV who can do it. To the scientists and the scientific method I invite you to invite me to put up or shut up. The job of science is discovery.

This is the decade of remote viewing.

If Ingo Swann was the Wright brothers of RV who taught us all how to fly, then I now lay claim to the right of teaching space travel. Those that went along for the ride, such talented folks as Mel Riley, Paul Smith, and my team at Matrix Intelligence Agency, are people I'll cherish my entire life. Together we journeyed through space and time in the cases documented in this book. I was the navigator on this wild ride and they the captains. What wonderful things we achieved and *will* achieve. And to those few commanders and enlightened souls who acted to protect the RV Unit from the wolves seeking to devour us—you did the right thing. It's in part because of your efforts that this fantastic voyage was possible.

The ability to remote view is the next step in the evolution of the mind. The human race may not be evolving, but on an individual level some of us are learning how to grow in consciousness and spirituality. What started out as a military tool based on the desperate need of warriors seeking to destroy their enemies in battle has now developed into an invaluable instrument in the search for enlightenment. Remote viewing is a teachable psychiclike skill anyone can learn. What is often overlooked is its potential to help us more deeply experience life. By experiencing a more direct and accurate psychic understanding, we move beyond belief and analysis into the realm of a poignant, life-altering universe. The world changes for us because we change the way we see it. The best way to experience the future is to create it.

On the other side of the coin, the ability to view and influence events and people from a distance is too tempting a talent for some to simply use for the good of mankind. Psi warfare was the initial goal of the governments who funded and supported it, and that remains the same to this day. As new and more deadly biological and nuclear weapons systems are developed, remote viewing their physical locations becomes less and less important. What will occupy the minds of those determined to dominate is remote influencing the military and political leadership in control of these systems. It won't matter how devastating or potent these ghoulish devices are, if you can manipulate the minds of those operating them to the point they serve your needs, then control shifts to you. This changes the whole game, the rules of engagement of how future wars are to be fought. It comes down to a simple equation: grab their brains and their bodies will follow.

The Chinese government is currently training remote-influencing fighters in clandestine research facilities spread across its vast borders. The implications of taking out key elements of an enemy's command structure and weapons sytems without firing a shot haven't been lost on them. Should they succeed, they would have in their growing arsenal a weapon of unparalleled capability. The die would be cast for the Chinese to become the next unrivaled superpower. The mind muscle to take down a missile, stop pacemakers, and intrude into someone's dreams to the point where they can no longer sleep are just a few examples of psychic attacks we would all be helpless against. It isn't too late to change this scenario, however. For us to wage war on the battlefields of the future, we must achieve a level playing field. We must develop these same superpowers as well.

But it doesn't have to be this way.

In Arthur C. Clarke's classic science fiction novel *Childhood's End*, which narrates humanity's transformation through psychic

The end of the "cold war"—at home in Lugansk, Ukraine, with my fiancée Natalia Tyupa.

links with a cosmic "hive mind," the role of man's unconscious in the context of the broader universe takes center stage—just as it does in remote viewing when we access the universal library for answers.

The book relates the tale of how mankind turns control of Earth over to a race of benign aliens who claim they will care for us and improve our lives. Who wouldn't want that? These aliens display a cautious interest in human enterprises involving the occult and psychic research. They also pay an unhealthy amount of attention to our children. To make a long story short, after the aliens, who have been hiding their true appearance, finally reveal themselves, selected human children begin manifesting telepathic and telekinetic abilities. Turns out only the little ones can merge with the hive mind and lead the rest of us to a higher plane of existence. They are the leaders of a new and younger world.

Let's hope that our children will one day do the same. That in classrooms from China to the United States, remote viewing will be taught to be used for the greater good, not for destruction.

If there's one notion this book has made apparent, it's that the mind can know anything. So why not look at everything?

You never know what you'll find.

# INDEX

Page numbers in *italics* refer to illustrations.

# ABOUT THE AUTHORS

*Diana Miller Photography*

Major Edward A. Dames, U.S. Army (ret.) is the world's foremost teacher of remote viewing, the ability to perceive people, places, and events without using physical senses or special equipment. In the late 1980s, he served as training and operations officer for the Defense Intelligence Agency's controversial psychic intelligence (PSIINT) unit and is currently executive director of the Matrix Intelligence Agency, a private consulting group. "Major Doom" (as he is affectionately known to his millions of *Coast to Coast AM* radio fans) was a technical consultant on the Tom Cruise–produced feature film *Suspect Zero* where he coached Sir Ben Kingsley and played the role of an FBI remote viewing instructor. His psi spy experiences were the inspiration behind George Clooney's hit movie *The Men Who Stare at Goats*. Dames now resides in Lugansk, Ukraine and California. He is fluent in Chinese Mandarin and an avid student of the Russian language. More about Major Ed Dames and remote viewing can be found at www.LearnRV.com.

*Lisa van Hecke*

Joel Harry Newman is a former staff reporter/editor for the Los Angeles *Herald Examiner* where he covered the crime, politics, and entertainment beats. He added business writing to his portfolio at *Adweek* magazine, where he generated award-winning coverage of the mad men and women of the advertising world. As a freelancer, he's contributed to such publications as the *Los Angeles Times Magazine, Details, L.A. Style, PDN*, and the *Hollywood Reporter*, among others. His screenwork includes serving as story editor on the hit motion pictures *John Carpenter's Vampires, Arachnophobia*, and *Hollow Man*. Joel and his wife, Feryat, divide their time between Los Angeles and their ranch near Joshua Tree, California. Please visit him at his Web site www.jhnewman.com.